EUROPEAN ADVERTISING STRATEGIES

The Profiles and Policies of Multinational Companies Operating in Europe

Rein Rijkens

With a Foreword by
Lord Cockfield

Vice-President of the European Commission 1985–1988

CASSELL

Cassell
Villiers House   387 Park Avenue South
41/47 Strand   New York
London WC2N 5JE   NY10016-8810
England   USA

First published in hardback 1992

Reprinted 1994

Paperback edition first published 1993

British Library Cataloguing-in-Publication Data

Rijkens, Rein
  European advertising strategies. The profiles and policies of
multinational companies operating in Europe.
  1. Europe. Advertising
  I. Title
659.1094

ISBN 0-304-31796-9 (Hardback)
ISBN 0-304-32813-8 (Paperback)

Typeset by Colset Private Limited, Singapore

Printed in Great Britain by Bookcraft (Bath) Ltd

CONTENTS

FOREWORD

The programme for the completion of the Internal Market – 'Europe 1992', as it is popularly called – is the key to Europe's future prosperity. But it is more than that. It is also the foundation on which the other policies of the Community are built. So, as the 1992 programme now reaches the point of achievement, we must look to the next steps along the road to European Union. The intergovernmental conferences launched at Rome, dealing with economic and monetary union and political union, point the way forward.

It is particularly important that everyone in trade and industry, in finance and commerce, should understand these developments, should support them, should take advantage of the opportunities opened up and should be prepared to meet the challenges created.

Advertising has a critically important part to play. It is the main channel of communication between the producer and the consumer, and ultimately it is the synergy between producer and consumer that translates opportunities into achievements: that translates growth potential into growth achieved.

Mr Rijkens's book describes how a number of multinational corporations operating in Europe have prepared themselves for marketing and advertising goods and services throughout Europe after 1992. It is a unique collection of views and experiences of senior practitioners in the field of communications, reporting on how they cope with the organizational and procedural problems of a single European market-place, and on how they have developed and executed their international advertising strategies.

In all fifteen chapters in this book the points that stand out are the companies' awareness of their responsibilities towards today's more critical, demanding and selective consumers and their understanding of consumers' attitudes and expectations. The success of all these companies clearly depends upon their being seen by the public at large as businesses of indisputable integrity, and on the quality of their products and services.

In all this, the interests of business and those of governments run largely parallel. Both share the same concern and need to share the same determination in ensuring that the Internal Market programme is completed, and is completed on time. It must therefore be a major concern of both business managers and political leaders to work together to achieve what are so clearly shared objectives.

This book deals with the many problems, including political ones, which today's managers face when advertising on an international scale. It should therefore be of interest not only to those involved in the international aspects of communicating messages across many countries, but also to those who can influence the effectiveness of these activities, particularly to politicians, civil servants and the consumer organizations.

In this way, Mr Rijkens's book makes an important contribution to ensuring that the benefits of the Single European Market are realized to the full.

Lord Cockfield

PREFACE

OBJECTIVES

The idea for this book and the timing of its publication may be attributable to the expected interest in the European market-place after 1992, but the book itself is not a collection of academic models to help those preparing themselves for new opportunities in the Single European Market, or in Europe as a whole, nor is it intended to provide a set of rules for those who will be involved in future advertising operations on an international scale. Instead, I thought that all those concerned with such activities, today and tomorrow, might be interested in the practical experiences of a number of companies which are already carrying out such operations and are doing so very successfully. In addition, by describing the principles underlying these activities, I thought that I would also have an opportunity to share with readers my long-held convictions as to why some international companies are more successful than others, and the confirmation of these beliefs that the preparation of these 15 case studies has provided.

The study that follows is also based on my own experience – more than 30 years in managerial, co-ordinating and advisory functions, at both company and advertising-agency levels. In addition to having run a Unilever company and one of the Lintas agencies, I have had co-ordinating responsibilities for companies and agencies within Europe. My later work brought me into contact with a number of other international companies in Europe and in the USA, giving me a valuable insight into the way in which these companies were operating internationally, particularly in the field of advertising, which is the subject of this book.

When I looked back on these experiences, a pattern of common denominators emerged. After careful scrutiny of many facets of international operations, I concluded that there were three major, closely integrated factors common to all cases. In my opinion, these were the decisive factors in the international operations of the businesses concerned. I have called them the 'Three Dimensions of Success', and they run as follows:

---

1. Quality of the product and its concept
2. Consistency of advertising policies
3. Ability to manage people and resources

Let me briefly elaborate.

Quality of the product and its concept

These factors are the top priorities for all managements and are attended to with infinite care, since advertisers know full well that in today's competitive environment only the best products will prevail. A product and its concept should form one indivisible whole, comprising, on the one hand, the product's physical properties and outward appearance and, on the other hand, the promise to consumers that it will deliver a benefit, whether concrete or emotional, usually conveyed through the medium of advertising. One element cannot exist without the other. If the physical properties of the product fail to deliver the expected benefit, the consumer will be dissatisfied and will not buy it again. However, if the benefit itself is of no interest, the consumer will not even try the product in the first place.

Many people will argue that these functional and emotional elements of a product or service belong to the make-up of a 'brand'. Whilst this may be so, the reason for calling the first dimension 'Quality of the product and its concept' is to differentiate between the intrinsic properties of the product or service and the idea behind its shape or form, the 'added value', the competitive edge – the concept – which will rarely realize its full potential without advertising, and which is the principal concern of this book. For example, although the advertisements for Lux contain the promise of a beautiful skin, whilst Marlboro offers the enjoyment of a pleasant smoke, the real uniqueness of the advertising for both brands is in suggesting that they will give their users sex-appeal.

However, apart from the significance of advertising in the total make-up of a brand, there are, of course, numerous other aspects that constitute a 'product' as defined in this book and that will affect its success in the market-place negatively or positively. Some of these factors are of more immediate relevance to the subject of this book than others. Consider, for example, the relationship between quality and price. Price is a relative factor and is better discussed in terms of 'value for money'. For example, a stay at the Club Méditerranée is considered by some to be 'expensive', but most visitors find that they get substantial value for their money, enhanced by the Club's advertising, which spells out all the Club's delights. Consequently, in the opinion of these visitors, the Club Med sells a high-quality product, and they are therefore prepared to pay the price for it.

There is one more factor that, in today's competitive and saturated markets, will often be of decisive importance. This, of course, is service, which can make or break a company's marketing and advertising operations, as is shown by the importance that KLM and Mercedes attach to it. In spite of all advertising efforts, one failed opportunity to provide good service can easily make the consumer turn away for good.

However, this book will concentrate on the advertising function as one of the principal elements contributing towards the 'quality of the product and its concept' and will show how to manage it on an international scale, by means of the case studies that follow.

Consistency of advertising policies

The 15 cases in this book emphasize the importance of this element. Without exception, the advertising strategies for all the brands and services discussed, and the means by which they have been implemented, have remained basically unchanged for many decades, irrespective of the international structure of the company and the relationship between it and its subsidiaries. Adaptations and small adjustments have been made; fundamental changes have not. All the companies studied have managed to overcome the usual dangers inherent in changes of personnel, such as the natural desire of newcomers to make their mark and to do better than their predecessors, which results in the unfortunate habit of making changes for their own sake.

Whether through clearly and precisely defined and laid down procedures, through manuals or 'Creative Guidelines', through frequent personal contacts, or through a combination of all three, the companies taking part in this study maintain careful control over advertising policies and their execution and ensure that their advertising agencies are fully integrated into the process. This represents managerial command of the first order. Product life-cycles are one thing, brand life-cycles are quite another; the successes of the long-standing brands discussed in this book prove my point that consistency in advertising policies will help to keep brands youthful and modern, if that is what managements want.

Ability to manage people and resources

This ability to manage and to lead is the key to success. 'Leadership is many things,' Peters and Waterman say in their book *In Search of Excellence*, and they continue:

It is being visible when things are going awry, and invisible when
they are working well. It's building a loyal team at the top that
speaks more or less with one voice. It's listening carefully most of the
time, frequently speaking with encouragement, and reinforcing words
with believable action. It's being tough when necessary, and it's the
occasional naked use of power.[1]

I have always maintained that the best definition of 'international advertising' is the ability to manage people and resources, and the writing of this book has reinforced this conviction. Given the fact that creative talent can be bought at a price, albeit at a high price, it remains the task of the leader, of the manager, to inspire people, to engender commitment, to unleash energy, in order to achieve success.

Combining creative and managerial skills, managing people and resources, will be the key to the future success of multinational operations and their international advertising. This thought is not new. Back in the eighteenth century, the British statesman and author Edmund Burke (1729–1797) put it as follows:

No men can act with effect who do not act in concert; no men can
act in concert who do not act with confidence; no men can act with
confidence who are not bound together with common opinions,
common affections and common interests.

This may be true, but does it still apply in the world in which we live? In reading most annual company reports, one will find the president or chairman expressing his exuberant appreciation for management and staff, whose devotion and loyalty have made such a decisive contribution to the results of the company . . . etc. etc. One sometimes wonders how genuine these statements are and to what extent, in today's tough business world, factors such as devotion and loyalty still have the meaning and value that they used to have in the past. On the other hand, when one learns that at Miele there is hardly any turnover of staff and that the contact between directors and their employees is of a most informal nature, one cannot help feeling that there must be a connection between the qualities of leadership apparent in such a business and its continuing success in the market-place.

Theory and practice

I realize full well that there are many other factors governing the success of international operations, but I still maintain that my three basic elements will always be at the root of successful operations of the kind described in this book. In fact, I do not expect my 'Three Dimensions' theory to cause great controversy. Most informed readers will readily agree with its significance, but there is an immense difference between what people say and what people actually do, between theory and practice. This point is particularly important at a time when international business is becoming much more complex, and when operational methods are getting more sophisticated. The need to remind ourselves of a few basic truths that are so easily forgotten would appear to be greater than ever.

In line with the entire concept of this book, instead of making my three dimensions into theoretical guidelines, I have chosen to ask experienced practitioners to explain how they plan and carry out their international advertising operations in an increasingly difficult and competitive environment.

In selecting the companies for this study, my overriding concern has been to demonstrate the difference between mediocrity and excellence in the running of a business. All these companies devote meticulous attention to literally every detail of their operations; nothing is left to chance, no risks are taken, quality comes first in everything that they do. This is why I feel confident that when readers have studied the 15 cases described in this book, they will agree that my 'Three Dimensions' are not merely theoretical concepts, but do indeed form a common and recognizable thread running through all of them. As advertising cannot be discussed in isolation, since it forms part of the cultural background and history of a company and the environment in which it operates, brief profiles of the companies concerned precede the discussion of their actual advertising policies.

Scope of study

In order to make this study as representative as possible of advertising on a European scale, the participating companies were selected because: (a) their success depends largely upon the effectiveness of their communications with consumers; and (b) they differ sufficiently in character and in the type of product or service that they provide to offer readers a wide choice of organizations with which to identify.

Having visited and studied the advertising departments of 13 companies (Unilever and Nestlé each provide two of the 15 cases), I feel more confident than ever that the selection presented in this book offers a 'choc des opinions' that will be difficult to match. Separately and collectively, these cases represent a wealth of experience that, as far as I know, has never been brought together in this way.

Definitions

The readers of this book will not need to be given one of the many available definitions of advertising. But, in order to avoid any confusion about the concept of 'international advertising', I shall simply cite the passage in the book co-written by Professor Gordon Miracle and myself, in which we defined international advertising as '. . . that which is created at, coordinated or directed from one central point, for execution, with or without local adaptations, in a number of countries'.[2]

Thank you!

This Introduction would not be complete if it did not acknowledge the contribution of those many people, particularly the executives of the participating companies, who so readily and generously made time available to share their experiences with me. Whenever possible, I have paid tribute to them in the notes at the end of each chapter, but the names of all the other colleagues and friends who were so helpful in giving me their valuable counsel have been included in the Acknowledgements section near the end of this book.

However, a few names require special mention here. I was, of course, extremely pleased that Lord Cockfield accepted my invitation to write the Foreword. He is, after all, one of the main architects of the Single European Market, and as the idea for this book was suggested by the Market, I feel that I could not have found a more prominent and authoritative person to introduce it to its readers. The book itself could never have been written without the invaluable assistance of Wendy van Os-Thompson, who helped me to overcome my difficulties with the English language. 'Take my word, English is a very difficult language', writes Frenchman Pierre la Mure on the jacket of his famous book *Clair de Lune*, and he has certainly convinced at least one person of how right he is! My wife developed an uncanny eye for spotting spelling errors at the many stages passed through by the manuscript, which could never have been produced without the help of my great friend Macintosh, graciously made available by the management of Apple Computer Europe, based in Paris. Neither could I have done without KLM, who, with equal kindness, enabled me to make the many necessary visits abroad.

The magic 1993 . . . and beyond!

This book appears at a crucial moment. Not only will the Single European Market accelerate trends towards greater centralization of decision-making, including in the field of advertising, but the destruction on 9 November 1989 of the Berlin Wall was an historic event with serious consequences for the entire business world. Since that date, and particularly since the unification of the two Germanys, it is not so much a question of principle but rather of time, albeit much time, before Russia and the other Eastern European countries become part of one immense European market-place. As if this were not enough, the development of electronic and computer technology will, in the long term, greatly influence the marketing and advertising of products and services; in my Conclusion, I shall come back to this important point.

In the short term, the Single European Market will not make a great deal of difference to the companies discussed in this book. They will all have been running their businesses on an international scale for a considerable period when the enlarged market-place comes about. Of course, they will be alert to changing circumstances and adapt their policies accordingly, and they will also prepare themselves to expand into Eastern Europe when the time comes, but, generally speaking, it will be 'business as usual' as regards their advertising policies for the European market-place. In fact, this was the very reason for inviting these companies to participate in this study. I felt that their experience could well benefit those to whom 1993 will indeed make a difference and who may wish to expand their businesses into many European countries. I also felt that, although in years to come the scope of operations will be bigger and more complex than today, the basic principles underlying advertising on an international scale would maintain their validity.

In my Conclusion, I shall have an opportunity to elaborate on the findings of this study, as well as to return to my 'Three Dimensions' and to a few thoughts about the future. At this stage, it should suffice to say how proud and pleased I am to be able to present to readers a study encompassing such a unique collection of successful international advertising operations, the results of visionary and entrepreneurial leadership.

The Hague
July 1991   Rein Rijkens

Notes

1. Peters, Thomas J. and Waterman Jr., R.H. (1982), *In Search of Excellence*. New York: Harper & Row, p. 82.
2. Rijkens, Rein, and Miracle, G.E. (1986), *European Regulation of Advertising*. Amsterdam: Elsevier, p. 3.

AFTER EIGHT

Wafer-thin Chocolate Mints

"The Ambassador's just like a thin mint... slim, square, and delicious!"

"My dear, I might have been Visiting Royalty, he was so
attentive! And the deliciously diplomatic way he monopolised my
After Eight Wafer-thin Mints... I just sat and watched them
vanishing before my eyes. And you know those nice
little envelopes they come in? Darling, he was practically
knee-deep in them!"

ROWNTREE MACKINTOSH LIMITED

AFTER EIGHT

After Eight

AFTER EIGHT
Wafer-thin Chocolate Mints

'Et ne dites pas, "ils sont fous ces Anglais", pas avant d'avoir goûté des After Eight,' was the somewhat unusual final text in the first French After Eight commercial, introducing this new product to the French market in 1971. As the remarkable story of the international advertising campaign for After Eight, the thin chocolate after-dinner mint, unfolds, we shall see how, thanks to a team of dedicated and involved people, prejudices were overcome and new habits were introduced, resulting in the achievement of common objectives. However, before looking at this brand in detail, let us first review the history of the company responsible for this successful international operation, which at the time upset current thinking about internationalizing the marketing and advertising of a food product.

MR ROWNTREE AND MR MACKINTOSH

The company started in York, where, in the early nineteenth century, Mary Tuke's grocery shop was doing a thriving trade in tea, chocolate and coffee. In 1869, Henry I. Rowntree, a Quaker like Mary Tuke herself, bought her chocolate business, acquired a factory in town and founded H.I. Rowntree & Co. in partnership with his brother Joseph. The company prospered and, in the course of time, launched a number of brands, such as Kit Kat, Black Magic and Smarties, that are still prospering in several markets.[1] However, the period in the company's history that is of primary interest to us begins in 1962, when Rowntree formed a 'European Market Committee', later to be called the 'European Division', to tackle what would be referred to as the 'Common Market'.

At that time, the Continent was as unknown to the company as the name Rowntree was to the Europeans, but this situation was to change rapidly. Rowntree initially established marketing and sales companies in Holland, Germany, Belgium, France and Italy, and then acquired manufacturing facilities on the Continent; first the German firm of Stockmann, in 1964, then, in 1971, the French company Chocolat Menier.

In the meantime, Rowntree had merged in 1969 with John Mackintosh and Sons Ltd, which originated in Halifax, also in Yorkshire. This company produced the well-known Mackintosh toffees but also sold the twist-wrapped Quality Street assortment, and Rolo sweets. Together, the firms founded Rowntree Mackintosh, whose principal business was the production of confectionery, a field in which the firm, in the form that it had then, was ranked among the top three manufacturers in the world. Thus, practically within one decade, Rowntree Mackintosh had established itself and many of its products within the Common Market and Europe as a whole.

The results of what was achieved in the early years can be seen in the firm's annual report for 1987, the last year of Rowntree Mackintosh's existence as an independent company, then employing 33 000 people in 25 factories in nine countries. This annual report shows that in 1987, out of a total net revenue of £1.4 billion, the firm's operation in continental Europe, with its head-office in Paris, accounted for approximately 20 per cent, North America for 30 per cent, the UK and Ireland for 40 per cent, and Australasia and the rest of the world for the remaining 10 per cent. In 1987, the company made a trading profit of £130 million, or almost 10 per cent of its net revenue; a result of which it could justly be proud.

Rowntree's confectionery business has always been the company's most important activity, representing about 75 per cent of its total sales. Its products in this business category include three mentioned earlier: Kit Kat, a chocolate biscuit well-known in many parts of the world and the company's most important single brand; Smarties, the coloured sweets for children; and Quality Street. In addition, of course, there is After Eight, which in 1987 achieved a worldwide turnover of more than £60 million from 83 countries.[2]

... AND THEN CAME NESTLÉ

In 1988, Rowntree Mackintosh became part of the Nestlé concern. Its acquisition by the Swiss company has 'to be seen within the broader context of the Single European Market, and, above all, of the general trend toward worldwide competition among large groups in the food industry.'[3] After the merger, the chocolate and confectionery responsibilities of Rowntree PLC were integrated into the general management structure of the Nestlé concern, which will be described in greater detail in the chapter on Nescafé. For the purpose of this chapter, a simplified organization chart has been drawn up, indicating the functions most relevant to the After Eight operation:

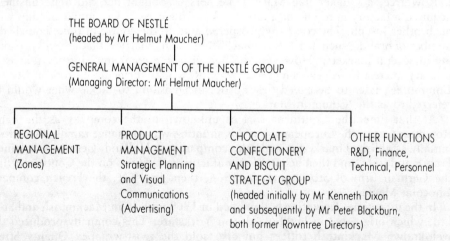

THE BOARD OF NESTLÉ
(headed by Mr Helmut Maucher)

GENERAL MANAGEMENT OF THE NESTLÉ GROUP
(Managing Director: Mr Helmut Maucher)

| REGIONAL MANAGEMENT (Zones) | PRODUCT MANAGEMENT Strategic Planning and Visual Communications (Advertising) | CHOCOLATE CONFECTIONERY AND BISCUIT STRATEGY GROUP (headed initially by Mr Kenneth Dixon and subsequently by Mr Peter Blackburn, both former Rowntree Directors) | OTHER FUNCTIONS R&D, Finance, Technical, Personnel |

The executive authority for the complete range of Nestlé and Rowntree products rests, in the main, with the managers of the national companies, who report to regional managers, based in Vevey. Each regional manager is responsible for one of Nestlé's 'zones': Europe; the USA and Canada; Latin America; Africa and the Middle East; and Asia and Oceania. These regional managements are assisted by a number of staff functions, also at general management level, such as product management, responsible for counselling regional managements on strategies for Nestlé's global products, for example drinks, cereals, frozen foods, ice creams and petfoods. However, there is one exception to this scheme. When Nestlé and Rowntree Mackintosh merged, it was decided that the confectionery interests of both companies would be combined into one 'International Chocolate, Confectionery &

Biscuit Strategy Group' (CSG), to be responsible directly to the general management of the Nestlé group and to be based in York. This was done to ensure the continuation of a large measure of independence for the existing Rowntree Mackintosh operation.

The visual communications department has advisory responsibilities for packaging, advertising, promotion and corporate identity. It is instrumental in counselling the national companies, the strategic planning groups and the CSG, on all aspects of communications representing the company and its products to consumers and the trade. It employs a staff of approximately 30 people.

The Nestlé policy of giving its national managers final responsibility for the results achieved in their territories, combined with central responsibilities for worldwide product strategies, was not very different from the way in which Rowntree PLC had run its business, except that Rowntree had exerted more control over the advertising of its international brands. Thus, generally speaking, apart from the usual problems inherent in any such mergers, the integration of Rowntree PLC in the Nestlé concern has taken place quite smoothly. This is particularly important because of the properties that Rowntree had vested in its great international brands. The considerable goodwill among consumers towards these brands may never be adversely affected by changes in the ownership of the company that made them into what they are, and what they should long continue to be. Probably the most important of these brands, from a marketing and advertising point of view, is After Eight, the after-dinner mint chocolate, that is the product studied in this chapter.

THE AFTER EIGHT CONCEPT

When Nestlé took over Rowntree, it acquired a product established by one of the most remarkable international marketing operations since the end of the Second World War. Many people have wondered how Rowntree successfully introduced a product so essentially British in character and in presentation to, for example, the French, to whom the combination of chocolate and peppermint as an after-dinner treat was almost sacrilege; or to the Germans, to whom the typical English after-dinner gathering did not mean anything at all; or to the Italians, who were accustomed to purchasing big boxes of chocolates as gifts for their mothers but who were not used to the combination of mint and chocolate, far less to the idea of an after-dinner mint chocolate. One might think that it was sufficient simply to tell the French, the Germans and the Italians what a good product After Eight was and to suggest that they should try it for a change. However, the operation was by no means as easy as that! Before going into its details, let us look at how the confectionery line was developed in its country of origin, the UK.

THE GAP IN THE MARKET

The consumption of chocolate and sugar confectionery in England is among the highest in the world, and in the early 1960s the Rowntree management identified a segment of the confectionery market in which the company was not represented: that of expensive and exclusive boxed chocolate. A wafer-thin chocolate mint was soon selected as one way of filling this gap in the market and in the company's range of products. Interestingly, the original idea for a product of this type had come from the USA,

> where the Wallace Corporation had a range of wafer-thin chocolates
> with a variety of cream centres – peppermint, coffee, orange, etc.
> Negotiations were conducted with the Americans to manufacture their
> product under licence in this country. These were rather protracted
> and finally stumbled over the question of royalties – Rowntree
> considering the Wallace demand excessive. It was, therefore, decided
> to ask our own Engineers and Development people to produce a
> wafer-thin mint. In a remarkably short period this was achieved.[4]

By the beginning of 1962, preparations were sufficiently advanced to support a test launch in Scotland.

'AFTER EIGHT' – WHAT'S IN A NAME?

By this time, J. Walter Thompson, a long-standing Rowntree advertising agency, had also been appointed to handle this new product, and one of the agency's first tasks was to suggest a name and produce a pack design. In this chapter and in the next, two very different, but extremely successful, brands are described, the names of which must have made a considerable contribution to their success in the market-place, though this can never be proved. These names were not arrived at by playing around with ingenious combinations of letters, or by just using the name of the company; they were developed spontaneously in moments of inspiration. One name was invented during a drive in a car, the other was suggested by an idea put forward during an informal brainstorming session. But what brilliant ideas they both were!

The brands referred to are Apple and After Eight. As regards the way in which the latter got its name, a former Rowntree Mackintosh executive writes as follows:

> Jeremy [Bullmore] told me that the clue was provided by an
> advertisement in some curious New York magazine . . . which was
> drawn to their attention by a visiting American copywriter. This was
> for a smart, for the day, sort of shirt, called, I believe 'After Six' . . .
> What a thought. Why not 'After Eight'?[5]

AND WHAT'S IN A PACK DESIGN?

The packaging for the new product had, of course, also to reflect its up-market nature and the fact that it was intended for special occasions. Once the name After Eight had been selected, it was decided that the pack should carry a symbol relevant to the product, its name and its usage. Thus, a complete trade-mark was devised, which was both verbal and pictorial; it consisted of the words 'After Eight' and the picture of a Louis XIV ormolu clock (ormolu being a moulded, embossed and gilded bronze used for decorative purposes), showing the time at a few minutes after eight o'clock. A distinctive green colour was adopted for the pack, and the trade-mark became the most important and memorable element in the final design. This has remained virtually unchanged since its introduction, apart from a couple of minor changes to the type-face. Another important aspect of the packaging was the use of brown glassine envelopes, bearing the trade-mark, to wrap the individual sweets in the pack. In 1976, the company was awarded the prestigious Bass Award for the most effective use of a trade-mark.

POSITIONING OF AFTER EIGHT

The positioning of the product in the UK has never been changed and was later adopted almost unaltered for international use. Having studied all the available documentation, this positioning can be described as follows:

> Consumers should perceive After Eight as a uniquely presented,
> wafer-thin, high-quality mint chocolate, which is enjoyed after a
> relaxed dinner or on comparable occasions. It should be associated
> with the elegance, sophistication and social status of the good hostess
> and of her guests. As an affordable token of friendship or
> appreciation, it reflects the good taste of the giver and will flatter the
> receiver.

What could be more British? Such positioning evokes the art of entertaining, the attention to detail in laying the table, the silver candelabra, the crystal brandy glasses, the black ties and cigars, all the refinement of an old English country house, complete with butlers, and with the Rolls-Royce and its chauffeur waiting outside. But would the concept still be credible in this day and age? Would it induce consumers to go and buy the product?

It is well known that no audience will take such emotionally loaded advertising too literally, but if it is done well, if the proper balance between truth and fiction can be found, it may give many people the feeling that members of the smart set are still living the kind of sophisticated life to which they perhaps secretly aspire. It is only a small step from such thoughts to actually buying one of the smart set's products, particularly if the product itself then conforms to the buyer's expectations.

AFTER EIGHT ADVERTISING

Developing the right kind of advertising for such a product required great skills on the part of those who made the advertisements and those who had to approve them; the advertising could so easily miss the mark. The tone of voice, choice of cast and selected scenarios all had to be ideal to avoid total failure. The test launch of the product, in Scotland in 1962, was initially supported by press advertising only, as was the extension of sales to the whole of the UK, but the real breakthrough occurred when the first TV commercial 'Dinner Table' was put on air in the Yorkshire Television area in the spring of 1964. It immediately resulted in a 64 per cent sales increase, as compared with 18 per cent in other parts of the country. This commercial, combining, in a most professional manner, all the elements making up the personality of the brand, has been used ever since as the standard against which all subsequent commercials, produced in the UK and on the Continent, have been judged.[6]

AFTER EIGHT GOES INTERNATIONAL

The success of After Eight in the UK soon resulted in the company's management giving serious consideration to launching it on the Continent. The decisive question was whether such an English product concept could be exported to countries where the added values that the brand represented might not be readily accepted.

In order to assist the company in assessing and carrying out such an operation, Rowntree Mackintosh appointed the Lintas advertising agency to handle the account on the Continent. J. Walter Thompson continued to do so in the UK but as it handled competitive business in other European countries, it could not take on the international assignment. Lintas had full service agencies in all European countries and was available to handle the account.

Germany - Holland - Italy - France

If ever there was a case for using one international advertising agency and its subsidiaries everywhere, then this certainly applied to After Eight. The subtleties, the nuances, the cast and the location required by the commercials made close collaboration and co-operation imperative. No risks could be taken. The UK experience and the excellent After Eight advertising that formed part of it were accepted as 'creative guidelines' for similar commercials to be produced elsewhere.

But why, one might ask, could the UK commercials not simply be taken as they stood, and dubbed into the local language, thereby saving a considerable amount of money? At the time, the answer was simple. If, in addition to introducing the new habit of having a mint chocolate after dinner, the advertisements had contained dinner tables or picnics unlike those to which Continental consumers were accustomed, one could not have expected their audiences to identify emotionally with the situations that they presented. This was all the more important because, in spite of the misgivings of many people on the Continent, the company's management had taken the brave decision that no concessions should be made to the 'Englishness' of the product's concept; the very British character of the brand, and its equally British name, were not only going to be maintained, but even highlighted. Thus, a virtue was made out of a necessity. What is more, the concept worked; though, of course, it worked better and more quickly in some countries than in others.

Germany

In the northern part of Germany, the very British character of After Eight was quite acceptable, but instead of producing a commercial centred around a dinner party, an occasion with which the German consumer could not easily identify, the advertisers chose to show a high-society soirée. In addition, although After Eights were produced in Germany, the formulation and flavour of the product, and its name and its packaging, in other words its total concept, were not only fully maintained but indeed emphasized. The text of the commercial ran as follows:

The lady says:
'Ah, Hubert - has the Consul once more brought some After Eight from London?'
The butler replies:
'No madam, we are now in the fortunate position of being able to obtain After Eight in Germany.'

She says:
'Oh, really!'
Voice-over:
'After Eight – extremely thin peppermint leaves.'[7]

This appeal to snobbery, also emphasized in magazine advertisements, had immediate success in the test market, in 1966. In 1967, After Eight began to be sold throughout Germany and by 1969 it had become a major brand leader.

Holland and Italy

After Eight was introduced to these two countries in 1969 and, in both, the basic strategy was maintained; while adaptations ensured acceptance of the product and its advertising by consumers and resulted in successful operations.

France

The quotation from the French commercial with which this chapter started is indicative of French resistance to the 'Englishness' of this brand and its advertising. In France, confectionery products were not associated with social activity, English food products were not taken seriously anyway, and peppermint in chocolate as an after-dinner sweet was simply unheard of.

Mr Anthony Mackintosh, at this time European marketing director of Rowntree Mackintosh, said on this subject:

Jointly with Lintas and our French management, we gently and persistently researched these opinions to see how firmly they were held and then find ways around them. Through qualitative research we found that, although the idea of chocolate and mint was strange and, in many cases, unattractive, the actual experience was less alarming and could easily become accepted. The unique presentation held a genuine attraction and, without being specific, Frenchmen could see no personal and social place for the product. The whole concept clearly puzzled them and a final explanation that it was English, produced the proverbial 'Ah voilà'. We . . . were gratified to find over 60 per cent of confectionery eaters thought it was excellent or very good. All we had to decide was whether to change the name and disguise the English origin of the idea. . . . We decided to maintain the uniform name, pack and presentation which we had in other countries and to deal with the problem of Englishness and the social function purely through advertising. We developed the following film – the text reads:
Voice over:
The English have always had a certain way of life – a sense of refinement if you like . . . Here is a new fashion from London for after dinner – After Eight. Fine leaves of chocolate filled with melting mint.
Yes, you heard – mint and chocolate. And don't say, 'They are mad, these English', before having tasted After Eight.[8]

This is a long quotation and it is included because it describes in simple, but very clear, terms all the steps that had to be taken for the introduction, not only of a new product, but of a new habit as well; a habit that might well meet initially with considerable resistance among the high-class audience at which it was aimed. After Eight was introduced to France in 1971 and has been doing very well ever since. Its success stemmed from a remarkable marketing and advertising operation, which deserves attention and study by everyone involved in international projects of this kind.

PRINCIPLES AND GUIDELINES

Rowntree Mackintosh gradually realized that in order to safeguard After Eight and its other successful international brands against any local deviation from agreed policies and actions it should lay down a set of 'International Marketing Principles', later to be followed by 'Advertising Guidelines'. In 1985, the marketing principles document for After Eight was introduced. It had the following headings and sub-headings:

Positioning	Product	Advertising
Target Market	Appearance	Target Group
Brand Characteristics	Type of Eat	Preferred Media
Competition	Packaging	
	Name and Motif	
	Price/Value	

The 'Advertising Guidelines' were recorded on tape. After being introduced by the person within Rowntree's European division responsible for overseeing marketing activities, the international account director and international creative director from the Lintas advertising agency explained the various creative elements of After Eight advertising. Aspects reviewed included the elegance required of actors and settings, how to portray the right life-styles, the use of humour, the required atmosphere of 'Englishness', the way that the product should be shown when being consumed and the importance of the right music. As we shall see in other chapters, many companies use such systems of documentation to ensure the proper adaptation of agreed policies and actions as well as to combat disruption caused by changes of staff both in the companies themselves and in their advertising agencies.

After Eight continued to do well, and, many years later, the following statement could be found in the manufacturer's annual report for 1987, the year in which Rowntree PLC was established as the holding company for what had previously been known as the Rowntree Mackintosh Group:

After Eight made strong advances in many countries and confirmed its position as one of Europe's leading boxed chocolate brands.
In Sweden more After Eight was eaten per head of population than anywhere else in the world.[9]

THE ROLE OF THE INTERNATIONAL ADVERTISING AGENCY

As already mentioned, in a case such as that of After Eight, when success in the market-place depends almost decisively upon perfecting the many different nuances in the presentation of an extremely sensitive creative idea, collaboration between company and advertising agency, at both national and international levels, is of great importance. Rowntree and the major advertising agencies that handled After Eight, J. Walter Thompson and Lintas, collaborated closely and continue to do so. As is usual in such circumstances, both Rowntree and Lintas, which handles After Eight advertising outside the UK, have appointed senior executives to guide and co-ordinate work in the various countries where the product is sold. Although, as we have seen, the basic strategy for advertising After Eight remained unchanged when it entered the European market, allowances had to be made for different opinions about the kind of festive occasion on which it should be consumed. For this reason, the advantage of economies of scale, which is so often important when firms employ uniform advertising in a number of countries, could hardly be obtained; the occasions, the choice of actors, their tone of voice, the overall directing, all necessitated local productions. There have been a few isolated cases when UK commercials have been used in one or two countries on the Continent, but Continental advertisements have never been used in the UK. However, it is a measure of the success of the French commercial quoted in part earlier in this chapter that, 18 years after it was originally made, it has been used again in 1990, for the launch of After Eight in Portugal!

REMUNERATION

Rowntree initially employed the commission system of remuneration for its advertising agencies, but, due to local pressures, alternative methods, such as fees, were subsequently introduced. After some time, the company returned to the commission system, using a sliding scale to take account of the differing natures of its markets. Since the Nestlé takeover, the basis of remuneration has again become largely a matter for negotiations between the company's local affiliates and the local offices of the agency concerned, but, like all matters regarding advertising, these negotiations take place in close consultation with Nestlé's visual communications department in Vevey.

LEGAL AND OTHER RESTRICTIONS

Fortunately, After Eight advertising does not suffer unduly from any important legal or voluntary restrictions as regards the way in which it communicates with consumers, nor does the Commission of the EC appear to take a great interest in confectionery advertising in general. The main controls are exercised by individual governments, which can introduce legislation regarding the advertising of certain products. For example, in the Netherlands a stylized toothbrush has to appear towards the end of every commercial for a confectionery product, reminding viewers, particularly children, that regular brushing of the teeth will help to prevent tooth-decay. However, there are indications that more stringent controls are impending. 'EC to tighten food claims law', announces an advertising trade magazine in an article discussing a European Commission paper mapping out new laws '. . . which would form an EC Directive on food claims, covers, presentation and advertising'.[10] One can only hope that any such directive, if it ever appears, will not affect the advertising of confectionery products, but the Commission will almost certainly ensure that it does.

COMPETITION

A successful concept such as After Eight almost invites imitation and competition. However, imitation is hindered by complex production methods and an equally complex mixture of raw materials and flavours; while straight imitation has usually been perceived as such by demanding consumers and has not been very successful.

In the field of confectionery in general, Nestlé has inevitably come up against important competitors, such as Mars, Ferrero, Hershey, Cadbury and Suchard, but with regard to After Eight, it is difficult to define its competition precisely. Any box of chocolates offered as a gift to a friend or hostess is, of course, competition for After Eight, but so are flowers and books!

AFTER EIGHT: AN ANALYSIS

The remarkable success of this product in Europe and elsewhere merits an analysis of the factors that have helped it to become an almost classic example of international brand marketing. These factors can be summarized as follows:

---

1. The fact that the right 'niche' in the market has been found and a product developed for it.

2. The superior quality of the product itself, based upon a careful selection of chocolate beans and peppermint flavour. These ingredients are the same all over the world, and the complicated production process makes imitation very difficult. At all stages there is rigorous control of production and quality.

3. The individually enveloped sweets, the green pack with the distinctive clock, not only illustrating the product's apt and original name, but also providing a reminder of the time of day when the chocolates will usually be consumed, plus the elegance and luxurious character of the product's total presentation. All these elements form one indivisible whole, of much greater value than the sum of the parts.

4. The fact that advertising for the product in the UK has underlined, enhanced and enlivened the snob value of the brand. The advertising addresses a select public to which many people would like to belong, and does so by means of high-class presentation, in line with the standing of the brand.

5. The management's conviction that, contrary to current opinion, it should be possible to introduce a product that has a novel taste and that requires new habits into markets with many different tastes and habits. This has been done with single-minded directness, with assistance from a dedicated and committed team

of people from the companies and advertising agencies concerned, at both national and international levels. This team has combined flexibility of interpretation with unfailing support for agreed basic policies and strategies.

1993 AND BEYOND

Like every responsible marketer, the CSG is continuously monitoring trends in the market and in consumer behaviour and habits. Could it be, for example, that today's generation has a different perception of what constitutes an 'exceptional occasion'? Is it possible that the modern woman no longer identifies, even in her dreams, with 'crusty lords and bejewelled hostesses', as the actors in the well-known After Eight commercials featuring candle-lit dinners and guests in black ties were described in one British newspaper?[11] Does today's consumer perhaps believe in a different set of values, in a different life-style, in which there will continue to be room for the 'special occasion', but for one of another kind? If such suggestions were shown by research to be correct, might this result in a revamping of the After Eight concept, without the abandonment of its basic positioning as *the* elegant product for *the* elegant occasion? And would such revamping stop at the brand's advertising, or should it include reviewing the physical properties of the product itself and its packaging, perhaps even its ormolu clock?

There can be no doubt that the management responsible for the future of this brand will ask itself these and many other questions, and one hopes that it will find the right answers to guarantee the continued success of this brilliant product concept. However, if the company wishes to maintain the international character of the brand and its advertising, the Nestlé management will have to insist on strict adherence by all its affiliates to the brand's 'International Marketing Principles' and 'Advertising Guidelines', as originally laid down by the Rowntree management. Since every detail of After Eight advertising is of equal importance, this might well require a control mechanism to guarantee the right treatment of the product in all the countries concerned. Whereas Rowntree tended increasingly to operate in this fashion, it has always been Nestlé's policy to leave considerable freedom to its affiliates in this respect. It will be of great interest to see how the new owners of an old idea will manage to maintain consumer goodwill for this highly successful concept and to what extent they may even succeed in combining new thinking and traditional values to the advantage of a brand that many people like to receive, or give as a present, on a 'special occasion'.

Notes

1. Nestlé, *Annual Report 1988*, p. 18.
2. Rowntree plc's *Annual Report and Accounts 1987*, pp. 10–13 and 43.
3. Nestlé, *Annual Report 1988*, p. 4.
4. Pearce, M. (1970), former Brand Manager of Rowntree plc, *After Eight in the UK*, a report, p. 2.
5. Letter to the author from Mr David Lamb, former Advertising Executive of Rowntree plc, York, UK, 11 May 1990.
6. Bottomley, F. David (1979), former Advertising Executive of Rowntree plc, 'After Eight in the UK', a presentation for Lintas Europe, 18 October, pp. 16–20.

7. Mackintosh, Anthony (1972), former European Marketing Director of Rowntree Mackintosh Limited, 'After Eight in Europe', a presentation to the Advertising Association Conference, London, 4 July, p. 5.
8. *Ibid.*, p. 7.
9. Rowntree, *Annual Report 1987*, p. 11.
10. *Campaign*, 'EC to Tighten Food Claims Law', 23 February 1990.
11. *Daily Telegraph*, 'Peterborough Column', 10 November 1990.

APPLE COMPUTER

'The Power to Be Your Best'

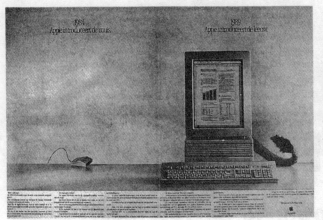

1984
Apple introduceert de muis.

1989
Apple introduceert de leeuw.

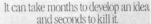

Una buona
presentazione
dovrebbe
lasciare chi
ascolta ad
occhi aperti.
Anche se
finisce tardi.

APPLE COMPUTER CO.

NEWTON... A MIND FOREVER VOYAGING THROUGH STRANGE... ALONE

Apple präsentiert den neuen Macintosh IIcx

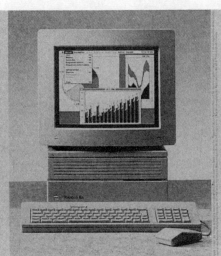

Apple Computer

The power to be your best™

APPLE COMPUTER
'The Power to Be Your Best'

Imagine one of America's best-known head-hunters, 'the ultimate C.E.O. power broker, a head-hunter extraordinaire',[1] trying to convince the president of Pepsi-Cola to give up his job for the top position in a small, relatively unknown computer manufacturing company situated about 30 miles south of San Francisco, in a town called Cupertino, in Silicon Valley (of which the head-hunter in question says, 'Silicon Valley is different from anything else I've ever experienced. It's like Florence must have been in the Renaissance.')[2] The computer company concerned must be a truly exceptional one, and, indeed, its founders claim that its computers are not just examples of a new technology but represent an entirely new approach designed to sharpen our intellects to benefit the future of mankind.

Apple computers – the owners, management and staff of the company maintain and reiterate – will revolutionize the world, one person, one computer, at a time; this will definitely happen, slowly but surely, one person, one computer, at a time . . . In an era of rational, one-track-minded thinking, with a lack of daring initiatives and courageous personal endeavours, such highly idealistic and emotional visions might seem too nebulous and mystical for the tough world of big business. Yet these visionary thoughts, this almost fanatical belief in a mission, are precisely what have made Apple Computer Inc. into a multi-billion dollar company. According to its annual report for 1990, the company's total sales are in the order of $5.6 billion and its net profit is around $475 million.

Considering the fact that this company was only founded in 1976 and thus has achieved its total annual sales figure of $6 billion after just over ten years (it reached the 'Fortune 500 List' more quickly than any other company has ever done), it is not surprising that its success story has made the headlines and inspired journalists and others to write about it.[3] Not all articles are equally complimentary, but life at the top is never easy, and, as Apple's senior executives happen to be extrovert, creative, emotional types, they are an easy prey for journalists.

APPLE'S BASIC PHILOSOPHY

Apple firmly believes that its success is due largely to the vision of its founders and to the business philosophy that it adopted right from the start: it does not sell a piece of complicated machinery that makes considerable technical demands on the user; it offers the public a tool, the handling of which does not require much greater skills than driving a motor car; a tool that enables users to improve their personal development and their contribution to the businesses that they are working for, enhancing their careers and stimulating their intelligence and imagination, giving them the ability to do things that they did not think that they were capable of doing before.

All this sounds idealistic and far-removed from the hard realities of people's personal lives and business concerns. And yet the philosophy makes sense:

We place the individual – not the organization – at the center of the
computing universe.
We believe that an organization can only be as productive as its
individual members, so improving the computer user's experience is at
the center of everything we do.
We build tools specifically designed to increase personal productivity.[4]

That is Apple's message, its statement of its mission, and it is totally different from
the sort of statements that other computer manufacturers make about themselves and
about their products, which are usually loaded with technical jargon and wrapped
up in masses of facts and figures.

[Advertising for computers would normally be considered as falling into the domain
of industrial advertising, but Apple, with its consumer orientation, seems more
likely to fall within the scope of advertising for consumer products.] In fact, this is
only partly true. When all is said and done, even today a computer is still a high-
technology instrument, so, despite Apple's desire to humanize the computer business
and to make its products part of their owners' personal lives, much has to be done
either to overcome people's inborn resistance to change or to convince the users of
other computers of Apple products' superior qualities; particularly since purchasing
these products still requires a substantial outlay of money. In advertising terms,
as well as in other respects, a delicate balance had to be found between purely
rational, intellectual arguments for buying an Apple and emotional overtones
emphasizing how the acquisition of an Apple would enable an employee to become
more than a mere number on his employer's payroll. Before we look at the details
of Apple's advertising policies, let us briefly examine the history of this remarkable
company.

HISTORIC PERSPECTIVES

The Apple Computer Company was established in 1976 by Steve Wozniak, an
ex-employee of Hewlett-Packard, and Steve Jobs, an ex-employee of Atari, who were
soon joined by Mike Markkula from Intel. All three were computer 'wizards' and they
sold their first personal computers, built in the garage of Jobs' parents' home, to
hobbyists and electronics enthusiasts.

Though Mike Markkula had been brought in to help in establishing the new
venture, someone was still needed to look after the business aspects of the company; in February 1977, Michael Scott joined the team and became Apple's first
president. That same year Apple moved to Cupertino and launched its first
advertising campaign, produced by the Regis McKenna advertising agency. In
1978, Apple Computer Inc. became one of the fastest-growing companies in the
USA.

Emphasizing the educational aspects of the computer industry formed an important element of Steve Jobs' 'mission', and in 1979 the company set up the Apple
Education Foundation. Its establishment at such an early date indicated the importance that the firm attached to teaching the younger generation how to use its products, and the Foundation made Apple computers available to any schools wishing
to integrate them into their curricula.

In 1980, Apple became a public company. By this time, it employed 1 000 people
and had the largest distribution network in the industry: 800 independent retailers
in the USA and Canada, plus 1 000 outlets abroad. Events continued to move fast.

In 1981, Chiat Day Advertising took over the Apple advertising account from Regis McKenna, and a European headquarters was opened in France. By then, Apple had 3 000 dealers worldwide and 2 500 employees. An Apple survey showed that public awareness in the USA had risen from 10 per cent to 80 per cent.

In April 1983, John Sculley, formerly the president of Pepsi-Cola, was brought in by Steve Jobs to run the business and became Apple's new president and chief executive officer. The appointment of a marketing man to head a high-technology company heralded a new era.[5] Unfortunately, the initially excellent and fruitful co-operation between Sculley and the brilliant Steve Jobs came to an end in 1986, when Jobs was asked to resign. As so often, having two dominant figures had proved to be impossible.

WHAT'S IN A NAME?

Before we continue with the story of this corporation, a brief word should be said about how it acquired its remarkable name. In a talk with John Sculley, Steve Wozniak recalled how Steve Jobs and he had discussed the setting up of a computer company:

> We were driving along the freeway once and started talking about
> maybe starting a company and he said, 'How about this? Apple
> Computer'. We started tossing names back and forth. I threw out a
> couple. He tried out a couple. It was clear nothing would beat Apple
> Computer for sounding so good.[6]

It not only sounded good, it symbolized, perhaps accidentally, the very personal character of the products that the company was going to produce and sell. The name of the company was later considerably reinforced by the design of the logo, which was produced in 1977 by Rob Janoff, then art-director of the Regis McKenna advertising agency, and is still in use.

Although brand names do not usually need an explanation and often only obtain their value and significance through the medium of advertising, it is intriguing to see the name of an ordinary fruit used for something as far-removed from food as a computer company. Some people felt that the name Apple and its logo were symbols of hope, innovation and pleasure, but Jean-Louis Gassée, a quintessential Frenchman who, until 1989, was a senior vice-president of the company, explained it in a somewhat different manner:

> One of the deep mysteries to me is our logo ... the symbol of lust
> and knowledge, bitten into, all crossed with the colours of the
> rainbow in the wrong order. You couldn't dream of a more
> appropriate logo: lust, knowledge, hope and anarchy ...[7]

Clearly, name and logo fulfil their purpose by leaving it up to each individual to use his or her imagination to apply the intellectual and emotional values represented by the simple shape of the apple, the colours running across it and the bite taken from it to the high-technology product itself. However, such a brilliant name can also have its negative side. For example, if it is not only used to identify the company, but is also given to some of its products, such as the Apple II, yet not to others, such as the

Macintosh, the uninformed consumer could easily get confused about what he is buying from whom. In these circumstances, the only beneficiaries will be Apple's competitors. But, with so many emotional associations attached to the name, it must be extremely difficult for the company's management to decide how much advertising support it wishes to give, respectively, to establishing the company name and to establishing the names of its existing and future products. In any event, the company's sensational and sweeping success during the first decade of its existence, meant that this question was not a top-priority issue at that stage. It is thus more appropriate to take a brief look at how that remarkable success was achieved, especially after the arrival of Apple's new president.

Many factors accounted for the rapid growth of Apple Computer Inc., for example the quality and uniqueness of its product and its distribution network throughout the USA, but the new president used some rather unorthodox methods to market and advertise the still relatively new venture. Some of the steps taken reflect the imaginative, entrepreneurial and almost adventurous way in which the company succeeded in creating considerable awareness of itself and what it stood for, resulting in soaring sales; as illustrated by the following examples:

---

1. In 1983, Apple introduced a new personal computer better than anything available at the time, to be launched under the name of Macintosh (which, incidentally, in the USA, is a variety of apple). The introduction of the 'Mac' was supported by a single sixty-second commercial, which cost $1.6 million to produce and was run only once, in January 1984, at a Super Bowl broadcast, but, because of its phenomenal success, was replayed many times by news and talk shows, and is aptly referred to as the '1984' commercial.[8] The commercial, produced by the Chiat-Day advertising agency, went on to win the Grand Prix at Cannes, as well as 34 other national and international awards.[9] It positioned the new product in a most dramatic way, representing it as a modern tool enabling every individual to break through symbolic walls of indifference and uniformity and to reject the hierarchy of traditional business computers, thereby improving his or her personal contribution to the success of his or her company and establishing his or her self-respect.

2. In further support of the Macintosh launch, in January 1984 Apple inserted a 20-page advertisement in major magazines, setting new records for readership and for recall scores.[10]

3. In November 1984, Apple ran a fold-out advertisement in Newsweek to launch a 'Test Drive a Macintosh' promotion, resulting in 200 000 people taking a Macintosh home for a 24-hour trial.[11]

4. In October 1986, after the company had gone through a bad spell, due to the resignation of Steve Jobs, a sharp fall in sales and the flop of a variant of the '1984' commercial, Apple invited well-known film critics to a press conference at the Plaza Hotel in New York, for a preview of 11 new commercials, with the theme 'The Power to Be Your Best'.[12] The commercials had been produced by the BBDO advertising agency, which had been appointed to represent Apple in the Pacific Region in 1983, in Europe in 1984 and, finally, in the USA in 1986. As the company was in considerable need of a morale boost after two critical years

in its short existence, it took the bold and unusual step of trying to create excitement about several new commercials and so gain free publicity for them.

These four examples reveal the inventive operational methods of the company, which has now fully recovered from its difficulties in 1984 and 1985 and is continuing to set itself extremely ambitious goals for the years to come. Meeting these goals will undoubtedly involve overcoming a number of obstacles; organizational and managerial problems are the inevitable consequences of a formidable growth record. Personalities will sometimes clash, and personal aspirations cannot always be met. However, Apple's main concern will be to continue its momentum at a time when the novelty of the personal computer has started to wear off. With competition growing fiercer by the day, Apple will have to try to exploit the work it has been doing to open up an entirely new era for the communications industry. Even allowing for the excellence of Apple's products, technical innovation is not an exclusive Apple property. It is to be hoped that the company will succeed in keeping its technological edge over its competitors, but more will be needed.

Advertising, whilst it is by no means the only tool for creating demand, will most certainly be one of the tools that will enable Apple Computer Inc. to establish an image of superiority in the minds of consumers. Also, in Europe, with its many different cultures, languages and levels of sophistication in the use of computers and with its current competitive scene, advertising should be able to create the desired uniform image for the company and its products. However, before considering this question in detail, let us first look at how Apple's European operations are organized.

APPLE'S EUROPEAN OPERATION

Although the first Apple was shipped to Europe during 1977, it was only in 1980 that the company started production in Cork, Ireland, with its European headquarters in Paris and a European distribution centre in Zeist, Holland. All three operations today service fully owned Apple subsidiaries in 13 European countries. Continuing growth of Apple's European business will require much larger production facilities in Cork and the removal of the support centre in Zeist to more spacious premises in Apeldoorn, also in the Netherlands.

In 1988, Apple's export markets were divided into three geographical areas, served by distinct operating units, each headed by a division president. Apple USA, Apple Europe and Apple Pacific.

Broadly speaking, about 50 per cent of Apple's European turnover is derived from small businesses, including legal and medical practices; while 25 per cent is accounted for by large businesses, '. . . thanks to a lengthening list of major sales to the continent's largest corporations, including Lufthansa in Germany, Plessey in the United Kingdom, and Volvo in Sweden'[13]; and the final 25 per cent comes from educational establishments (to be discussed later).

Apple Europe accounts for almost 30 per cent of the company's total business and is run from Paris. As is clear from the following organization chart, the president of Apple Europe can seek assistance from a team of people who, between them, are responsible for the business in 12 countries, of which France,

Germany and the UK are the most important. Other responsibilities of Apple's headquarters in Paris include research and development, legal work, finance and, of course, marketing and corporate communications. It is of interest to note that although the advertising function is of such vital importance, the responsibility for corporate communications is devolved to a relatively low level in the hierarchy.

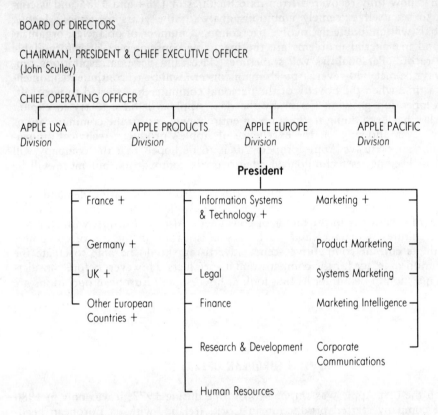

BOARD OF DIRECTORS

CHAIRMAN, PRESIDENT & CHIEF EXECUTIVE OFFICER
(John Sculley)

CHIEF OPERATING OFFICER

| APPLE USA *Division* | APPLE PRODUCTS *Division* | APPLE EUROPE *Division* | APPLE PACIFIC *Division* |

President

France +	Information Systems & Technology +	Marketing +
Germany +		Product Marketing
UK +	Legal	Systems Marketing
Other European Countries +	Finance	Marketing Intelligence
	Research & Development	Corporate Communications
	Human Resources	

+ Preparing subjects for decisions by the complete board, meeting once per month.

Apple Europe is run on the basis of a so-called 'multi-local' policy, as introduced by Michael Spindler, who was, until 1989, head of Apple Europe, but is now the company's chief operating officer at its headquarters in the USA. Spindler says the following on this subject:

> The multi-national format has two drawbacks. . . It means too much jurisdictional influence from corporate headquarters and too much of a nationalist approach. Multi-local means you have a network model that adapts to local markets. You behave and act like a local company, yet you are within the network of the mother company back home. The whole world can thus become one big shopping chart for ideas and capital.[14]

This 'multi-local' policy of loosening central control, of leaving final responsibility for local operations largely in the hands of local managements, would appear to be in line with the company's basic philosophy, centred around every individual person's contribution to the business that he or she serves. Since it says on the cover of Apple's annual report for 1988, 'The individual is at the center of everything we do', it would be something of a contradiction if the company were to lay down hard and fast rules for its marketing and advertising in European countries, instead of expecting its managers in Europe to produce solutions ideally suited to local problems and to the special circumstances of each case.

This policy of relative freedom for Apple's subsidiaries of course also applies to the domain of advertising. As we shall see later, local managements receive from European headquarters in Paris the internationally agreed strategy for the advertising of Apple and its brands, but, when it comes to translating this strategy into action, the affiliates need not follow central recommendations. This important point will be discussed later in some detail, but the advertising strategy and its execution should be reviewed first.

APPLE'S ADVERTISING STRATEGY

Given the company's promotional activities in the mid-1980s, readers might well have the impression that Apple Computer Inc. is an exciting, but perhaps somewhat amateurish, type of company, whose marketing and advertising activities depend more on short-lived publicity stunts than on solid positioning and strategy. Nothing could be more wrong. Despite the sometimes boisterous nature of the operation, the company adheres strictly to a basic philosophy, expressed by its president, John Sculley, as follows: 'Our goal has always been to create the world's friendliest, most understandable, most usable computers – computers that empower the individual.'[15] As far as Europe is concerned, this philosophy has been translated into an overall advertising strategy for Apple Computers, which states that:

> 'Apple is the only brand that makes the power of personal computing accessible to each and everyone, such that they may change the way they work, learn, think and communicate.'[16]

As already explained, the role of Apple's headquarters in Paris is to infuse life into this strategy, in close collaboration with its subsidiaries and with its advertising agency. As has also been pointed out, Apple's management clearly distinguishes between centrally agreed strategy and the local implementation of this strategy; the corporate communications manager in Paris writes as follows:

> The European headquarters of Apple establishes the positioning statement and creative guidelines and on that basis every country develops its own advertising campaign. There are regular meetings between the countries to try and ensure that ads seem to come from the same 'sender'.[17]

EXECUTION OF ADVERTISING STRATEGY

There are, of course, many international companies, some of them discussed in this book, that will allow their subsidiaries considerable freedom in the execution of local advertising; indeed, some will even allow national managements to appoint an advertising agency of their own choice. Apple Computer Inc. does not go that far; it has appointed BBDO as its international advertising agency, to be used everywhere. One of the advantages of this way of operating is that it will ensure full co-operation between the European head-offices of both company and agency, as regards the implementation of agreed policy and the execution of such policy by Apple's subsidiaries, as well as by BBDO's local offices.

Clearly, a procedure such as this makes considerable demands on the managerial skills and advertising experience of all concerned. This is certainly true of the advertising for Apple's products, which is so different in character from the advertising of other brands of computer. The task undertaken by the company and its agency is to explain to its subsidiaries the long-term gains to be expected if advertisements of Apple's products concentrate on appealing to every individual's desire 'to be somebody', instead of trying to compete with other computer manufacturers by using purely technical arguments. Such a task is by no means an easy one, and it is rendered even more difficult if there is only an internationally agreed strategy, without any hard and fast recommendations for its execution. Without proper controls, creative advertising minds can easily run wild, or else the value of a unique strategy may be watered down as a result of day-to-day sales pressures. From an advertising point of view, and in spite of the company's general policy of decentralization, Apple might well consider exerting more control over the way in which its emotional advertising message is presented to the European public, particularly in view of the highly competitive nature of the European market. This is not so much for the sake of standardizing the advertisements themselves, even though that could save considerable amounts of money, as to ensure, above all, that one uniform image of Apple and its products is presented throughout Europe. If the best available creative talent from BBDO offices throughout the world were concentrated on producing the highest quality advertising for use in all European countries, and if that bane of all international advertising, the 'Not Invented Here' syndrome, could be overcome, Apple's objectives might be achieved more simply and speedily. As a result, Mr Spindler's 'multi-local' policy might well become a little more 'multi' and a little less 'local'!

THE ROLE OF APPLE'S INTERNATIONAL ADVERTISING AGENCY

The agency is fully aware of these complexities in the execution of Apple's advertising but also appreciates its responsibilities towards its client and towards consumers. Consequently, it has compiled an elaborate presentation (which has already provided some of the quotations cited in this chapter) for its own offices and for the company's subsidiaries.

Apple's 'mission' to put man above systems and structures and help him to optimize his personal creativity and imagination must, in an advertising context, be expressed through a combination of rational and emotional arguments. In BBDO's presentation, all this is explained in great detail, and clever use is made of what is called 'The BBDO Buying Cycle'. This provides a model of the thoughts that pass through the minds of potential consumers at various stages in the buying process, emphasizing considerations such as the need to overcome indifference, to create awareness, and to eliminate intimidation barriers, making people sufficiently interested and confident to try out or purchase the product. It also points out that, once the product has been bought, an initial 'honeymoon period' is followed by a period of waning pleasure, after which the consumer begins to look around again for other offerings. Apple's subsidiaries and BBDO offices are taken through this presentation to make them fully aware of the complexities of this particular advertising problem, but central influence goes no further than that. The Apple and BBDO affiliates take the final decision regarding the way in which they will spend the total European advertising budget of approximately $15 million; while media selection is also a local responsibility.

ADVERTISING APPLE'S MAC

Much has been said in this chapter about the unusual character of Apple's advertising, which does not concentrate on any of the product's technical innovations, but tries to convey an impression of the results that one can achieve with an Apple or a Macintosh. A passage quoted earlier is again of relevance: 'We build tools, specifically designed to increase personal creativity'.[18] To elaborate briefly on this point, just imagine looking at a commercial showing an elderly gentleman and his son sitting in the back of a car and driving past what clearly are the old man's factories. 'One day', the elderly gentleman says, 'all this will be yours – the factories – the machinery – but remember, when taking decisions you will be alone – don't count on all those others working for you – they are there to carry out orders, not to think for themselves – if they did, they would want to change things – which is not within their competency – never forget that everything depends on you.' The voice-over says, 'There are different ways to run a business. This is one. Fortunately there are others.' The commercial finishes by showing the Apple logo.

Another commercial, referred to as 'The Nightmare' and so far shown only in France, portrays a modern company president, a 'tycoon', in his executive office. When he presses a button to summon his secretary, she does not appear. Irritated by the silence around him, he presses all the different buttons on his telephone, but still nothing happens, nobody answers. In desperation, he gets up and walks through the other offices; nobody is there, the building is totally deserted. Yet it is a normal day of the week. The man is now shown back in his office, sitting in his chair and waking up. Unsure that he has just been dreaming, he again presses the button; his secretary responds immediately. He takes a deep breath, and seems reassured, but seems also to understand that if he does not change his thinking pattern, this nightmare could one day become a reality. The voice-over says, 'Those who still believe that a company's worth depends solely on machines, will come to realize sooner or later that its worth also depends on human beings. Apple had this in mind when it created Macintosh.'

It is not my intention to explain the advertising discussed in each chapter of this book; it should speak for itself. However, in this chapter I am making an exception, and, having read the previous paragraphs, readers will understand why. The commercials described here presuppose perfect understanding of their message on the part of Apple's staff and complete acceptance of Apple's basic business philosophy and advertising strategy. They also required sound advertising judgement and considerable courage on the part of the managements that decided to run them.

Naturally, the commercials are only part of the total media-mix. They serve to overcome any indifference on the part of their viewers and to make them understand that an Apple can do something for them. But more is needed to clinch a sale. Direct marketing, for example, fulfils an important function for a product of this nature, which requires so much explanation. Thus, Apple's subsidiaries have to pay much attention to using the right media at various stages in the 'BBDO Buying Cycle' for computers, as well as to the important area of after-sales service.

The advertising for Apple and its products is as unusual as the entire approach of the company to the production and selling of its products, making high demands upon all involved at the various company and advertising agency levels.

APPLE AND EDUCATION

We have already touched on the importance to Apple, as a computer company, of becoming closely involved in matters concerning education, but some further discussion of this subject is appropriate. Probably as a logical consequence and continuation of Apple's basic policy to change people's attitudes to themselves and the world, the company has always been a pioneer in education; hence its policy of introducing computers to schools, universities, scientific institutes, research establishments etc., enabling young people to become acquainted with the unlimited opportunities that the computer can offer for widening horizons and discovering and developing untapped skills.

Worldwide, Apple Computer Inc. has over two million of its products installed in primary and middle schools; Apple's Macintosh can be found on more than 3 000 college and university campuses, and millions of dollars are being contributed in the form of direct grants and computer equipment to the educational community as a whole. This is a formidable programme, and it is most regrettable that it has proved difficult to introduce it to Europe. The reason is that, in most European countries, education at main school level is the responsibility of governments, which will usually give preference to local manufacturers when computer equipment and the like has to be acquired.

1993 AND BEYOND

Discussions about the future with Apple staff are quite different from discussions on the same subject with staff from other companies simply because, since it was founded, the Apple company has done little else than talk about the future of personal computers and how these will change mankind and the world at large. For Apple's staff, the future is not a distinct subject in its own right, it is the very basis of Apple's philosophies and business objectives. The company is constantly adapting itself to new circumstances, changing from week to week, from day to day. Consequently, it would be rather futile to try to set out how Apple expects its business to develop. New generations of computers will come and go, new managers will come and go, new organizational structures will come and go; but the company, which now employs more than 14 000 people, will still merely want to be the most innovative, the most creative, and, above all, the most successful, of all computer companies in the world.

One can only hope that Steve Jobs' vision will not turn out to have been too optimistic. Will the day really come when every individual possesses a personal computer, just as so many individuals now own a telephone? The company's 1990 Annual Report says on its cover, 'Our goal is to put Macintosh computers in the hands of as many people as possible,' indicating that the company's objectives have indeed become a little less ambitious than in previous years.

In fact, Apple's president, John Sculley, whilst still committed to the company's original 'mission', as described earlier in this chapter, now realizes that, 'It's dangerous to have a company defined by religion without a little pragmatism'. The company has therefore set itself a new target: to introduce, as soon as possible, a low-cost Macintosh, and a micro computer the size of a pocket calculator.[19]

Nonetheless, Sculley does not easily relinquish his visionary long-term plans. In one of his provocative statements, he has said: 'A future generation Macintosh, which we should have early in the twenty-first century, might well be a wonderful fantasy machine called the Knowledge Navigator, a discoverer of worlds, a tool as galvanizing as the printing press.'[20]

Notes

1. Sculley, John, and Byrne, A. (1988), *Odyssey, Pepsi to Apple*. Glasgow: William Collins, p. 89.
2. *Ibid.*, p. 531.
3. Freiberger, Paul, and Swaine, M. (1984), *Fire in the Valley*. Berkeley, CA: Osborne/McGraw-Hill; Moritz, Michael (1984), *The Little Kingdom, The Private Story of Apple Computer*. New York: William Morrow.
4. *1988 Annual Report*, Apple Computer Inc., Cupertino, CA, p. 5.
5. *Corporate Timeline* (1988), Apple Computer Inc., Cupertino, CA, 1976–1983.
6. Sculley and Byrne, p. 198.
7. *Ibid.*, p. 380.
8. *Corporate Timeline*, p. 6.
9. Sculley and Byrne, p. 248.
10. *Corporate Timeline*, p. 6.
11. *Ibid.*, p. 7.
12. *Ibid.*, p. 10.
13. *1989 Annual Report*, Apple Computer Inc., Cupertino, CA, p. 4.
14. Sculley and Byrne, p. 442.
15. Apple Computer, *1988 Annual Report*, inside cover.
16. Gilson, Peter (1990), 'Directions for the 1990's', a presentation of strategies for Apple Europe, prepared for BBDO, Paris, February.
17. Written reply from Ms Helen Goossens to questions from the author, Paris, 3 March 1989.
18. Apple Computer, *1988 Annual Report*, p. 5.
19. Schlender, Brenton R. (1990), 'Yet another strategy for Apple', *Fortune*, 22 October.
20. Sculley and Byrne, p. 540.

UNILEVER'S 'CAPTAIN' RANGE OF FROZEN PRODUCTS

Captain Birds Eye
Captain Findus
Captain Iglo

UNILEVER'S 'CAPTAIN' RANGE OF FROZEN PRODUCTS
Captain Birds Eye
Captain Findus
Captain Iglo

In June 1971, the following obituary appeared in one of the personal columns of *The Times* in London:

Birds Eye, Captain – On June 7th, after long exposure, life just slipped through his fingers. Celebrity and gourmet. Mourned by Sea-Cook Jim and the Commodore, in recognition of his selfless devotion to the nutritional needs of the nation's children.

To some it may have come as a surprise that Captain Birds Eye, a fictitious character invented by the Unilever company in the UK to advertise the fish products in its Birds Eye frozen foods range, who was only 'born' in 1967, could have done so much in the four years of his life, for 'the nutritional needs of the nation's children'. Perhaps even more remarkable, though, was the fact that, after such a successful career, his creators had decided to let him quietly pass away. However, his spirit continued to haunt them and, only a few years later, the Captain rose from his grave and has been 'alive and kicking' ever since in a number of European countries, more recently even in Japan.

UNILEVER AND ITS 'CAPTAIN'

The products to which the name 'Captain Birds Eye' has been attached are successful and profitable, so Unilever can be justly proud of the way that the Captain is being presented to the public and of his contribution to Unilever's financial results. Indeed, the concept of using someone who is portrayed as a universally accepted authority on life at sea to recommend a range of fish products to consumers is one of those brilliant ideas that emerge all too rarely, but often result in a remarkable degree of commercial success. Of course, Unilever can boast a number of similar ideas, thereby apparently contradicting the view that large conglomerates – which are often perceived as over-organized, slow and impersonal – can hardly ever produce anything original and creative. In fact, the development of successful ideas has little to do with an organization's size; they are usually the result of good thinking, hard work and a bit of luck on the part of a small group of people, irrespective of whether those people are employed by a big or a small business.

Nonetheless, as Unilever does happen to be one of the largest companies in the world selling mass consumer goods and is also quite a complex organization, it might be helpful to the readers of this book to summarize briefly how it is structured and managed, with special reference to the way in which the 'Captain' range of frozen products fits into the overall operation.

Unilever was founded in 1930, when a group of Dutch margarine businesses combined with a group of English soap businesses to form one concern, consisting of two parent companies: Unilever N.V., based in Holland, and Unilever PLC, based in the UK. This Unilever concern now employs some 304000 people and, in 1990, achieved a total turnover of Dfl.72 billion. The structure and organization of the upper echelons of the company are as follows:

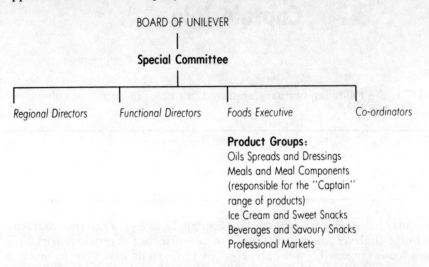

BOARD OF UNILEVER

Special Committee

Regional Directors   Functional Directors   Foods Executive   Co-ordinators

Product Groups:
Oils Spreads and Dressings
Meals and Meal Components
(responsible for the "Captain"
range of products)
Ice Cream and Sweet Snacks
Beverages and Savoury Snacks
Professional Markets

The eighteen members of the boards of Unilever N.V. and Unilever PLC include a chief executive, known as the 'Special Committee', comprising the chairmen of the two parent companies and a third senior director, who, together, have overall responsibility for the entire Unilever business. Reporting to the Special Committee are a number of regional directors and functional directors, as well as several product co-ordinators. The regional directors carry varying responsibilities for allocated parts of the world, while the functional directors look after the various services, such as accounting, finance, corporate development, personnel, research, etc., and the co-ordinators are responsible for the many different product categories, such as detergents, personal products and chemicals. Unilever's food interests are now united in a separate group.

UNILEVER'S FOODS EXECUTIVE

Until the 1990s, Unilever's food business comprised three separate Foods Co-ordinations – (a) edible fats and dairy products; (b) frozen products; and (c) food and drinks – together accounting for approximately 50 per cent of Unilever's total business. However, opportunities for further growth, with existing and new products that are convenient, healthy and appetizing, are of such magnitude that in 1990 this structure was no longer considered to be adequate and sufficiently attuned to new product strategies and growth in many markets, particularly overseas. Unilever therefore decided that it needed one central organization, providing the opportunity for coherent strategic focus, according to region and product, making the best use of all available resources and enabling rapid transfer of product and of technology.

The three Foods Co-ordinations mentioned earlier have, therefore, in the course of 1990, been replaced by one 'Foods Executive', consisting of three members of the Unilever board, who will, between them, carry profit responsibility for Unilever's food business in Europe and the USA and will work closely with overseas regional directors to develop food business overseas. Members of the Foods Executive will individually have responsibility for profit in a certain region, but, collectively, they will all have responsibility for developing worldwide foods business.

To support the Foods Executive in the implementation of its strategy, five product groups have been established, each headed by a senior executive who will report directly to the chairman of the Foods Executive.[1] These group executives also carry responsibility for the advertising of the group's products, but decisions about advertising agency alignment are reserved to the Foods Executive. The group executives will provide the regions with specialist support, which will include support in the field of advertising, thereby continuing a function that has always existed in Unilever's product co-ordinations.

FROZEN PRODUCTS

As already mentioned, of a total Unilever turnover of Dfl.72 billion in 1990, products coming under the responsibility of the Foods Executive accounted for Dfl.35 billion, of which frozen foods and ice creams have produced Dfl.9 billion. Of this Dfl.9 billion turnover, the 'Captain' range of frozen products represents an important share, mainly derived from Europe, but more recently also from Japan.

In Europe, the products previously handled by the Frozen Products Co-ordinations are exclusively marketed by companies that specialize in the production and distribution of goods that lend themselves to deep-freeze treatment, such as fish products, pizzas, vegetables, ready-made meals, soups, meat products, snacks, and, of course, ice creams, in many different varieties.

Not all of these products are based upon international positioning or an international marketing strategy; some have a purely local character, and the Foods Executive will therefore not consider them as having a high priority from the point of view of international co-ordination. It is, of course, a different matter when a product, or a range of products, introduced in a number of countries either simultaneously or over a longer period of time, is concerned. The fish products discussed here had already been on the market in the UK for some time, when, in 1967, the 'Captain' idea was introduced. In the mid-1980s this range of products also became available in a number of European countries, thereby qualifying for the full attention of the co-ordinating body.

CAN FOODS BE INTERNATIONALIZED?

Before dealing with the 'Captain' and his products, the general question of the internationalizing of the marketing and advertising of food products should first be discussed briefly. It is a somewhat controversial issue, but a very important one, particularly in the light of the growing internationalization of marketing and advertising. Clearly it is hard to generalize, but many experts on internationalization will automatically reject it for foods; tastes, cultures and habits differ so much between nations that international uniformity of such products would only rarely seem feasible; or, as Mr Ronald Beatson, director-general of the European Association of Advertising Agencies, put it:

> The Belgians drink beer, lots of it, but they do not like English beer.
> They do not like the temperature of English beer, and they do not like
> the taste of English beer. The French not only dislike the taste of
> English beer, they also dislike the look of English beer . . . If you
> want to sell a glass of beer to the French, at least a third of it must
> be a foaming head: la mousse.[2]

Accepting that, in some instances, it may be extremely difficult to internationalize food products, Unilever has certainly been successful in establishing the 'Captain' products in a number of markets, so it should be of interest to those involved in international operations of this kind to analyse Unilever's policy and its execution in some detail.

INTERNATIONALIZING THE CAPTAIN

Leaving questions of production, sales and distribution aside, and looking at the 'Captain' products from a consumer point of view only, it would seem that there are a number of factors relevant to the process of internationalization – such as: (a) formulation; (b) name; (c) packaging; and (d) positioning – in addition to actual advertising.

Formulation

Unlike a product such as Colgate Dental Cream, to be discussed elsewhere in this book, with a uniform composition and flavour worldwide, the 'Captain' products are carefully adapted to the different tastes of the various countries in which they are sold. It is argued that as long as the product's basic positioning can be maintained and as long as the product fulfils consumers' expectations, based upon its advertising, the composition of the product need not be exactly the same everywhere. Naturally, the main ingredients of each of the 'Captain' products are, to a large extent, similar in every country, fish being the most important, but adaptations are also made in order to optimize the chances of local acceptance.

Name

One would expect it to be an absolute prerequisite for a product to have the same name everywhere if the label 'international' is to be attached to it. However, this is not necessarily so; but, before discussing this further, here is a list, showing in which European countries the 'Captain' products are being marketed, by which companies and under which names:

Country	Name of company	Name of range
Austria	Eskimo-Iglo GmbH	Captain Iglo
Belgium	Iglo-Ola S.A.	Captain Iglo
France	Cogesal S.A.	Captain Iglo
Germany	Langnese-Iglo GmbH	Captain Iglo

34

UNILEVER'S 'CAPTAIN' RANGE OF FROZEN PRODUCTS

Ireland	Birds Eye HB Ltd	Captain Birds Eye
Italy	Sagit SpA	Captain Findus
Netherlands	Iglo-Ola B.V.	Captain Iglo
Portugal	Iglo Industrial de Gelados	Captain Iglo
Spain	Frigo S.A.	Captain Iglo
United Kingdom	Birds Eye Wall's Ltd	Captain Birds Eye

Interestingly enough, the name Iglo has been registered in all European countries, but different names are used in the UK, Ireland and Italy. The reasons for these decisions need not be discussed here; Unilever's Foods Executive does not seem to attach great significance to them. In its opinion, as long as the concept, and the presentation of the concept, are practically identical everywhere, it is not essential to have the same brand names everywhere. The executive believes that consumers will not identify the Captain with a particular name, but rather with their notion of what a captain personifies and should look like; hence Captain Birds Eye in the UK and in Ireland, Captain Findus in Italy and Captain Iglo everywhere else will all be seen as archetypal seafaring fatherly figures, ensuring a uniform international image.

In this belief, Unilever's Foods Executive is not alone. Unilever's Detergents Co-ordination has among its many brands an extremely successful fabric softener, sold under many different names, but always using the identical symbol of a teddy-bear. The then chairman of the Detergents Co-ordination addressed an international conference on the subject of 'Global Brands but Local Consumers' and made the following statement regarding the use of brand names:

> I have left out of this discussion the question of the brand name. There is no doubt that it is easier if your brand name is Sony, or Levi's, or Marlboro. But this is not always possible. We have many brands that have global names. Lux Toilet Soap for instance. But in some cases the brand name varies from country to country . . . We developed in Germany in 1968, in response to Procter & Gamble's domination of the market with a brand called Lenor, a fabric softener which had two things going for it: it was cheaper and it put over the idea of softening via the brand name and the image of the teddy bear on the pack. The brand when we launched it nationally was called Kuschelweich, which means 'cuddly soft'. The brand did pretty well and it moved next into France, where it was called Cajoline, which has similar connotations in the French language to Kuschelweich in German, and there the teddy bear moved from the pack into the advertising. We then launched in Italy, where it was called Coccolino, and in Spain (Mimosin) and in the US, where it is called Snuggle, and it is now sold in more than 20 countries around the world, including Japan . . . It is a highly successful *international brand*, clearly identically branded, and in no two markets do we use the same brand name.[3]

Symbols such as a teddy-bear can, indeed, play an important role in branding a product. In 1990, Mr Howard Belton, then marketing member of the Detergents Co-ordination, wrote: 'A very good use of a symbol is Shell – if the brand name were a translation of the word "shell" in each language I suggest that the integrity of the brand would be maintained.'[4]

Whilst one cannot but accept the logic of these arguments, it is also interesting to learn that if Unilever's Detergents Co-ordination had been free to use one brand name everywhere, it would certainly have done so. One assumes that growing international cross-border communication would have been an important consideration in this respect.

Packaging

What has been said earlier about the importance of symbols is certainly reflected in the packaging of the 'Captain' products throughout Europe. As we shall see later, a wide range of products, which differs from country to country, is sold under the unifying name 'Captain'. Although the packaging of these products is not the same everywhere, the packs display two identical elements: (a) a picture of a smiling captain looking through a porthole; and (b) a picture of the product and a description of it – the captain, in this case, being the product's symbol and providing the connecting link in various markets.

Perhaps, before long, the remaining elements of the packaging, such as its overall lay-out and colour scheme, will also become identical, in order to support the international operation as much as possible. However, when all is said and done, probably the most important factors in any international operation are the positioning of the brand in the consumers' minds and how such positioning is expressed in terms of advertising.

Positioning

Within the frozen foods category, fish products, and particularly fish fingers, have always made an important financial contribution to the Unilever companies marketing them. Fish fingers are considered by the Birds Eye company in the UK, which created the product, as being primarily intended for families with small children. Fish fingers are healthy and nutritious, and their positioning has therefore always been based on emphasizing that they are a natural seafood with an excellent taste, that is easy to prepare and especially favoured by mothers, who want only the best for their children.

INTERNATIONAL BRAND OR INTERNATIONAL CONCEPT?

Having discussed how Unilever successfully introduced a food product on an international scale, one final question remains on the subject of internationalizing the marketing and advertising of any product, food or otherwise: could some of the controversies or misunderstandings perhaps be avoided by referring in the appropriate cases to international 'concepts', rather than to international 'brands'? Although the question may seem a little theoretical, Mr H. Eggerstedt, a member of the board of Unilever, and, until recently, the frozen products co-ordinator, is of the opinion that, strictly speaking, the Captain is not an international brand, but an international concept:

Coca-Cola, Marlboro, Lux Toilet Soap, are international brands – they have the same name, the same packaging and the same advertising everywhere – our 'Captain' products have practically uniform advertising everywhere, but they do not have the same name and the same packaging everywhere. However, they are based on the same concept and I would therefore not call them international brands, but see them as part of an international concept.[5]

It is an interesting distinction, to which we shall return in our chapter on Lux Toilet Soap, a truly international brand. Suffice it to say here that, to Unilever, the most important aspect of this issue appears to be that consumers throughout Europe, indeed, throughout the entire world, should be able to identify themselves equally well with a product, irrespective of its name and presentation, and should recognize it as a product with the same intrinsic quality, offering similar benefits and fulfilling similar promises everywhere.

We have looked at the name, packaging and positioning of the 'Captain' products, but how does the Foods Executive deal with the international aspects of implementing agreed strategies?

PROTECTING THE CAPTAIN'S IMAGE

Understandably, the implementation of agreed strategies for the marketing and advertising of the 'Captain' products is one of the main concerns and top priorities of both the Foods Executive and of Lintas, the international advertising agency handling this brand. The precious concept, described in previous paragraphs, must be protected carefully, one of the most crucial considerations being the need to include under the Captain's recommendation only those products that fully conform with this concept and will be seen to do so by consumers. The point is an important one, because there is always the risk that the popularity and strength of the idea might be watered down by the inclusion of products that have little to do with the original concept; the credibility of the Captain's recommendation could easily be stretched too far.

Again, one must beware of generalizations, and much depends upon awareness of the Captain, his reputation and the advertising devoted to him in any one country. In the UK, for example, where he has been in existence for a long time, his prestige and authority can encompass a wide range of products that – although they are invariably fish products – might not normally be recommended by a sailor or a seaman. In the other European countries, the assortments will vary, but, as in the UK, the 'Captain' range will only include fish products.

Apart from acting as a guardian ensuring the suitability of the range of products covered by the Captain's recommendation, the Foods Executive is, of course, just as closely involved in the actual presentation of this range through advertising.

ADVERTISING THE CAPTAIN

In view of mounting pressures on its dominant share of the fish-finger market, mainly from supermarkets' own-brand fish fingers, Birds Eye decided in 1966 that a new advertising campaign was needed that would also offer the sales force promotional opportunities. Lintas was briefed accordingly.

The creative team developed the 'Captain Birds Eye' concept, which was 'quite unlike anything they'd had before',[6] and therefore not immediately received with great enthusiasm. However, making a sea-captain, with his accepted authority on the subject of seafood, recommend a range of fish products, was as ingenious as it proved to be effective. The advertising presentation of the ideas, using the popularity of a sea-captain among children, with their love of adventure, could reinforce the positioning of the product as a whole. The outcome might then be an exclusive marketing and advertising property that, one could assume, would be equally well received and effective in many markets throughout the world.

When the 'Captain' idea was tested together with three other approaches, it won only narrowly. However, when it was discovered that an important competitor was about to use a similar idea, the first four commercials were swiftly produced, with a carefully selected British actor taking the role of the Captain. The commercials appeared on television in February 1967, and the success of the new campaign was instantaneous. Though it was briefly abandoned between 1971 and 1974, the campaign is still maintaining its impact and effectiveness in a number of markets, with the same actor still portraying the Captain in his inimitable way. In fact, although children had previously never really liked fish, the fish-finger concept and the popularity of the Captain, have helped to make it more acceptable to them. Admittedly, for a long time, Continental countries had serious misgivings as to whether the values that the typically British Captain stood for would be acceptable elsewhere. Indeed, Unilever's affiliates in other countries paid little attention to the success of the first advertising campaign in the UK, and it was not until central co-ordination had persuaded those on the Continent to study the idea of the Captain seriously that the other companies gradually took it up. Today, the very Western-looking Captain has become totally accepted even in Japan.

THE ROLE OF THE INTERNATIONAL ADVERTISING AGENCY

When international brands have been unusually successful, as in the cases of Marlboro, Coca-Cola and Lux Toilet Soap, it is interesting to note that their advertising is often handled by one international agency and its offices in the countries concerned. For example, Lux Toilet Soap is handled by J. Walter Thompson, Marlboro by Leo Burnett, Martini by McCann, and Unilever's 'Captain' Products by Lintas, all on a worldwide basis.

Although there are multinational companies that hold the view that no international agency is perfect everywhere and that their local subsidiaries should select the agencies that best meet their requirements, there is considerable evidence to suggest that close co-operation, at all national and international levels, between the advertiser and one international advertising agency will produce a combination of formidable strength. The success in the market-place of the brands just mentioned provides cogent confirmation of this point of view.

One of the main reasons for the one-agency alignment practised by the companies mentioned earlier is the possibility that it provides a way of concentrating the best creative talent available anywhere in the world on finding an optimal solution for a given problem, thereby benefiting the company's operations in all the countries involved. Another advantage lies in the economies of scale that can be achieved, for example by shooting one top-quality commercial to be used everywhere. The cost of producing first-class commercials is soaring and few national subsidiaries can now afford to mount them on their own. However, most experts will agree that quality is of paramount importance. The one-agency approach is only possible if intensive consultation and co-operation take place right from the initial planning stages until the job has been finished. And, as always, the details count. We shall be discussing them in the paragraphs that follow.

CO-ORDINATING THE CAPTAIN'S ADVERTISING

For the benefit of the Lintas agencies handling the 'Captain' account in their respective countries, the creative director of Lintas International, who has been personally involved in the production of this campaign at all stages, developed video-taped guidelines in which he explains in great detail the criteria for adapting the centrally produced 'Captain' commercials to local circumstances. He insists that the Captain's voice, which has to be dubbed into many different languages, should always have a serious, authoritative, low-pitched intonation, making his recommendations sound pleasant and credible to both mothers and their children. The voices of the children in the commercials, the use of music, the packshots, the final editing – all are factors that can make the difference between a good and a poor adaptation, and the guidelines contain all the advice necessary to achieve the right result. However, mutual consultation between advertiser and agency begins earlier than this. To ensure optimum efficiency in the shooting of the many different scenes in each commercial, it is important for the producers to know in advance what each country's special requirements are going to be. The Captain, his ship, the location, the children and the music are evidently fixed elements in any 'Captain' commercial, but the emphasis on one scene or another, and, of course, the packshots, can be planned and, if necessary, modified, in accordance with the wishes of the local company.

LEGAL RESTRICTIONS

There are often a number of voluntary or legal restrictions in any particular country regarding the use or depiction of children in advertising, especially on television. In order to avoid problems at an advanced stage in production, when changes would be very costly, subsidiaries in the countries concerned must be consulted in advance about what is, and what is not, permissible. Examples of what this means and how it can affect the work of the advertising agency are as follows:

Austria	Children have to be accompanied on the set by a parent or other person authorized to supervise them; children are not allowed to make any advertising statements or handle the product in any way, except to eat it; children are not allowed to have any advertising on their clothes; no adult is allowed to address children with advertising statements.
France	The child is not allowed to promote a product but may be shown in a commercial or film actually consuming a product.
Netherlands	Children can be used more actively, provided that they are accompanied on the set by adults.
Portugal	Children can be used more actively when the product is directly related to them.

This all shows the importance of having a close working relationship between the company, and all its affiliates in European countries, and the advertising agency, with its offices in the same countries. This co-operation is not restricted to the production of commercials; clearly it also applies to all other forms of advertising produced in any one country, including newspaper or magazine advertisements, point-of-scale displays, consumer promotions etc. Considering the total volume of work executed and co-ordinated throughout Europe, the international advertising agency can make a significant contribution to the success of such multinational operations and will, in varying degrees, share the responsibility with the manufacturer of acting as custodians of the property that they have either created themselves, or that has been entrusted to them.

THE CAPTAIN AND HIS COMPETITORS

The range of products sold under the 'Captain' name is the undisputed market-leader in its field throughout the world. This is principally due to the quality of the products themselves, which is always of prime concern, but also to their wide availability and, of course, to their advertising. It does not mean, however, that there is not serious competition: Nestlé and the D.O.B.s (distributors' own brands) are important, and, in years to come, their significance may well increase; nor does competition stop there. Just as a gift of flowers for a dinner hostess is considered to be serious competition by the makers of After Eight, so too the makers of the 'Captain' products are concerned by the popularity of baked beans.

1993 AND BEYOND

As has been explained in this chapter, the formation of a Foods Executive has been one of the steps that Unilever has taken in order to be well prepared for the years ahead, particularly as regards optimizing its exploitation of existing and new opportunities in the very important area of foods. There are a number of countries inside and outside Europe where this successful range of fish products has not yet been introduced, but where it may well be introduced in the future. The 'Captain' as a marketing and advertising idea would appear to offer almost unlimited opportunities for further development of its successful formula: Captain – ship – children – fun – good food, expressed in such an entertaining, lively and colourful way that the sales-pitch seems quite natural. What is extraordinary is that the producers of this advertising idea have succeeded in developing it in such a truly international way that the very British character of the Captain is not seen as British in other countries; in France he is seen as a Frenchman, in the eyes of the Germans he is a German, in Holland he is a typical Dutchman. It is not surprising, then, that in Unilever and in Lintas circles there is no discussion about how long the Captain will survive; he is simply immortal!

Notes

1. *Unilever Magazine* (London) (1990), 'A new recipe for the future,' 3(77), pp. 37–9.
2. Beatson, Ronald (1990), 'EC Regulations/Product Category Bans in Europe', a presentation at the Annual General Meeting of the Danish Advertising Agency Association, Copenhagen, 1 February.
3. Dowdall, Mike (1989), 'Global Brands but Local Consumers', a presentation at the 'Wide Open World' conference, Manila, 23–28 October.
4. Personal letter from Howard Belton to the author, London, 12 March 1990.

5. Personal discussion with H. Eggerstedt, then Unilever's Frozen Products Co-ordinator, Rotterdam, 28 February 1990.
6. Spicer, Bernard (1989), *The Origin of Captain Birds Eye*, an outline, London, 10 October.

CLUB MÉDITERRANÉE

'Happiness Is Our Business'

CLUB MÉDITERRANÉE
'Happiness Is Our Business'

For many people visiting a Club Méditerranée holiday resort it must be quite an experience to be greeted on arrival by someone who is not referred to as the manager, or the chef de réception, or the hotel's hostess, but who is known by staff and guests alike as a 'Gentil Organisateur', or G.O. for short. This G.O. will, in turn, not talk about 'guests', but about 'Gentils Membres', G.M.s – and visitors will soon find out that the G.O.s are versatile and capable people, international in outlook, professionals in their various fields of sports, organization or management, always helpful and friendly, always there when needed, full of energy and spirit. There are more than 8000 G.O.s., with an average age of 28 representing more than 65 different nationalities and specializing in various aspects of the running of the Club, such as management, entertainment, sports, tours, housekeeping, child care etc. Some are graduates who do this job for a couple of seasons, others make a career of it and can become managers in the Club Mediterranée organization and its resorts.[1]

The G.O. is one of the unique features of the Club; the 'village', of which the Club runs around 100 in about 35 countries on five continents, is another. Ideally situated in beautiful natural surroundings, each village accommodates between 600 and 1500 G.M.s and forms . . . a world in itself: 'where everything is readily available and within easy reach: restaurants, boutiques, bars, theatres, nightclubs, excursions . . . tennis . . . golf . . . watersports . . .'[2]

These two unique features are the main reasons for the success of the Club Méditerranée. The Club itself is often referred to simply as the 'Club Med', and it is to be hoped that people realize that the two Clubs are one and the same. Officially, there is a Club Méditerranée S.A. for Europe, Africa and South America, and a Club Med Inc. for North America and Asia, but the company likes to be referred to universally as the Club Med, and one wonders why it risks confusion by having different names in different parts of the world.

THE BEGINNING

The company began its existence in 1950, when Gérard Blitz established the Club Med at Alcudia, on the northern shores of Mallorca, receiving 2300 visitors in that particular year.[3] Blitz, who died in March 1990, was born in Antwerp in 1912. He was a diamond-cutter until the outbreak of the Second World War, when he joined the resistance movement, subsequently receiving several decorations. After the war, his dissatisfaction with the enclosed nature of Western society and his dream of creating havens where people could establish human contacts free from social barriers amidst wide horizons and under sunlit skies led him to start the Club Med on a non-profit basis. He strongly believed that by encouraging people from all over the world to vacation together and mix in a relaxed fashion, he could help to increase the happiness of future generations.[4] Happiness became his business, and the formula proved so attractive and successful that, after forty years of unabated zeal, the Club Med became one of the world's largest operators of holiday resorts.

Or, as Blitz once put it himself, 'Le Club Med est aux vacances ce que Frigidaire est au réfrigérateur et Kodak à la photographie'.[5]

To return to the early days of the organization's existence, in 1954 Gilbert Trigano joined the Club, adding his particular business abilities to the special qualities of the founder, who, as we have seen, was an idealist and a philosopher, but who had little financial expertise. In 1957, the Club was made into a limited company, and in 1961 Edmond de Rothschild became its major shareholder. Village resorts were founded in Morocco and in the French West Indies, and in the 1970s the Club took over, or acquired shares in, other ventures in the same field of business. In addition, it also entered an increasing number of markets and in 1980 it opened its first US village, at Copper Mountain in Colorado.

In 1982, it was decided to decentralize the company into major geographical zones. The business continued to grow and expand, and between 1989 and 1990 the Club's total revenue rose to Frs. 8.2 billion, with group earnings at Frs. 395 million. The Club employed around 25 000 people, looking after 1 226 000 Club members, giving an occupancy figure of more than nine million hotel days.[6]

THE PRESENT

As has already been mentioned, one of the most important features of the Club Med is the 'village', which initially provided somewhat primitive tent-style accommodation in huts with bamboo walls and thatched roofs, which were entirely in line with Gérald Blitz's original concept of what the Club Med should be. Telephones and television were taboo. Much later, the villages developed into communities offering everything a holiday-maker could wish for and accommodating their G.M.s in pleasant bungalows with all the facilities of a house. In addition to the traditional dinner tables for eight, designed to encourage people to get together at meal times, tables for two and for four were introduced.

All expenses are usually included in the cost of a stay at the Club Med, except those for certain extras, such as excursions, drinks at the bar and purchases of non-essential items. In accordance with the original concept of the Club, money is not allowed to change hands, so payment for these extras is made using the Club's own currency, consisting of a necklace of coloured beads that the G.M.s pay for at the end of their stay. To modernize the system, the necklace is gradually being replaced by a kind of credit card, but the principle of settling all these expenses on departure remains the same.

NEW DEVELOPMENTS

Two recent developments designed to create a modern image for the Club and upgrade its reputation among a wider audience deserve attention. The first concerns a new village that was opened in June 1990 in Opio, near Grasse, in the South of France. It caters especially for those who want to combine leisure with study or business in pleasant surroundings, and for those who run seminars and conferences or wish to attend them. Equipped with cable-television, personal computers, telex and fax, the Opio village offers the Club Med's renowned package of services, in beautiful surroundings and in the right kind of luxurious environment, to a clientele that will consist of traditional vacationers, business executives and those engaged in study.

The other development concerns the launch of a 'floating village' aboard a new sailing ship. This vessel is the largest of its kind in the world, with 200 cabins and all modern facilities, swimming pools, bars and restaurants, and is called, appropriately, the 'Club Med I'. It cruises in the Mediterranean during the summer and in the Caribbean during the winter.

THE CLUB MED'S TOTAL ACTIVITIES

Apart from the villages, which form the heart of the Club Med's activities, the company also runs around 12 traditional hotels, which it prefers to call 'villas', because they offer the same hospitality as the villages and also have small teams of G.O.s. However, its diversification has proceeded further. Since January 1986, The Club Med has run The City Club in Vienna, which covers more than 22 acres and offers a contrast to conventional life in the city in the form of tennis courts, a tropical lagoon, a health and fitness centre, etc. This establishment has 450 bedrooms and ranks as a five-star hotel. Through financial participation in other ventures in the same general field of business, the Club Med has become involved in the time-share real-estate market and also has a place in the leisure-rentals market. Finally, the Club Med is one of Europe's leading tour-operators. Nonetheless, the Club's main source of income remains its villages, accounting for approximately 90 per cent of total sales.

THE COST OF PLEASURE

The price of a vacation at one of the Club Med's resorts may seem higher than average. For example, a one-week cruise on the new Club Med I in the Mediterranean, will cost at least Frs.10 000 per person, excluding flights. Similarly, spending one week in the new, luxurious Opio village in the South of France will cost anything between Frs.5 000 and Frs.7 000 per person. So a stay at the Club Med could never be described as a low-cost 'special deal' holiday. However, what is important is the fact that the price is all-inclusive, and the Club Med appears to be living up to its reputation for providing good value for money.

LOCATIONS

Naturally, climate is one of the key factors in deciding on a location for a holiday resort, so the French West Indies and the Bahamas, as well as the southern European countries, were obvious choices for the Club. However, Club villages have been established in more than 30 countries all over the globe, and provide a total of approximately 90 000 beds. The countries where Club Med villages can be found are listed overleaf.[7] Interestingly, the list does not include countries such as Germany, Holland, Belgium or the Scandinavian nations, or, for that matter, Argentina, generally because of their climatic conditions. Nevertheless, the coverage is impressive.

Bahamas	Indonesia	Portugal
Bermuda	Israel	Saint Lucia
Brazil	Italy	Senegal
Bulgaria	Ivory Coast	Spain
Dominican Republic	Japan	Switzerland
Egypt	Malaysia	Thailand
France	Maldives	Tunisia
French Polynesia	Mauritius	Turkey
French West Indies	Mexico	Turks and Caicos Islands
Greece	Morocco	United States
Haiti	New Caledonia	Yugoslavia

THE 'GENTILS MEMBRES'

As one would expect, about 35 per cent of all visitors to the various villages are French nationals. The Club Med is, after all, and in spite of its international presence, still very much a French operation. In addition, most of the management in Paris is French, though the G.O.s do, of course, speak other languages and so assist communications between the various nationalities residing at the villages. This is essential, because more than 25 per cent of visitors are from European countries other than France; about another 20 per cent are from the USA, and the remaining 20 per cent from other parts of the world.[8]

Over the years, the characteristics of the Club Med's membership have altered significantly. In the past, the Club and its members were regarded as rather frivolous. In fact, the Club was considered to be the ideal place for amorous encounters, with the sunshine, the beaches and the wonderfully relaxed atmosphere giving it a 'sun-and-sex' image. Gilbert Trigano and his son Serge, together with their colleagues on the Club's board, realized that if they wanted to attract a different clientele and capture a share of the very important and increasingly popular all-inclusive holiday market, the positioning of the Club Med had to be redefined. Thus, over the last five years, the management has tried to upgrade the Club's image, whilst maintaining the basic formula of relaxed holidays in perfect surroundings, providing excellent food and first-class service. The opening of the Opio village and the launch of the cruise ship Club Med I have helped considerably in the achievement of this objective.

ORGANIZATION

The board and general management of the Club Med have their offices in Paris. As mentioned earlier, there is also a Club Méditerranée S.A. with offices in Paris, responsible for Europe, Africa and South America, accounting for 64 per cent of the Club Med's total turnover of Frs.8 billion. In addition, there is a Club Med Inc., with offices in New York and Tokyo, which attends to North America, the Caribbean, Asia, the South Pacific and the Indian Ocean and which accounts for the remaining 36 per cent of the Club's business. A simplified organization chart looks as follows:

CLUB MÉDITERRANÉE GROUP

CLUB MÉDITERRANÉE S.A.	CLUB MED INC.
International Office, with its head office in Paris: Overall Strategy, Finance, Administration, Computerization, Human Resources, Real Estate, etc.	Head office in New York City
Villages and villas in:	**Villages and villas in**
Zone Europe & Africa (Paris)	Zone North and Central America (New York)
Zone South America (Rio de Janeiro)	Zone Asia and Pacific & Indian Oceans (Tokyo)

Interests in other ventures.

Although the Club Med decided in 1982 to decentralize its operations into the four zones shown above, 'certain operations, however, remain centralized in Paris: the general definition of Club strategy and its human relations, financial, real-estate and computerization policies'.[9]

It is interesting to note that advertising is not mentioned as one of these central functions, although, in practice, the central office in Paris is very much involved in advertising for the Club Med in Europe, to which we shall refer later. Gilbert Trigano is the président directeur général and chairman of the two companies; his son Serge is the chief executive officer and is responsible, among other things, for the various staff functions at headquarters, as shown on the organization chart. The general management of the Group consists of twelve people while the board of directors also comprises twelve people, and a further eleven people act as advisors to the board.

HOW TO BUY THE 'PRODUCT'

Those who would like to visit any of the Club's villages or enjoy other Club Med facilities have to start by becoming members of the Club for a nominal entrance-fee. The club has sales offices in 39 countries, but one can also make a booking through any of the 33 000 travel agencies that are directly linked to the Club Med computer system.

IS CLUB MED AN INTERNATIONAL ADVERTISER?

The Club Med is a French company, selling probably the most international, indeed the most global, 'product' of all the companies discussed in this book: happiness. Yet, in spite of its uniqueness, the concept of this global product has not yet been translated into a form of expression that is consistent in terms of both content and presentation, to be used everywhere in the world. In Paris, where central responsibilities include the Club Med's worldwide strategy, which also covers communications, the management has decided that 'happiness' should be its universal basic promise everywhere, but that its local offices should be entitled to express this basic theme in accordance with local preferences.

Mr Gilbert Trigano explains as follows:

> While the same unique image is promoted everywhere in the world, Club Med carefully tailors its advertising campaigns to local markets. French holiday-makers respond to 'La plus belle idée depuis l'invention du bonheur', while Americans are drawn to 'The antidote for civilization', and vacationers from south-east Asia find 'Absolute Paradise' irresistible.[10]

One cannot help feeling that it should not be too difficult to find a single way of expressing this unique theme that is acceptable to everyone everywhere. This would not only help to obtain the financial advantages of economies of scale, but would also enable the best available creative talent to concentrate on finding a global expression for the unique property that would have the desired impact on consumers everywhere. As we shall see later, the company has already achieved much greater uniformity in most of its advertising in Europe, so it will probably not be too long before the Club's advertising covers wider areas in a uniform manner. Until then, though the Club Med is certainly an international operator, selling a most unusual international product, it will not be a genuinely global advertiser.

CLUB MED'S COMMUNICATIONS STRATEGY

Before discussing how the Club Med's basic promise of happiness could best be presented in terms of an advertising campaign, let us review its advertising strategy, which could be formulated as follows:

> Club Med makes available to vacationers from all over the world a selection of different holiday resorts, situated in attractive surroundings with pleasant climates, offering a wide variety of activities and entertainment to its visitors of all ages, under the leadership of an enthusiastic management, responsible for the well-being of its guests and rigorously maintaining the highest quality of comfort, food and service.

CLUB MED'S INTERNATIONAL ADVERTISING EXECUTION

Club Med's total communications budget is close to Frs.400 million per annum, representing about 5 per cent of the Club Med's total revenue; of this budget approximately 40 per cent will be spent in Europe. Here, as already mentioned, the management is seriously endeavouring to develop uniform advertising for use throughout the continent. The French advertising agency Roux Séguéla Cayzac Goudard (RSCG) is responsible for creating commercials and posters to be used in France, Italy and a number of other European countries, all conveying the basic message of happiness. The poster advertising portrays relaxed and happy holiday-makers and always uses a similar pay-off: 'Le bonheur . . . si je veux'; 'Happiness . . . as I like it'; 'Felicità . . . come ti va'; or 'Das Glück . . . zu tun oder lassen'.

The Club Med's policy of leaving much of the responsibility for local advertising to its offices in the countries concerned, is gradually changing to a more centralized approach, and, as a consequence, RSCG handles the Club Med account in most European countries. Indeed, this advertising agency appears to be well on the way to becoming the internationally aligned agency for all Club Med advertising. Apart from the more conventional media, selected by the national offices of the company, Club Med uses another very important medium that is elusive and abstract, but extremely effective, in both positive and negative terms. The advertising business is sometimes inclined to underestimate its significance, but there are certain types of product that depend on it very heavily for their success in the market-place. It is sometimes referred to as 'word-of-mouth' advertising and in the case of the Club Med it undoubtedly makes a greater contribution to the success of the total operation than could ever be measured statistically.

1993 AND BEYOND

In 1988, the Club Med celebrated its 40th anniversary and it still appears to be going from strength to strength. Its special formula has been remarkably successful and, as the amount of leisure time in people's lives is increasing dramatically, there is no reason to believe that this success will not continue. When I asked to which three main factors the management of the Club Med attributed these remarkable results, I was not surprised to find that the originality of the Club Med concept and its execution came first. This was immediately followed by the quality of the Club's human resources, which is also understandable, since the reputation of the Club clearly depends crucially on the professionalism, the involvement and the enthusiasm of the people running it, particularly those responsible for the villages. Finally, the management also feels that its worldwide strategy is also an important factor contributing to the success of its business. This is probably true, but to the consuming public, strategies as such do not mean much. People are more affected by what they actually see or hear in the press or on television, in other words by the way in which the strategy is presented. At the moment the presentation of the Club Med's strategy can differ widely from continent to continent. Although the Club Med management is considering this point carefully, it has not yet actually decided to introduce a uniform scheme for the worldwide presentation of its strategy. The main criterion determining when such a scheme can be introduced is that markets around the world should be equally mature and should share the same attitudes towards matters such as holidays and leisure.

In other respects, the management is extremely alert to any new developments. The Club Med will continue to expand its range of villages, villas, 'city clubs' and cruise ships, whenever it sees an opportunity to do so. In addition, according to a Dutch newspaper, since the collapse of the communist regimes in Eastern Europe, the Club has taken over the running of a holiday centre near Varna in Bulgaria in co-operation with a local organization and also plans new villages or villas in Central Europe.[11]

That the management of the Club is not resting on its laurels is also apparent from its continuing efforts to perfect the facilities of its existing establishments and the services that it offers. In 1986, it drew up a ten point 'Quality Charter', laying down the duties of the G.O.s in each village. In addition, it distributes questionnaires among its visiting members, asking them which aspects of the Club and its facilities and services have given them particular satisfaction or dissatisfaction. About 200 000 of such questionnaires are returned to Paris every year, providing valuable tips and recommendations.

As far as advertising is concerned, the Club Med will probably eventually join the core of advertisers who run truly global advertising campaigns, for example by showing mostly non-verbal television commercials throughout the world and making use of satellites to do so effectively and efficiently. This is particularly feasible for the Club, because the industry to which it belongs has the good fortune of not being hampered by legal or voluntary controls or restrictions in the advertising of its product.

The future of the Club Med looks highly promising, and Gilbert Trigano may well have been right when he said that future generations would look at the villages of the Club Med as 'des ateliers de vie'.[12] In any case, provided that the Club Med successfully and continuously adapts Gérard Blitz's formula to meet new conditions and new expectations on the part of increasingly critical and demanding consumers, it will live up to the promise of its founder to provide a little happiness for the many people in search of relaxation and relief from their everyday personal and professional responsibilities.

Notes

1. *Happiness Is Our Business* (undated), a brochure published by the Club Méditerranée, Paris, p. 13.
2. *Ibid.*, p. 4.
3. *Ibid.*, pp. 32–3.
4. Ranganath Nayak, P., and Ketteringham, J. M. (1987), *12 Idées de génie auxquelles personne ne croyait* (Twelve Brilliant Ideas in Which Nobody Believed), Chapter 2: 'Club Méditerranée: Des Rêveurs qui savent compter' (Club Méditerranée: Dreamers who know how to count). Paris: Editions First, p. 48.
5. *Ibid.*, p. 48.
6. *Annual Report 1989–90*, Club Méditerranée, Paris, 29 April 1991, p. 24.
7. *Annual Report 1988–89*, Club Méditerranée, Paris, p. 27.
8. *Ibid.*, pp. 31–41.
9. *Happiness Is Our Business*, p. 26.
10. *Annual Report 1987–88*, Club Méditerranée, Paris, p. 5.
11. *Het Parool* (Amsterdam), 'Club Med in "party-dorp" ' (Club Med in party-village), 26 May 1990.
12. Nayak and Ketteringham, p. 54.

COLGATE
TOOTHPASTE

'World Leader in Oral Care'

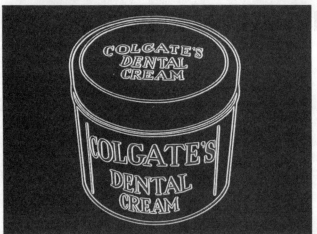

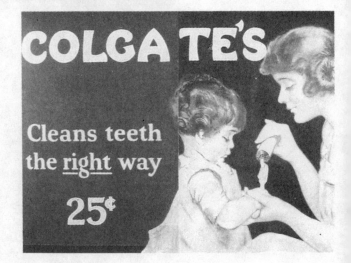

COLGATE TOOTHPASTE
'World Leader in Oral Care'

It is difficult to say if it is an advantage or a disadvantage for a company to be named after two worldwide brands, but, in any case, the Colgate-Palmolive Company combines the name of the world's top-selling toothpaste, with a market share of more than 40 per cent, with that of a toilet soap that also comes very close to being the world wide market-leader in its field. In 1990, the company's total turnover was just under $5.7 billion, of which the USA accounted for 33 per cent and Europe for 34 per cent, the remaining 33 per cent coming from the Western Hemisphere, the Far East and Africa. During the same year, the company's operating profit was $584 million, or 10.3 per cent of the net value of its sales. Colgate-Palmolive has operations in 65 countries and employs close to 25 000 people. In 1990, the company's five 'core' product categories, and their relative importance in terms of percentages of turnover were as follows:[1]

ORAL CARE (Colgate dental products)	21 per cent
BODY CARE (Palmolive toilet soap, etc.)	18 per cent
HOUSEHOLD SURFACE CARE (Ajax, Fabuloso, etc.)	19 per cent
FABRIC CARE (Fab, Dynamo, etc.)	23 per cent
DIETARY CARE (Hill's Pet Products, etc.)	12 per cent

Before we discuss Colgate Toothpaste in detail, we should first review the history and background of what originally started as a soap manufacturing business.

AN HISTORIC PERSPECTIVE

The Colgate-Palmolive Company started as a genuine family business, or rather as a combination of three family businesses, belonging to the Colgates, the Johnstons and the three Peet brothers. The history of the Colgate element goes back to 1806, when a 23-year-old Englishman called William Colgate, who had arrived from England only three years earlier, started a starch, soap and candles business at 6, Dutch Street in New York. He named it the Colgate Company, and was both its president and its only employee! Between 1806 and 1928, when the Colgate Company merged with what was then the Palmolive-Peet Company, the firm remained in the hands of the Colgate family, with control passing from William to his son Samuel in 1857. Samuel ran the business until he died, in 1897, when control of the company passed into the hands of his five sons, in those days sometimes referred to as the 'most famous quintet in American business'. Richard, the eldest of the five, became president of the company and when he died, in 1919, his brother Gilbert took over, to be replaced by another brother, Sidney, in 1925. It was Sidney who began the first systematic programme of advertising and who, in 1928, signed the merger deal with the Palmolive-Peet Company, an important soap manufacturing business. This had been founded only one year earlier, on 1 January 1927, as a partnership between the Palmolive Company and Peet Brothers. The Palmolive Company itself had started as the B. J. Johnston Soap Company, but it had changed its name to the Palmolive Company because of the great success of its toilet soap, Palmolive. The three Peet Brothers had been running a laundry-soap business, and it had been felt to be a logical step for them to merge with a maker of toilet soap.

In 1930, after the death of Colgate's fifth president, Sidney Colgate, S. Bayard Colgate became president of the new combine, but it was not until 1953 that the present name of the company was adopted. By that time the presidency of the company was no longer in the hands of the Colgate family and the fascinating story of an era in which the leadership of the business had been passed on from generation to generation had come to an end.[2]

AND WHAT ABOUT TOOTHPASTE?

Remarkably little is known about the reasons why those highly successful soap manufacturers the Colgates also started to produce toothpaste. However, it was not until 1873 (when the company's founder, William Colgate, had already died) that the first aromatic Colgate toothpaste, then sold in jars, was launched. Perhaps the link between toilet soap and toothpaste is furnished by the importance that the founders of the business always attached to bodily cleanliness. This was once expressed by Sidney Colgate, a consummate marketing man, as follows: 'We exist not for the purpose of selling this or that kind of soap, but for the purpose of keeping people and their houses clean, healthy, comfortable and attractive'.[3] It could be the company's motto even today!

COLGATE-PALMOLIVE'S ORGANIZATION

The company has an interesting organizational structure, combining horizontal and vertical responsibilities in a most effective manner. The president and chief executive officer and the chief operating officer share between them line-responsibilities for five regions, covering the entire world, each region being accountable for its own financial results. In addition, there are, at the same level, five so-called 'Global Business Development Groups' (G.B.D.G.s), responsible for developing and controlling worldwide policies for the major product categories of the concern, oral care, household care, fabric care, body care and animal dietary care products. As already indicated, these five groups form the company's core business and in each of them the following basic strategies are pursued: (a) the development of new products within the individual group itself; (b) the application of aggressive global marketing to all the group's operations; (c) the making of strategic acquisitions to strengthen the company's global presence; and (d) geographical expansion, Eastern Europe being one of the latest examples of a region offering the company new and exciting opportunities.[4]

In support of these important regional and global responsibilities, there are a number of staff functions, placed under one Vice-President who also reports to the chief operating officer. This Vice-President has responsibilities for worldwide sales, marketing effectiveness (to be discussed later) and certain advertising functions, such as corporate media and corporate design. The organization can be simplified into the following chart form:

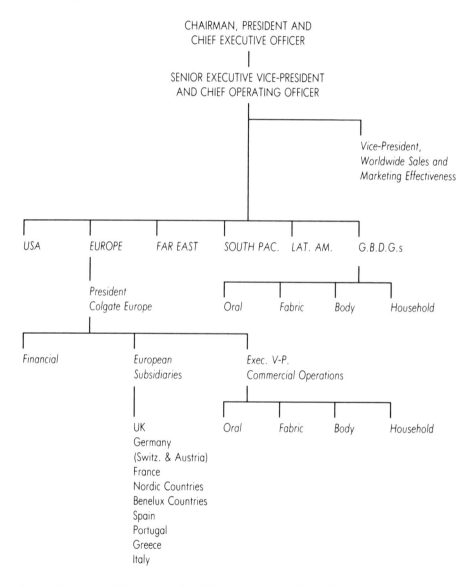

It may be noticed that the animal dietary care products have not yet been integrated into a fifth Global Business Development Group; because of the channels of distribution, this group is run on a separate basis.

It is also interesting to note that horizontal and vertical responsibilities appear to work very well together, and the chief operating officer's help as an arbitrator in conflicts between regional presidents and the Global Business Development Groups, be they at headquarter or regional levels, is only rarely enlisted. This is certainly a compliment to all involved in the complexities of internal procedures and communications. These require much experience and goodwill at all levels, as well as tolerance and patience. But, above all, they require leadership and managerial abilities from those at the top.

'INTERNATIONAL' OR 'GLOBAL'?

The word 'global' frequently appears in this chapter, not only to describe certain functions but because it is also often used in the annual reports and other official publications of the company. Although one sometimes wonders if those employing the word 'global' have not succumbed to the advertising profession's rather gimmicky use of the term to describe what are really international operations, there can be no doubt that Colgate is fully justified in describing its operations as 'global'. Its core products are indeed global in the sense that their names, packaging and basic positioning are virtually identical all over the world. There are not many brands for which such a claim can be made, but Colgate, Martini, Marlboro and Lux Toilet Soap, all of which are discussed in this book, are among them.

THE ADVERTISING FUNCTION

There is no doubt that, like many other manufacturers of mass consumer goods, Colgate-Palmolive puts advertising among its first priorities.

William Colgate started advertising his soap in newspapers back in 1817, but it was Sidney Colgate who, in the 1920s, raised the company's advertising to a higher professional level. He also introduced the slogan 'Truth in advertising implies honesty in manufacture', not a bad slogan by any standards at any time![5] Now that approximately 10 per cent of the value of the company's net sales is spent on media advertising alone and another 12 per cent on sales promotional activities, it is not surprising that the top management devotes much thought and time to the subject. This is also apparent from the company's business principles, philosophies and ethics with regard to its employees, its shareholders, governments, and, of course, consumers. As regards the latter, the company says:

> Since our business is consumer products, our success depends upon consumer satisfaction, trust and goodwill. . . . Consumer needs are constantly changing. So we must continually listen to what people want and use our creativity to satisfy these changing needs. . . .
> One of the most important aspects of our business is advertising our products. Advertising should be creative and competitive but at the same time honest and not misleading. . . .
> Advertising creates more than a product image. It creates our reputation for reliability, dependability and trustworthiness.[6]

COLGATE'S TOOTHPASTE

Calling this product simply a toothpaste rather undervalues its importance and standing in the world of dental care and hygiene; the company therefore prefers to speak of its oral care product category, which has top priority. As we saw earlier, toothpaste production started in 1873, when Colgate launched an aromatic dental cream in jars. This was followed in 1896 by the introduction of collapsible tubes similar to those in use today. Only in the early 1980s did a new type of packaging emerge, in the form of a pump, which rapidly gained popularity in large parts of the world.

THE PRODUCT

Unlike other toothpastes, often sold on their cosmetic appeal, Colgate has largely been advertised on the basis of its health enhancing qualities, supported by medical evidence. As far back as 1896, cartons holding the first collapsible tin tubes carried an endorsement from Professor Henry Leffman of the Pennsylvania College of Dental Surgery, stating that he had found the toothpaste a 'pleasant and agreeable stimulation for the teeth and gums', and also that it gave 'an agreeable fragrance to the breath'.[7] This testimonial from a professor of dental medicine carried sufficient weight to make the toothpaste become more and more successful.

Thanks to continuous development of the product, its packaging and its advertising, Colgate Ribbon Dental Cream was to grow in popularity among adults and children. Later, the flat orifice producing a ribbon of toothpaste was replaced by a round orifice, allowing more toothpaste to be put on the tooth-brush so that more active ingredients would come into contact with the teeth. However, the real breakthrough occurred in the USA after the Second World War, when young men returning from the armed forces brought the habit of proper dental care home with them. Toothpaste became a mass consumption phenomenon, with many competitors trying to get their share of this new and vastly expanding market. Toward the end of the 1950s, ammoniated and chlorophyll toothpastes became temporary fads. Competition became really fierce in 1960, when Procter & Gamble introduced Crest with fluoride, receiving the Seal of Approval of the American Dental Association. To exacerbate the situation, a new brand – Maclean – appeared on the market, using cosmetic appeal to gain a competitive advantage, though it was later successfully challenged by Colgate-Palmolive with its product called Ultra Brite. However, in the late 1960s Colgate succeeded in obtaining official recognition for its monofluorophosphate (MFP) formula, which, in clinical tests, proved to give better protection against decay than Crest.[8]

After its introduction, in 1984, of a new pack in the form of a pump, which rapidly gained popularity, as well as of a very successful gel intended to extend its product line, also in the mid-1980s, Colgate obtained important medical support for its new Tartar Control Formula, specially formulated to help fight tartar build-up on teeth. The product received the American Dental Association Seal for Tartar Control and was launched in the UK in 1986; while by the end of 1988 it was in use in 41 countries, including the USA.[9]

Finally, in 1989, the company launched its Colgate Gum Protection Formula (GPF), combining a proven plaque-fighter with long-lasting protection and now marketed in 25 countries with more to follow. In the same year Colgate was the world's best-selling toothpaste with a global share of the toothpaste market of 42 per cent.[10]

COLGATE'S ADVERTISING

When past Colgate toothpaste advertising is reviewed, it should be remembered that until the late 1920s print advertising was practically the only available means of communicating with consumers. Radio became a medium in the 1930s, whilst television advertising only became popular in the 1940s.

Colgate was introduced throughout Europe in 1920 and became well known for its 'strip' advertisements, emphasizing its efficacy at combating bad breath with the words, 'Nobody makes a pass at *me*. . . . . . .'; but after the 1950s Colgate concentrated its advertising on television, using health claims as its main selling point, with fresh breath as a subsidiary promise. For example:

1950	'Colgate Ribbon Dental Cream stops tooth-decay best, it cleans your breath and cleans your teeth.'
1953	'Just one brushing with Colgate Dental Cream removes up to 85 per cent of decay- and odour-causing bacteria.'
1955	'New Colgate contains Gardol, an invisible protecting shield, giving surest protection all day long; Colgate cleans your breath while it cleans your teeth.'
1957	'Colgate Dental Cream with Gardol gives an invisible protective shield; just one brushing brushes bad breath away.'
1963	'Colgate with Fluoride shows in a university-supervised test that it is a leader in reducing cavities and it stops bad breath.'

It is interesting to observe how, at this date and during the subsequent launches of new products in the 1980s, the company has sought to maintain its strong market position by constantly improving the medical properties of its product. Following on from Gardol, the MFP Fluoride Formula, the Tartar Control Formula or the latest Gum Protection Formula, there will always be new developments to keep the momentum going. In an indirect way, the strong advertising for these new Colgate products will also support other Colgate products, such as Colgate Regular, Colgate Junior, the Colgate mouthwash, the Colgate tooth-brush, Colgate dental floss or the Colgate pump, which may receive less advertising coverage or none at all.

COMMUNICATION BUDGETS

According to the company's 1988 annual report, total marketing and selling expenses are in the order of $1.2 billion per annum.[11] Of this expenditure, approximately $1 billion is spent on advertising and promotions, covering both consumers and the trade; 40 per cent of this $1 billion being devoted to media advertising and 60 per cent to promotional activities.

In view of the importance of trade promotions, the company has formed a 'Worldwide Marketing Effectiveness Group', which reports directly to the chief operating officer at headquarters in New York. Its task is to liaise closely with all the subsidiaries to help them to obtain better returns on their trade-promotion spending. The subsidiaries are responsible for choosing which advertising media they use, but, because choice of media is a crucial aspect of the company's overall advertising policy, the vice-president, worldwide sales, also has a corporate media function. His task is to oversee the quality of the media strategy development and planning at the subsidiary level and, in doing so, he works closely with the offices of the company and the relevant advertising agencies in various countries.

It is interesting to note that the vice-president, worldwide sales, also has corporate responsibility for the package designs of the company's products; most package design is done in-house, but major projects are handled by outside consultants. The company often uses Landor Associates, now a subsidiary of Young & Rubicam.

COLGATE-PALMOLIVE'S ADVERTISING AGENCIES

The company follows a strict agency alignment policy, to which all subsidiaries have to adhere. Young & Rubicam is the aligned agency for Palmolive in Europe and for Colgate globally, except in Latin America; Foot, Cone & Belding is the aligned agency for Palmolive globally, except in Europe, for Colgate in Latin America and for Ajax globally. The appointment of an advertising agency is the final responsibility of the chief operating officer, who reaches his decision after consultation with the leader of the GBDG concerned and the Colgate-Palmolive managements in the most important countries taking part in a given project.

The case for adopting an agency-alignment policy is particularly strong when the advertising concerned is for a product such as Colgate toothpaste, with the same name, packaging, formulation, flavour and – most importantly – basic promise to consumers, all over the world. When the advertising for a toothpaste is based upon an endorsement of the American Dental Association, the expression of its basic promise and the formulation of the toothpaste itself will have to be the same everywhere, because such an endorsement is given for one clearly specified formula and one equally precisely agreed description and text. In these circumstances, the aligned advertising agency also fulfils an important role as the custodian of the brand and of the way in which it is presented to the public.

THE 'BUNDLE'

Colgate-Palmolive operates on the basis of the lead-country system, which means that advertising intended for use on an international scale will be developed and created in one country, with collaboration between the subsidiary, the advertising agency concerned and the global business development leader. When final agreement on the advertising has been reached, the details will be sent as a 'bundle' to all countries involved. Such a bundle will usually include: (a) the product formulation; (b) details of the form and design of the packaging; (c) a positioning statement, which will include the advertising strategy; (d) the media strategy; (e) a professional support package, such as the endorsement of an official medical authority; and (f) recommendations for any public relations activity. For example, in the case of the new Colgate Tartar Control Formula, the lead-country selected was the UK, the international advertising agency was Young & Rubicam and the bundle was subsequently shipped all over the world, including to the USA. The 'Wall I' commercial introducing the Tartar Control Formula was included, to be dubbed by each country into its own language.

Whether in the lead-country or an adopting country, the 15 per cent commission arrangement will apply, subject to the agency concerned making a contribution of 0.5 per cent to advertising research to be carried out in each country. This contribution is held by the local agency and paid out for advertising development research after consultation with their local client. It is an interesting system and one that deserves special attention.

COLGATE'S ADVERTISING RESEARCH

As those involved in international operations of this kind will know from experience, a problem frequently encountered when conducting research on an international scale is that figures from various countries cannot always be compared, as methods for collecting them often differ greatly from one country to another. To overcome this problem, Colgate appointed an ad-hoc committee, consisting of: (a) company research and marketing directors from six subsidiaries around the world; (b) several corporate research staff from headquarters; and (c) account management and research people from both the national and international levels of the two aligned agencies. This gave a most interesting combination of advertising practitioners and research specialists. The brief was to develop 'Advertising Research Guidelines', to be used by subsidiaries and their advertising agencies in all countries where research on a given project would have to be carried out. The drawing up of these guidelines has helped considerably in overcoming the problems mentioned at the start of this section.[12]

LEGAL RESTRICTIONS

In other chapters much attention has to be given to the problems for advertisers that arise from government controls on the advertising for certain products, which can often take the form of severe restrictions. Toothpaste manufacturers find themselves in the enviable position of not being unduly hampered by such controls (apart from those relating to comparative advertising). Consequently, Colgate-Palmolive leaves the defence of its interests in this respect to its national and international trade associations.

1993 AND BEYOND

As we have seen, the company is ready for the introduction of the Single European Market by 1 January 1993. In particular, it has established a pan-European group, as shown on the organization chart. This operates from Brussels, and it is interesting to note that the president of Colgate Europe is responsible both for its national company managements and for the European Business Development Groups, the latter reporting back on an informal basis to the leaders of the G.B.D.G.s in New York. This way of operating underlines the importance that the concern attaches to the acceptance and implementation of agreed global strategies for their core products, at all levels.

The chairman, and president and chief executive officer, of the company must have had these developments in mind when he made the following statement: 'For the first time in nearly two decades, our energies and resources are now focused solely on our global consumer products business.'[13] In its 1989 annual report, the company develops this point further. It explains its leadership advantage in the rapidly changing global consumer products industry, by listing a number of key characteristics, such as: (a) its competitive advantage because of its understanding of the consumer; (b) its commitment to what it calls 'total' quality; (c) its technological leadership; (d) its decision to focus its resources on areas in which the company is the market-leader or has a major presence with powerful global brands; (e) its global business growth, and its view of the entire world as Colgate's market-place; and (f) its acceptance that its staff constitutes Colgate's most important resource, forming a multinational pool of talent.[14] Indeed, few firms appear to have reached as advanced a stage in their international operations as Colgate-Palmolive has.

In an advertising context too, the success achieved in the market-place by using two aligned advertising agencies for most Colgate-Palmolive products would seem to confirm the efficiency and effectiveness of marketing a genuinely 'global' brand in this manner. As a past vice-president of the company has said: 'Enormous savings can be made on production, packaging and advertising by producing one product based on one formulation.'[15]

As senior executives of the parent company not only oversee package designs and media strategies but are directly responsible for the appointment of the aligned advertising agencies and for the development of the international advertising campaigns, the influence of the centre of the company on all communications must be one of the reasons for the company's continuing success.

William Colgate would indeed have been proud if he could have witnessed the fantastic development of what had, for four generations, been no more than a small family business. After all, the firm that he founded is now one of the most prestigious and successful consumer products companies in the world, with an understandable pride in its achievements. In its 1990 Annual Report the Chairman's statement says:

I cannot stress enough the contributions of our 25 000 people around the world. . . . They have made Colgate a better company today than it has been in the past. . . . Indeed, all of us enter 1991 with a sense of excitement about Colgate and its prospects. On a global basis we are optimistic about our ability to continue our upward momentum.[16]

Notes

1. *1990 Annual Report*, Colgate-Palmolive Company, New York.
2. Hardin, Shields T. (1959), *The Colgate Story*. New York: Vantage Press, pp. 47–75.
3. *Ibid.*, p. 47.
4. *Colgate in the '90s . . . Accelerating Our Global Growth* (1990), Annual Meeting and First Quarter Report, Colgate-Palmolive Company, New York.
5. Hardin, p. 70.
6. *Code of Conduct: Partnership in Principles* (undated), Colgate-Palmolive Company, New York, p. 14f.
7. Meehan, Connie (1981), 'Birth of a toothpaste,' *Marketing Communications*, October, pp. 28–30.
8. *Ibid.*
9. *1988 Annual Report*, Colgate-Palmolive Company, New York, p. 7.
10. Colgate-Palmolive, *1989 Annual Report*, pp. 5 and 7.
11. Colgate-Palmolive, *1988 Annual Report*, p. 19.
12. Personal discussion with Clay Timon, past Vice-President for Worldwide Advertising of the Colgate-Palmolive Company, London, 16 November 1989.
13. 'Chairman's Statement', by Reuben Mark, Chairman, President and Chief Executive Officer, Colgate-Palmolive *1988 Annual Report*, p. 3.
14. Colgate-Palmolive, *1989 Annual Report*, p. 16f.
15. *Adformatie* (Amsterdam), 'Totalitaire marketing Colgate-Palmolive,' 18 January 1990.
16. Colgate-Palmolive *1989 Annual Report*, p. 3.

KLM

ROYAL DUTCH AIRLINE
'The Reliable Airline'

"I always thought I knew
the heights of comfort."

"Until KLM raised them again."

KLM
ROYAL DUTCH AIRLINE
'The Reliable Airline'

'When travelling, think of blue,' said Toon Woltman, then director of KLM Holland, proudly referring to the prominence of this colour in all the visual devices currently used to distinguish Holland's successful airline.[1] The colour blue has played an important part in the history of KLM, and has become an increasingly significant factor in establishing KLM's identity around the world. Recalling blue skies with their white clouds so often depicted in masterpieces by famous Dutch painters, it now helps to give KLM a unique and memorable image, being used for the decoration of the company's planes and their interior furnishings, for the uniforms of the cabin staff and, of course, in KLM's advertising. Nonetheless, choosing colours was not Albert Plesman's main concern when, on 7 October 1919, this proud and sturdy Dutchman founded the 'Royal Airline for Holland and Colonies', as it was then called, which was to become the first regular airline in the world when it started operations, in May 1920. This was not the only occasion on which this well-known and internationally respected protagonist of air travel was the first to take a bold initiative. In September 1929, KLM was the first airline to start a regular service between Holland and Indonesia, and after the devastating years of the Second World War, it was again KLM that, on 21 May 1946, opened the first regular service to North America.[2]

THE RISE OF KLM

The Dutch airline company has developed fast since its pioneering days, so a brief review of its current position, including its standing in relation to its main competitors, is certainly needed. It may come as a surprise to discover that, despite having been the first to start a regular airline service, KLM was only ranked fifth among the major carriers operating in 1989 in terms of size, based on ton-kilometres transportation on international scheduled services. However, it should be borne in mind that KLM does not have the advantage enjoyed by many of its competitors of a large home market; in fact, only about 25 per cent of KLM's turnover is derived from Holland itself. For this reason KLM extensively promotes Holland and 'surprising Amsterdam', offering a variety of package tours, designed to persuade people to start their European holidays in Amsterdam, or at least to encourage transit passengers to visit Holland as a stop-over. Nonetheless, the fact that in 1989 KLM carried more than 7 million passengers in about 60 aircraft to almost 150 destinations in nearly 80 countries, and employed 25 000 people to do so, represents no mean performance by any standards. It resulted in a net turnover of approximately Dfl. 6.5 billion (15 per cent of which was provided by freight) and a net profit of about 5 per cent.[3] These results are all the more remarkable if the size of the Dutch population and KLM's turnover is related, for example, to the size of the UK and the turnover of its national carrier, British Airways. The UK's population is about four times as large as that of Holland, but the turnover of British Airways is only a little over twice that of KLM. Similarly, American Airlines, the biggest airline in the world, had a turnover only three times as great as that of KLM.

Naturally, over a number of years, fluctuations in the results of KLM are bound to occur. The airline business is extremely susceptible to economic and political factors, which will almost immediately be reflected in the income and profit figures of airline companies. Although in 1990 and in 1991, in part because of the Gulf War, KLM's financial results were most disappointing, the long-term aim of the company is still to return to a net profit level of at least 5 per cent. In any case, KLM has certainly come a long way since the days when its founder, Albert Plesman, would personally shake every passenger by the hand and wish him or her a good flight in the name of the entire KLM organization, which then employed the grand total of 12 people![4]

STRUCTURE AND ORGANIZATION

Giving particular emphasis to the place of advertising within it, the company's organizational structure can be simplified as follows:

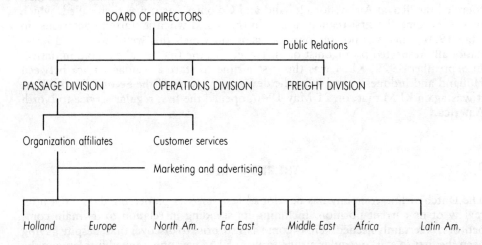

As can readily be seen, marketing and advertising are staff elements in the Passage Division, which is responsible for KLM's seven operating regions. These regions and the individual KLM offices within them, carry responsibility for their own marketing and sales results, but are supported by the staff departments just mentioned, which will exert their influence on the KLM offices to comply in principle with agreed policies, strategies and executions.

One might be inclined to assume that, as the advertising department is rather far removed from the top of the organization, directors do not give a high priority to advertising activities. However, the importance of advertising in contributing to the success of a business cannot simply be measured by the place of the advertising department in the firm's organization chart; the time devoted to this function will often depend upon the personal backgrounds of the top executives, who may have a considerable interest in it. In the case of KLM, its senior management – and particularly its most recent ex-president, Mr Jan de Soet – has always paid direct attention to the way in which the company positions itself and presents itself to its public and its stakeholders all over the world. It wishes to have a clear identity and image among the flying public, obtained through the rigid maintenance of a set of communication principles, to which everyone in the organization strictly adheres. These principles cover all aspects of internal and external communications, from the company's advertising and public relations activities to the many other visible ways in which KLM presents itself to the world at large. The totality of these activities – KLM's corporate identity – is based upon a clearly defined and carefully protected KLM house-style.

KLM AND ITS HOUSE-STYLE

In the early years of KLM's existence, attention to its corporate identity was restricted to the outward appearance of the aeroplane, its colours and the way in which the name KLM and its logo were presented. The first president of KLM, Mr Albert Plesman, decided that the words 'The Flying Dutchman' should be painted on the body of the plane, because the text was not only highly appropriate but also associated KLM with the well-known legend. In 1920, this descriptive title was used on a poster, and today it still appears on all KLM aircraft.

In the years that followed, more and more attention was given to the effective presentation of KLM in what was already becoming a competitive market. Towards the end of the 1950s, the need for greater unity in overall style and presentation resulted in the commissioning of the British designer J.F.K. Henrion to create a house-style that would give KLM a clear and distinctive identity in an increasingly competitive environment. Since then, the scope and significance of the KLM house-style have grown considerably; a corporate design group, chaired by KLM's president and in which all departments are represented, ensures that the instructions of the house-style manual, updated as and when required, are strictly applied to all visual aspects of KLM's operations.[5]

This also applies to KLM's advertising, which constitutes a most important means of implementing the corporate design group's intentions, by establishing the desired identity and image for KLM on a worldwide basis.

KLM AND ITS ADVERTISING

When studying KLM's advertising between the years 1948 and 1978, one sees a variety of different promises and presentations, covering the whole gamut of any airline's possible qualities. However, KLM's advertising was not alone in lacking a consistent theme, for most airline advertising was suffering from the same inability to find something unique to say about the service provided by the airline concerned.

For KLM, the breakthrough occurred in the early 1960s, when an advertising agency then called Ogilvy, Benson & Mather tried to acquire its prestigious account. David Ogilvy writes about the events as follows:

We were the first on their tour of inspection. I opened the meeting by saying 'We have prepared nothing. Instead we would like you to tell us about your problems. Then you can visit the other four agencies on your list. They have all prepared speculative campaigns. If you like any of them, your choice will be easy. If you don't, come back and hire us. We will then embark on the research which always precedes the preparation of advertisements in our agency.[6]

The agency got the account, and its thorough research resulted in the promise of 'reliability' being introduced for the first time into KLM's advertisements as a basic characteristic of the airline and an important argument for using it. It has remained one of the cornerstones of KLM's advertising ever since. However, the character of KLM's worldwide advertising was still somewhat haphazard and it was not until the early 1980s, again under pressure from increased competition, that a new attempt was made to bring more substance and consistency to KLM's communications policy.

A NEW COMMUNICATIONS CONCEPT

It is not easy to find a benefit that only one airline company can offer; they all seem to offer a similarly wide range of advantages to all passengers. And although there is a difference between just offering a benefit and making it into an exclusive property by concentrating all advertising on it – for example by emphasizing 'reliability' – it remains an extremely difficult task to come up with something that is really new and unique.

Identity

When Ies Hoogland, head of advertising & sales promotion, was asked how he would describe KLM's uniqueness, its identity, his spontaneous answer was, 'KLM is the no-hassle airline,' an apt way of summarizing the more formal definition that would appear in KLM's manual (to be discussed later): 'KLM is a dependable, no-nonsense all-round airline. KLM is at home in all markets. Reliable, careful, punctual, friendly.'[7]

The word 'reliable' could well be interpreted as including the other qualities mentioned, but one could also define KLM's characteristics from a product and from a service point of view; the product is reliable and punctual, the service is careful and friendly. Mentioning the four characteristics separately might in any case help the advertising agency in writing pointed copy!

Positioning

Together with its newly appointed advertising agency, Prins, Meijer, Stamenkovits, van Walbeek/Young & Rubicam (PMSvW/Y & R), in 1982, KLM turned the brand-identity statement just quoted into a positioning statement along the following lines:

KLM would like to be seen by frequently travelling business passengers, as the all-round, reliable specialist in air travel. Its experience and expertise as the oldest airline in the world, its punctuality, the friendly attitude of its staff, the service it provides and its worldwide network, give meaning to the claim: KLM – Royal Dutch Airlines – the Reliable Airline.

Strategy

This positioning statement resulted in the development of an advertising strategy, formulating communications objectives, whereby apt and relevant conversations, preferably between businessmen, would be used to present the rational and emotional arguments for flying KLM. These dialogues, which were carefully written and researched, formed, separately and collectively, the total message that KLM wanted to convey to the flying public.

Execution

Even more important than the rationale behind KLM's new strategy, which did not include any claims of great originality or uniqueness, was the need to develop a presentation of this strategy that would make the campaign stand out from all other airline advertising; and this KLM's agency succeeded in doing. Having discarded many ideas and suggestions, it found a basically simple, but most effective, solution: it created a campaign that featured the blue skies and white clouds reminiscent of paintings by Dutch masters that have become the most visually striking and recognizable elements of KLM advertising. The combination of pointed dialogues and a background of blue skies, constituted a new, original and distinctive way of advertising an airline. Used with great consistency ever since, it has achieved notable results in terms of its powerful and lasting impact on the public and certainly has contributed substantially to KLM's excellent reputation among business travellers, as confirmed by research to be discussed later.

KLM AND ITS ADVERTISING AGENCIES

Before the national and international implementation of KLM's new advertising campaign is reviewed in some detail, KLM's policy with regard to the employment of its advertising agencies should be discussed.

Although one would expect that PMSvW/Y & R, as an international agency with a large network of offices, would handle the KLM account on a worldwide basis, this is not the case. The PMSvW/Y & R agency has developed what KLM likes to call its 'umbrella' campaign, aimed at frequent business travellers in the most important markets; this international campaign forms the backbone of KLM advertising worldwide and is placed in a selective media list of about twenty titles. In order to adapt the international campaign to national media, or to use its basic elements to announce local special offers, KLM offices use advertising agencies in their respective countries; but these agencies must adhere strictly to the accepted format for KLM advertising in general. It is to be hoped that this freedom to use the format of KLM advertising for announcing special local deals will not distract local offices too much from the basic strategy and the instructions on how it should be expressed laid down in the company's guidelines.

This raises the question of why KLM does not use one international advertising agency to create and supervise all its advertising, from the 'umbrella' campaign to its various local projects. KLM argues that its national budgets are not always high enough to expect top-level service from the offices of the well-known international agencies. It maintains that, with a limited budget, it is better to employ a smaller agency, which will regard KLM as a major client and so give its prestigious account all the attention that it requires. Another reason is that KLM is not convinced that all the offices of an international agency chain will always be equally professional and equally well equipped to deliver the services that it requires. The counter-argument, that it is the task of the agency's head-office to make certain that its clients receive optimal service everywhere, is not disputed, but the company nevertheless prefers its existing arrangements. As a consequence, KLM's regional offices in about 70 of the 80 countries in which the airline is represented have appointed their own agencies, the remaining ten being served from headquarters in Holland, with the help of the Dutch Vaz Dias advertising agency in Amsterdam. Whilst KLM's competitors appear to be showing sound business sense in following the one-agency-alignment policy, generalizations in this respect are futile; there are too many factors involved for the choice of approach. The fact of the matter is, that the KLM system of operating appears to be working satisfactorily, probably again because of the controls exercised by KLM's central advertising department, designed to optimize advertising investments at both national and international levels.

In view of the work done by the PMSvW/Y & R agency in Amsterdam and the considerable input from KLM's central advertising department itself, the local agency's commission will usually remain below 15 per cent, but arrangements in this respect are left largely to the managements of the national KLM offices, who will usually act in close co-operation and consultation with KLM's central advertising department.

IMPLEMENTING KLM'S ADVERTISING

KLM's new advertising concept was one of total integration of national and international communications strategies. Visual uniformity became essential; KLM would in future show one face, and would present one basic message, to the entire world. To implement this policy, the KLM advertising & sales promotion department employs four co-ordinators, who maintain regular contact with all KLM offices around the world. The scope and depth of the service that they will provide will, of course, depend upon the size and importance of the office concerned, but, in general, planning, budgeting, media-selection, production-control and the appointment of advertising agencies are all activities in which the central staff will often wish to become involved. In the case of the appointment of a new agency, the co-ordinator concerned will always be present during the final stages of selection. In addition, extensive documentation supports the advertising department in its efforts to achieve the greatest possible uniformity of advertising throughout the world.

THE MANUAL

Two voluminous binders, together forming the 'KLM Advertising & Sales Promotion Manual', contain all the necessary information on how to use the centrally developed campaign as effectively and efficiently as possible. Starting with the 'Communication Concept', it runs through all aspects of the 'umbrella' campaign and of its local adaptations, with clear instructions on every detail. It also contains an extensive 'Dialogue Bank' and information on available artwork and photographic material, as well as guidelines for sales promotions, direct marketing and the selection of advertising agencies. It is a most comprehensive document, which is updated regularly and is of great help to all KLM offices and their many advertising agencies in the implementation of agreed policies. The most interesting feature of the manual is that those who compiled it managed to deal with the basic principles of the campaign in no more than three pages.

Elsewhere in this book, readers will find that those companies that do employ one international advertising agency for all their advertising, very often delegate control over matters such as local adaptations of campaigns to these agencies and their local offices. However, in the final analysis, all that counts is that the company should obtain its desired results as effectively and efficiently as possible, and KLM obviously feels that it succeeds in doing just that.

KLM'S ADVERTISING BUDGET

Advertising expenditure for national and international campaigns and for the special 'Holland Promotion' is covered by one budget, which will usually fluctuate around 3 per cent of the company's total turnover. Of this budget, 60 per cent will be spent on national advertising, 30 per cent on the 'Holland Promotion' and the remaining 10 per cent on the international campaign.

It is interesting to note that in 1988 KLM's expenditure on its international advertising campaign in the press was roughly on a par with that of British Airways and Lufthansa, but these airlines also use television advertising, which is not monitored internationally. If we look at the ratio between KLM's national and international advertising, KLM's central advertising department proves to have executive control over only a small part of the total budget. The responsibility for national advertising rests, to a large extent, with KLM's regional offices. This could easily result in the 'tail wagging the dog' and have an adverse effect on the authority of headquarters over the execution of national advertising campaigns. Fortunately, however, the working relationship between head-office, national offices and the many different advertising agencies is such that serious friction is avoided.

KLM'S MEDIA POLICY

Reference has already been made to the list of 20 titles used for the 'umbrella' campaign; this list includes publications such as *Time, Newsweek*, the *Wall Street Journal, The Economist*, the *Financial Times, Fortune* and the *International Herald Tribune*, all read by business travellers.

In individual countries, it is the local KLM offices, in consultation with their advertising agencies, that decide in which media KLM advertising will appear, whether the project involves an adaptation of the international campaign or the announcement of special offers for flights to attractive destinations. Generally speaking, television is rarely used, since KLM does not believe that this is the best medium with which to reach its target audience efficiently. Nonetheless, in 1989, KLM Holland ran a three-minute commercial four times in combination with a contest in the daily press. Not only did it win a prestigious advertising award, but the contest drew no fewer than 150 000 entries!

ORCA

The need for optimum internal co-operation in all matters concerning KLM's communication policy has already been emphasized. To enhance such co-operation between the centre of the company, the KLM offices and their advertising agencies, KLM organizes an annual workshop, attended by the large offices and a rotating selection of smaller ones. Experiences are exchanged, KLM's own advertising and that of its competitors are reviewed, and recommendations are made. On this occasion, an Orchestrated Communication Award (ORCA) is presented to the office that, in the opinion of a jury consisting of representatives of KLM's public relations and central advertising departments, has made the greatest contribution to KLM's integrated advertising, sales-promotion and public-relations policy and its execution.

It is, of course, of increasing importance that all KLM's communications with the public should carry a similar message. This not only applies to the disciplines covered by ORCA, but also to important areas such as the company's response to comments and complaints from passengers, or the behaviour of cabin personnel. It is cabin staff who make the final impression on KLM's customers and they can thus considerably strengthen or weaken all the company's preceding efforts to encourage passengers to fly with it. No wonder, then, that KLM spends up to Dfl. 200 million annually on the training of its personnel, trying to improve the quality of their total performance as much as possible.[8] After all, one more passenger on every flight means an additional annual income of Dfl. 40 million! In fact, KLM's president takes such an interest in passengers' reactions to the airlines service that he answers most of their letters personally.[9]

KLM AND ITS RESEARCH PROGRAMME

Much can, indeed, be learned from passengers' comments and complaints; interestingly, air travel still seems to inspire people to write about their experiences, particularly if they are unfavourable. The nature of the complaints will, of course, vary, but it is quite clear that the public expects considerably fuller service from airlines than from any other transport facility – much to the relief of managers of railway companies! However, KLM does not depend upon this source of information alone. It runs two important research surveys on an annual basis: (a) an internally organized survey among the members of the so-called 'Flying Dutchman Programme', consisting of 50 000 Dutch businessmen who fly frequently; and (b) an air travel survey, carried out by KLM in co-operation with the magazines *Time* and *Newsweek*, among the 175 000 readers of these periodicals who are regular business travellers.

The first survey does not draw any direct comparisons with competing airlines, concentrating entirely on the opinions and comments of Dutch businessmen who fly with KLM. In 1988, 4 000 members of this group responded, sometimes expressing serious criticisms of various aspects of KLM's operation, ranging from checking-in procedures at Schiphol Airport (still identified by many people with KLM itself) or on-board service and the attitudes of KLM staff to questions of value for money – a subject of perennial interest to the Dutch! Whilst this survey cannot be considered as representing the opinions of all business passengers, whether from Holland or elsewhere, it has been carried out every year since 1983, so that the trends and persistent opinions that emerge from it, should not be, and are not being, underestimated. 'The service-industry must pay attention to every detail, it should not accept any restrictions with regard to on-going and follow-up care. The consequences of ignoring this will be disastrous', writes the research and planning department of KLM Netherlands.[10]

The *Time-Newsweek* Survey has, of course, a much wider scope. In 1989, 9 000 questionnaires were sent to subscribers in 18 countries, collecting opinions from respondents on many aspects of air travel with KLM, British Airways, Lufthansa, Swissair, Air France and Scandinavian Airways. The response ratio was 27 per cent, and, generally speaking, KLM scored well, one of the most important findings being the following:

Preferred Airlines for Business Travel

	1988	1989
Air France	5%	6%
British Airways	10%	13%
KLM	10%	14%
Lufthansa	11%	9%
Scandinavian Airlines	6%	6%
Swissair	17%	19%

The fact that in 1989 KLM ranked second among such formidable competition must be interpreted as a compliment to its image and advertising. It is particularly gratifying that appreciation for two aspects of air travel that KLM has strongly emphasized in its advertising, shows a marked increase over the years: appreciation for KLM's punctuality increased between 1984 and 1989 from 9 to 16, and appreciation for its reliability rose in the same period from 10 to 18.[11]

As we indicated at the beginning of this chapter, KLM has a much smaller home market than most of its competitors. This is particularly unfortunate considering the positive attitude of business travellers towards the Dutch airline, as confirmed by the various research reports. Its second place in the airline preference rating for 1989 suggests that, if KLM's home market were only a little bigger, the (blue) sky would indeed be the limit! What is also abundantly clear from the research carried out, is the critical importance that must be attached to service. As there are so few unique and rational reasons for preferring one airline to another, the scope and quality of service offered to the flying public will ultimately make the difference between success and failure. Like all airlines, KLM attaches supreme importance to this aspect of its operations.

KLM AND ITS PASSENGER SERVICE

The subject of service is vast and complex, because service does not mean the same thing to everyone; some passengers will appreciate the showing of a film during intercontinental flights, others will loathe it; some will enjoy the captain's chit-chat over the intercom, others will reach for their earplugs! It may be argued that these are small points, but in air travel small points count, and, despite KLM's excellent ranking, there is no room for complacency. Nor has KLM shown it; the company has recently announced a number of improvements in the services that it provides, such as better checking-in facilities and baggage handling, more comfort in the cabin itself, roomier seats, more leg-room, champagne not only for first class passengers but also for business class ones and, finally, better meals – always bearing in mind that the catering for one first class passenger on an intercontinental flight costs approximately Dfl. 250 and that over half of the food provided on such a flight remains unconsumed.[12]

However, the provision of the highest quality service should start long before the actual flight, and, in this context it is interesting to note that KLM, together with a number of other airlines, will be participating in a company called 'Galileo Distributions System Ltd.', based in the UK and intending '. . . to bring about a joint, advanced and automatic bookings system'.[13] Its services will not be exclusively available to KLM, but its establishment will still be seen by KLM's business passengers as another step towards easier and quicker booking procedures. In addition, to eliminate the need for passengers to queue up at check-in counters, airlines will open such facilities at railway stations with connections with the airport; British Airways has established one at Victoria Station, in London, and KLM has done the same in The Hague and Rotterdam, with other major cities to follow. As KLM's president has said, indicating the importance that he attaches to the attention that travellers receive while they are at the airport itself, '. . . the airline which is fastest on the ground, will be among the winners'.[14]

The battle for the traveller's final choice of airline will continue to increase in intensity; and the flying public should benefit. All other things being equal, it may indeed be quality and scope of service that proves to be the critical factor. However, even if airline companies do try to excel each other in this respect, there will be a limit to the amount of service that can be provided. In the end, therefore, differences between airlines may again become marginal. At that point, the quality of an airline's advertising may become of even greater importance in influencing passenger choice.

1993 AND BEYOND

KLM's high standing and image in the domain of air travel have, to a large extent, been achieved through consistency in its communications policy, in which advertising has played such an important part. No wonder, then, that KLM and its principal advertising agency will do their utmost to maintain this 'edge' acquired over most of KLM's competitors. This will not be an easy task. Although the dialogues used in the advertisements offer much room for variation, the latter's format and visual presentation do not allow for much flexibility, and the fact that the campaign's uniqueness is largely based upon its visual qualities, rather than on the strength and originality of its promises, exacerbates this problem. Of course, the PMSvW/Y & R agency will regularly update the content and presentation of KLM's advertising, in order to bring it in line with the latest developments, but the investment in KLM's total communications programme has been so considerable that fundamental changes would, for the time-being, seem unlikely. In addition, preserving the continuity of this programme would appear to be even more important, at a time when changes in so many other aspects of air travel are likely to occur – indeed, already are occurring.

An example of these changes is the policy of liberalization of tariffs, pursued by the European Commission in Brussels, which should give the public greater choice and lower fares. Though desirable, in principle, 'there is a danger that this free market will be stifled by the stranglehold of the Brussels bureaucracy', as KLM's president put it.[15] On the ground, KLM will pay great attention, as remarked earlier, to the quality and speed of service at Schiphol Airport, which is often referred to as the 'Gateway to Europe' and is of pre-eminent importance to KLM itself.

All these, and many other, factors affecting the future of air travel in general and of KLM in particular, make it even more desirable that the company should not significantly alter its communications programme, all of which has been a proven success. When asked to list the three main reasons for the continuing success of the Dutch airline, KLM president De Soet said that they could be expressed in the single word 'reliability', with all its many connotations, relating to safety, punctuality, friendliness and service. 'The Nineties will probably see the most exciting period in the development of commercial aviation so far', Mr De Soet said recently, and he continued, '. . . KLM is firmly set on a course to position itself as an airline operating world-wide from a European base, placing it among the world's three top quality carriers . . .'[16]

Notes

1. Personal discussion with T. H. Woltman, then Director, KLM Netherlands, 31 May 1989.
2. Kampen, Anthonie van (1969), *Plesman, Grondlegger van de Gouden KLM*. Bussum, Holland: Unieboek, pp. 99 and 202.
3. *Annual Report KLM 1989/1990*, pp. 4 and 6.
4. van Kampen, pp. 76 and 78.
5. Smit, Gees-Ineke (1985), 'Een proces van voortdurende aanpassingen' (A process of continuing adaptations), *Industrieel Ontwerpen in Nederland*, No. 5, pp. 6–12.
6. Ogilvy, David (1987), *Confessions of an Advertising Man*. London: Pan Books, p. 52.
7. *KLM Advertising and Sales Promotion Manual* (May 1986), p. 01.00.00.
8. *KLM Wolkenridder* (1989), fortnightly publication of KLM, 12 August, p. 6.
9. Personal discussion with J. de Soet (immediate past president of KLM), 16 October 1989.
10. *Onderzoek naar de Kwaliteit van het KLM Product* (Research into the Quality of the KLM Product) (1989), KLM Nederland, Onderzoek & Planning, February, p. 14.
11. *Brief Summary Results Air Travel Survey 1989 KLM (Time-Newsweek)* (1989), PMSvW-Y & R, 2 June.
12. See note 9.
13. *Annual Report KLM 1987–88*, p. 6; *Galileo Distributie Systemen Nederland* (1988), 'Het Systeem van de Toekomst' (The system of the future), Maarssenbroek, Netherlands, September.
14. Kroese, Wim, Interview with J. de Soet, *Weekeinde De Telegraaf*, 7 October 1989.
15. See note 9.
16. Soet, J. de (1990), 'New Year message,' *Holland Herald Magazine*, January, p. 6.

LEVI'S

'Quality Never Goes out of Style'

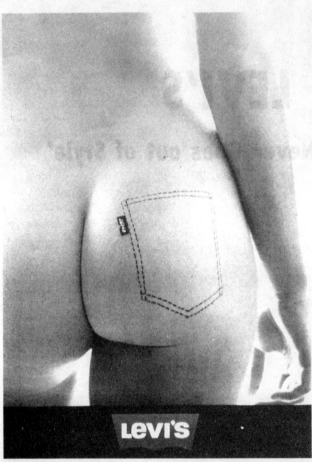

Levi's

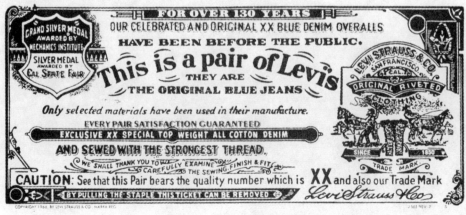

LEVI'S
'Quality Never Goes out of Style'

'They're guaranteed to shrink, wrinkle and fade,'[1] runs the recommendation for a product that can best be described as a pair of trousers, that appears at first sight easy to make, but in fact requires a minimum of 33 complicated steps to produce. The trousers have a simple shape, with double inner seams for strength, and are furnished with five pockets – two at the back trimmed with stitching in a double bow pattern and three at the front with reinforcing rivets at their corners. A leather label carrying the two-horses trade-mark and a tiny red tab with the name Levi's on it, on the right back pocket, guarantee that the buyer will receive a genuine pair of Levi's jeans, of undisputed superior quality and unusual longevity.

The above description has been taken from various publications concerning the history of the jeans, but a French author has expressed their unique appeal more elegantly and succinctly:

Parmi toutes les créations de la mode, le Jean, entre autres, s'est fait
le champion des sages raffinements de la sensualité visuelle.[2]

It is a product that has existed for almost 150 years and is still as popular as ever. The jeans were named after the man who, in the mid-nineteenth century, started making and selling them: Löb Strauss, later called Levi Strauss, who had been born in Buttenheim, northern Bavaria, Germany, on 26 February 1829, but emigrated to the United States in 1847.

LEVI'S EARLY LANDMARKS

When he travelled to the USA, Levi Strauss took with him some rather heavy brown canvas intended for making tents to be sold to gold-diggers, who at that time were flocking to California to make their fortunes. He soon found, however, that the men 'who spent their days scratching the soil or wading through streams, were not particularly concerned with comfort while asleep'[3]; they preferred to have something to protect their bodies while at work. As a consequence, Strauss replaced his stock of brown canvas with a cotton fabric made in Nîmes in France and called 'Serge de Nîmes' – soon shortened to 'denim' – and started to make overalls from this special fabric; when an indigo dye was developed, the brown colouring of the cloth was altered to the now familiar blue.

In the mid-1930s, well after Strauss' death, his company started to refer to its overalls as 'jeans', a name derived from the cotton trousers worn by sailors from the Italian port of Genoa, the name of this city in French being 'Gênes' which in English was corrupted to 'jeans'.

THE START OF THE '501'

This, then, was the background to the development of Levi Strauss' flagship product, the '501' jeans – thus named because it was the fifth production model, made of 01 denim – which has retained its phenomenal popularity throughout the world, regardless of changes in fashion and despite having always remained basically unaltered. Having started out as a peddler, first selling his tent material to miners, and then enjoying considerable success with his overalls, Levi Strauss established himself in San Francisco, where his business prospered over the years. An important development affecting the company's history occurred in 1928, at the time of the Wall Street Crash, when rich people from the East Coast of the USA became aware of the benefits of a cheaper, but fulfilling, way of life. They replaced their expensive trips to Europe by taking up ranching in the Far West, and, as a consequence, jeans not only obtained respectability but even acquired a certain snob appeal.

During the aftermath of the Second World War, American G.I.s took to wearing jeans in their leisure time, giving the product a further boost; while it also became increasingly popular among the younger generation outside the USA as well. When celebrities such as Marilyn Monroe, James Dean and Marlon Brando made jeans a standard part of their outfit, the wearing of jeans became an expression of a lifestyle, giving people a feeling of freedom, of adventure and of independence. People of the younger generation adopted the garment and made it their personal symbol of freedom and equality, not only in the USA, but all over the world, not least in Europe. Levi Strauss started to export jeans to Europe in the 1960s and now has fully owned affiliates in Austria, Belgium, Denmark, Finland, France, Greece, Holland, Italy, Germany, Norway, Spain, Sweden, Switzerland and the UK with a European headquarters in Brussels.

LEVI STRAUSS AND THE WORLD OF FASHION

One of the first questions that comes to mind when one studies this company is whether Levi Strauss is in the fashion business or simply in the clothing trade. Levi Strauss does not profess to being among the top fashion-houses, let alone to taking the lead in fashionable trends, but it certainly wants to be seen by its 15-year-old to 25-year-old buyers as closely following these trends and adapting its products accordingly. If it fell behind in this respect, Levi Strauss would lose credibility as a company selling modern, up-to-date garments. Thus, although the so-called 'core' products, such as the 501 and other 'Red Tab' jeans, like the 'Silver Tab' and the 'Orange Tab' jeans, sold at different price levels, will basically remain the same, the fabric, fit and finish will vary according to the latest fashion trends. In the shops, one may find 12 or even more varieties of Levi's jeans, of different shapes and finishes, not only in the traditional blue, but also in more fashionable colours, such as red, white and black.

Since fashion does play an important part in the Levi Strauss operation, the company will follow the custom of the fashion business and run seasonal sales campaigns, offering a 'collection' to its retailers, and taking advance orders. With this background in mind, a brief review of the company's past and present organization and of some of its performance figures might be appropriate.

SCOPE AND ORGANIZATION

When Levi Strauss died, in 1902, at the age of 73, rich but never having married, his four nephews took charge of the company, the eldest, Jacob Stern, becoming its president. He was replaced in 1921 by his brother Sigmund, who had earlier invited his son-in-law, Walter A. Haas, to join the management of the company. During the following decades, the business continued to expand, as its products became more and more popular. In the 1960s, Levi Strauss surpassed one sales milestone after another and in order to finance this expansion, it became a public company in 1971. Ten years later, it was the largest clothing company in the world – a position that it still retains. In 1985, one of the third Haas generation, Robert D. Haas, who was also a relative of Levi Strauss, joined with other family members to repurchase the publicly held stock and turn Levi Strauss once again into a privately owned company, with himself as its chief executive officer. In 1990, Levi Strauss achieved a worldwide turnover of $4.2 billion, showing a net income of $251 million. The turnover is not only derived from the sale of jeans; the company also produces children's clothing and casual sports wear, such as trousers, shirts, shorts, skirts, blouses, sweaters and dressy slacks and coats. In 1990, the breakdown of sales according to type of product and geographical region, was as follows:[4]

		(in millions of dollars)
Men's Jeans	(USA)	1 260
Women's Wear	(USA)	240
Men's Wear	(USA)	451
Shirts	(USA)	123
Youth Wear	(USA)	345
Britannia Sportswear Ltd.		134
Other		2
Total USA		2 555
Europe		1 028
Asia Pacific		316
Canada		196
Latin America		143
Total International		1 683
GRAND TOTAL		4 238

The above figures show that Levi Strauss International represents about 40 per cent of total turnover, while, within the international division, Europe accounts for 64 per cent of the business. Levi Strauss products are sold in more than 70 countries around the world; the firm employs 32 000 people, of whom 8 000 are with Levi Strauss International.

Levi Strauss International

From an organizational point of view, the following simplified diagram shows how the international business is controlled:

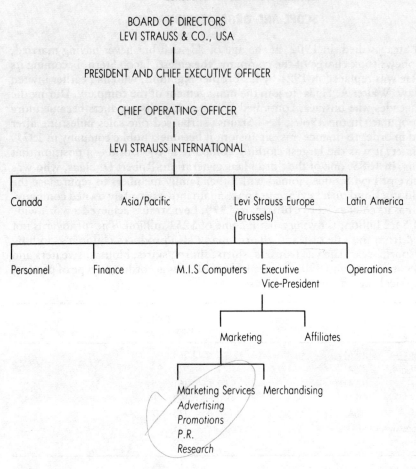

However, organization charts give only a limited indication of the way in which a company really operates. In the case of Levi Strauss Europe, the management likes to emphasize the 'shared responsibilities' of all concerned, both at the centre and in the subsidiaries, so that in fact, there should only be a small number of dotted lines on the organization chart, or better still, no lines at all!

True, Levi Strauss fully owns the local offices through which it operates, and, as far as Europe is concerned, it exerts its control through its head-office in Brussels. However, once financial plans have been agreed upon, the responsibility for achieving them rests firmly with the managements in the individual countries. Since, as we have seen, the garment industry is affected by the world of fashion, with its national characteristics and overtones, close collaboration between senior management, its staff at head-office, the managements of the local offices and the company's clients is an absolute prerequisite for success. Consequently, meetings between all the parties involved in the various aspects of the Levi Strauss operation are held quite frequently, to make the policy of 'shared responsibility' come to life. Naturally, the amount of influence from Brussels varies, depending on the nature of the product concerned; core products, such as the 501 jeans, may well receive more attention from the central management than other Levi Strauss' garments, which account for approximately 40 per cent of total turnover. It should also be remembered that Levi Strauss does not sell through wholesalers, but only direct to retailers, who often act as good barometers for measuring fluctuations in the tastes of the buying public. Levi Strauss offices are therefore in an ideal position to adjust their national policies to meet the tastes and needs of the market-place.

Levi's stores

An important element in the Levi Strauss operation is the Levi Strauss Stores, which are expanding rapidly in all European markets. They not only sell the full range of Levi jeans, but also a large collection of Levi's shirts and other casual tops. Interestingly, these stores, which sell only Levi's products, have contributed to an increased total European sales volume for the clothing categories concerned, rather than leading to reduced sales of Levi products by neighbouring retailers.

LEVI STRAUSS AND ITS ADVERTISING

As shown on the organization chart, Levi's marketing function is a little different from its conventional equivalents in other firms, which normally cover product development, research, consumer promotions, advertising and sales. In the case of Levi Strauss, selling, and implementing overall company strategies are very much a local responsibility, so that the central marketing function concentrates on identifying consumer trends and on developing marketing strategies for Levi's main products, including all the related activities mentioned on the organization chart. The main products, of course, always include the 501 jeans, and it is remarkable that although the characteristics of the wearers of 501s may differ widely in many respects from country to country, when it comes to buying a pair of jeans, their motivations, tastes and preferences are very similar; they enjoy aspects of the same life-style and an appreciation of freedom and adventure. Levi 501s are so popular in discothèques throughout the world that, on entering one, it is difficult to remember exactly where you are, or to establish the nationalities of the dancers. Not many other products have achieved such a universal and consistent user-profile and image, though Coca-Cola and Marlboro are also examples. It is, therefore, not surprising that the basic positioning of Levi's advertising is virtually the same all over the world.

Positioning of Levi's jeans

The audience to which Levi's advertising addresses itself can best be described as follows:

Levi Strauss would like to be seen as the maker of products for straightforward, honest, independent, adventurous, perhaps even a little rebellious, men and women between 15 and 25 years of age. Levi's wearers care for what is genuine, enjoy one another's company, feel attracted to the opposite sex and will express their sense of freedom and enjoyment in a manner acceptable to all, irrespective of age.

This description of the jeans' 'personality' applies worldwide and although, in theory, it should be possible to use exactly the same advertising everywhere, in practice, this cannot be done. Mainly for ethnic reasons, '501 youth' is represented in American advertising in a way that differs so much from what would, for example, be convincing in Europe that 'global' advertising for Levi's jeans is not yet possible. An American commercial was once tested in the UK but the test failed and the commercial was never run.

Another important point affects this issue. The price level of the European jeans market is considerably higher than that of the same market in the USA; in Europe, Levi's are positioned in the upper end of the jeans market, in the USA, in the middle. Naturally, this difference is reflected in the way in which the product is presented in the different regions. However, within Europe, there is no reason at all for developing different versions of the same basic strategy, and, consequently, the production of Levi's commercials for release in Europe is commissioned and controlled by the management of the company in Brussels.

Levi's non-verbal commercials

Levi's advertising in broadcast media and cinemas consists solely of moving pictures and music, because the combination of these two elements is sufficient to create the desired image for Levi Strauss and its products in a most convincing manner. Whereas, in the past, much emphasis was placed on demonstrating the strength of the jeans, sometimes under most unusual circumstances, the present approach shows the role a pair of jeans can play in encounters between members of the opposite sexes. Again, the situations are rather unusual. For example, one commercial shows a young man on a motorbike riding out of a lift into a stockbroker's trading room. He stops where his girlfriend is at work and throws a pair of 501 jeans onto her desk. The girl does not hesitate for one moment, she pulls off her skirt, puts on the jeans, climbs onto the back seat of the motorbike, and off they go. There is no dialogue, simply music by Steve Miller. Unworried by problems of language, complicated dubbing procedures or the need for different packshots for every country, the advertising agency in London can produce Levi's 501 commercials for use throughout Europe.

This is an interesting way of advertising a product, particularly at a time when television companies using satellites to reach wide, multi-national audiences are trying hard to encourage advertisers to use their services to send messages to consumers throughout Europe. Leaving aside the quality of the programmes, which still needs considerable improvement, these companies have found that the many different languages spoken in Europe are a much more formidable barrier than anticipated, so that the number of advertisers who can televise the same commercial in several different countries is still small. However, the director-general of the European Association of Advertising Agencies has made the following statement:

> What satellite broadcasting is going to mean for us, apart from reach, is greater emphasis on non-verbal communication: the big visual idea, and the use of visual symbols. Where the message transcends national frontiers, it will often transcend national languages. Remember, we have 9 different, national languages within the EC. This is going to put a premium on the visual and musical content of commercials, with less emphasis on verbal communication; and, as brands develop expertise in non-verbal communication, I think we shall see this phenomenon appearing in print media too, with much more emphasis laid on graphics than on copy.[5]

In this connection, Levi Strauss is certainly among the front-runners; the company will study carefully all developments in the international media scene, particularly those involving new opportunities to advertise throughout Europe via satellite, and will act upon them, provided that it is satisfied about the audience reached, the quality of the programmes involved and the price it must pay.

According to the company's annual report for 1990, its worldwide expenditure on advertising amounts to about 6 per cent of the value of its sales, that is approximately $250 million per annum. The percentage of advertising expenditure in Europe is a little lower in relation to the level of European sales but, as might be expected, the larger part of this budget is spent on broadcast media. In Europe, the British advertising agency Bartle Bogle Hegarty is responsible for the production of the all-important television commercials and cinema films. Levi Strauss Europe's marketing director briefs the agency and ensures uniformity in the presentation of Levi's image to the European audience. The alarming costs of these productions, often reaching seven-figures when expressed in dollars, are a continuing concern to all international advertisers, including Levi Strauss' management in Brussels. Its only solace is that they may prevent competitors from entering the jeans market. Apart from the broadcast media and, of course, commercials in cinemas, an important subsidiary medium for Levi's advertising is provided by outdoor hoardings while further support comes from the publication of magazines for the trade, such as 'Levi's Contact' in France, and, of course, from numerous merchandising schemes designed to help traders to sell Levi products to the public.

LEVI STRAUSS AND ITS ADVERTISING AGENCIES

As far as Levi Strauss' advertising in individual European countries is concerned, the local Levi Strauss offices, in close consultation with Brussels, appoint their own advertising agencies, which include international ones such as McCann as well as purely national agencies. This, again, is in line with the company's policy of leaving the responsibility for local matters in the hands of its local managers. The agencies make recommendations about the media to be employed and buy the necessary time for showing the international commercials or cinema films; in addition, they conduct all local advertising, as commissioned by their clients.

In such a situation, it is not unusual for head-offices to provide clearly defined instructions about the way in which an overall theme and its presentation should be adapted to local circumstances. However, the Levi Strauss management in Brussels does not favour such guidelines. Naturally, there will be regular consultation, and the policy of 'shared responsibility' applies fully, but initiatives for local advertising and promotions are taken by the managements of the affiliates, who will also negotiate terms of remuneration with the local advertising agency. As Levi Strauss pays in full for the commercials and films produced by BBH in London and does not charge its affiliates for their share in these costs, the agency commission will usually be less than 15 per cent. BBH works on a fee basis.

LEVI STRAUSS AND ITS COMPETITORS

The importance of advertising in establishing Levi's in its position as the leading brand of jeans in the American and European markets becomes even more apparent when one examines the competitive scene. The production of jeans is labour intensive, but does not require excessive capital investment. Because of this, and because it is not inordinately difficult to produce garments that superficially resemble those made by Levi Strauss, there are thousands of small manufacturers who are exploiting the goodwill created by a relatively small number of companies that are trying to establish brands with strong personalities.

In the United States the main jeans producers, in addition to Levi Strauss, are Wrangler and Lee. Between them, the three firms have approximately 40 per cent of the total market of 500 million units per annum; Levi's alone accounts for approximately 50 per cent of this smaller branded market. In Europe, the situation is different. Levi's is the only important advertiser in the market, which comprises about 500 manufacturers, and, in some ways, Levi Strauss Europe would be quite happy if one or two other leading jeans manufacturers were to join in its efforts to build up the total European jeans market, which still produces unit sales equivalent to little more than one-sixth of the total unit sales level achieved in the USA. As already mentioned, European price levels are considerably higher than those in the States; in Europe 20 per cent of all jeans are sold at a premium, with Levi's accounting for more than half of this market sector.

FAKES

Imitation may be the sincerest form of flattery, but Levi Strauss would rather not see too much of it! Yet, as we have seen, in view of the apparent ease with which jeans can be produced, many companies will be tempted to try to imitate the market-leader. In this respect, their miniscule tab is little help in distinguishing Levi's jeans from similar products, and, as a consequence, counterfeiting groups are actively trying to penetrate European markets, creating a serious problem for the company. The management in Brussels therefore employs a detective-in-residence, whose task it is to track down these activities and put a stop to them. He works closely with the local police, and, together, they have traced and seized many thousands of pairs of fake denim jeans. Although many thousands more have still been sold, the deterrent significance of such seizures should not be underestimated.

LEVI STRAUSS AS A COMPANY

The foregoing discussion illustrates the company's concern for consumers and its appreciation of its responsibility to produce and sell jeans and other garments of the highest quality. All its activities are based on high ethical standards, to which it wishes to adhere strictly. They are expressed in a kind of 'credo', which describes the values that Levi Strauss represents and stands for. In the company's Annual Report for 1989, the board devoted much attention to this aspect of its operation in explaining its 'Mission' and its 'Aspirations'; its 'Mission' runs as follows:

We seek profitable and responsible commercial success creating and
selling jeans and casual clothing. We seek this while offering quality
products and service – and by being a leader in what we do. What
we do is important. How we do it is also important. Here's how: by
being honest. By being responsible citizens in communities where we
operate and in society in general. By having a workplace that's safe
and productive, where people work together in teams, where they

talk to each other openly, where they're responsible for their actions, and where they can improve their skills.[6]

In the section on 'Aspirations', the company describes its four most important aims under the headings 'New Behaviors', 'Diversity', 'Empowerment', and 'Ethical Management Practices'. These aims cover the company's relationships with outsiders as well as with its own staff; its business conduct is based upon a 'Code of Ethics'.[7] The idealistic trait in this 'credo' can be traced back to the founder of the company, Levi Strauss, who, as far back as 1897, devoted much time and resources to charitable and philanthropic purposes. Not only was he a member of the board of the Californian School for the Deaf, but, during his lifetime, he established 28 scholarships at the University of California. In 1974, the company followed his example by establishing the Levi Strauss Foundation, which conducts social responsibility programmes with the help of 'Community Involvement Teams', and is now at work in many parts of the world: 'Employees volunteer their time to identify local needs and work with fellow employees and others in local non-profitmaking and public organisations, carrying on the tradition of people helping people – directly and personally.'[8] In 1984, Levi Strauss & Co was the recipient of President Ronald Reagan's Award for its outstanding national corporate volunteer programme.

ITS PUBLIC RELATIONS

The activities described above can, of course, be considered as forming part of the company's efforts to create the right image for the totality of its operations, by presenting itself and what it stands for to its own staff, its shareholders and the public at large. Another typical example of such activity was the exhibition about the firm organized in September 1990 by the French Levi Strauss office in Paris. Few companies will be able to present such a complete picture of their histories as Levi Strauss can and did. Starting in 1850, the entire development of the venture was reviewed, using paintings, pictures, posters, original materials, literature, a video presentation etc. But then, how many companies can claim such success with one and the same product, introduced before the very first motor car and still going strong!

1993 AND BEYOND

Levi Strauss Europe has formed a study-group under the chairmanship of its financial director, which analysed its operation and will eventually make recommendations regarding all aspects of its European business. The company certainly has a strong base from which to start. Firstly, it is the market-leader in the clothing business and has already made considerable progress as regards its pan-European strategies, resources and production. It has a number of core products that are, by any standards, distinctively European. This, however, is no reason for complacency, so the company is studying in which respects further improvements might be possible. The one factor governing all considerations is the need for close links with the company's customers – the Levi retailers – since service is the first priority under all circumstances. There are, indeed, areas deserving of the company's special attention, such as the future of the organized clothing business, or the harmonization of price policies. Fortunately, unlike the manufacturers of tobacco and alcoholic or phar-maceutical products, clothing companies are not under the constant threat of EC regulation, but Levi Strauss nevertheless believes that stronger representation of the clothing business at international level is called for.[9]

As far as advertising is concerned, the company will continue its policy of central production of non-verbal commercials and cinema films, to be shown throughout Europe and intended to establish a uniform identity for Levi Strauss as a business and for its products. Advertising produced locally by the Levi Strauss subsidiaries will respond to local circumstances and to the local competitive scene. This formula, also applied by other companies marketing a uniform product and using one advertising strategy on an international scale, has proved successful and may well be further developed once the Single European Market has come about. Most importantly, however, much of the company's planning for the future concerns the developments in Eastern Europe, where 'we think people will want to buy Levi's'; after all, 'Visitors to the Soviet Union, for example, have long been able to sell their jeans for high prices on the black market'.[10] A Hungarian joint venture is already in operation. Nor do the company's plans for the future stop there. In its 1989 report, Levi Strauss com-ments on its plans for the twenty-first century:

We'll want . . . to be successful through being profitable and
ethical . . .
We'll want to harness technology – for example computers and
automation . . .
We'll want to be ready to do business in any market anywhere on
earth and to out-perform any competitor . . .
We'll want to reduce the time it takes for us to meet our customers'
needs . . .
We'll want to be known for fulfilling our promises . . .[11]

Maybe all this can be summed up by referring to the final paragraph in the company brochure, from which we quoted at the beginning of this chapter, dealing with Levi Strauss, the man:

Well, everyone knows his first name. His ideals and visions live on,
embodied in a corporation that survives and flourishes – and in
millions of pairs of pants around the world that are guaranteed to
shrink, wrinkle and fade.[12]

Notes

1. *Everyone Knows His First Name* (undated), brochure published by Levi Strauss & Co., San Francisco.
2. Rachline, Michel (1988), *La Grande Épopée du jean*. Paris: Orban Communication Industrielle, p. 13.
3. Dupuy, Pierre (1990), *Le Fabuleux Roman du jean*. Geneva and Paris: Editions Minerva, p. 3. (Quotation translated from French.)
4. *The World of Levi's*, 1990 report of Levi Strauss & Co., San Francisco, p. 2.
5. Beatson, Ronald, 'Europe 1993,' a presentation to the Point-of-Purchase Advertising Institute Marketplace '89, New York, 31 October–2 November 1989, p. 15.

6. *The World of Levi's*, 1989 report of Levi Strauss & Co., San Francisco, p. 10.
7. *Ibid.*
8. *Levi Strauss & Co.* (undated), brochure published by Levi Strauss S.A./N.V. Brussels, p. 16.
9. Personal discussion with Kenneth S. Sirlin, Director of Finance, Levi Strauss & Co. Europe S.A., Brussels, 22 February 1990.
10. 'Where once there was red, Levi sees blue,' interview with George James, Levi Strauss Inc., San Francisco, in the *International Herald Tribune*, 1 March 1990.
11. *The World of Levi's*, 1989, back page.
12. *Everyone Knows His First Name.*

LUX TOILET SOAP

'The Beauty Soap
of International Stars'

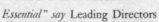

LUX TOILET SOAP
'The Beauty Soap of International Stars'

When, back in 1973, Brigitte Bardot said, 'There are no really ugly women. Every woman is a Venus in her own way,'[1] it would have been difficult for her to foresee how, almost twenty years later, the team working on the continuation of the film-star advertising for the best selling toilet soap in the world, would take these words to heart and carefully ponder them! No longer do the stars of the 1970s, such as Sophia Loren, Raquel Welch, or, indeed, Brigitte Bardot, have the appeal they used to have, no longer do today's young women aspire to the beauty, glamour and sexuality that made these stars famous and epitomized the kind of life that every young girl dreamt of. A little more is needed to make the stars of screen and stage appeal to today's generation, though it has not lost its interest in beauty, glamour and mild eroticism, as long as these are presented in a contemporary fashion.

All this will be discussed later; at this stage, it is simply worth recalling that the momentous idea of using endorsements by Hollywood movie stars to sell a bar of toilet soap was supposedly developed by a woman whom David Ogilvy once called the greatest copywriter of her generation, a strong personality and the wife of Stanley Resor, the man who created the J. Walter Thompson Company.[2] This form of advertising, first devised in the mid-1920s by Helen Lansdowne Resor, has enjoyed increasing favour with all those involved ever since, for several reasons. Firstly, and most importantly, the fact that a film star's qualifications to judge a beauty product could not be questioned made the use of film-star endorsements one of those great advertising ideas that only occur a few times in a century. Secondly, the film studios, which, in those days, had exclusive contracts with their artists, valued the considerable free publicity for their stars. Thirdly, the stars themselves also appreciated the publicity and became even more amenable when the original system of payment in free soap was later supplemented by a handsome fee. And, finally, the advertiser had the undoubted boon of a continual growth in sales. The combination of showmanship and business acumen gave satisfaction to all concerned!

LUX TOILET SOAP AND UNILEVER

Before we continue this saga of beauty and glamour, and their value in the toughest of commercial contexts, a sober, down-to-earth review of some of the organizational and financial aspects is called for. Elsewhere in this book, the Unilever organization has been described in some detail, and special mention was made of Unilever's 'co-ordinations', which have worldwide responsibilities for its various product categories.[3] Lux Toilet Soap is one of the important international brands of Unilever's Detergents Co-ordination, which in 1990 accounted for 21 per cent of the concern's total turnover of Dfl.72 billion, a figure of 15.4 billion, and made a profit of Dfl.1.184 billion, representing 18 per cent of the concern's total operating profit of Dfl.6.6 billion. Later in this chapter, we shall return to certain organizational aspects of Detergents Co-ordination and examine how it is preparing for the Single European Market in 1993 and beyond; but, at the moment, it should suffice to say that Lux Toilet Soap is not only the world-leader in its field (with Palmolive as a strong second), but is also one of those rare products that seem truly to deserve the often misused title of an 'international' or a 'global' brand.

LUX TOILET SOAP: INTERNATIONAL BRAND OR CONCEPT?

Elsewhere in this book, we have discussed the difference between an international brand and an international concept. In doing so, we have argued that the designation 'international brand' should only be applied to products that are intrinsically and visually totally identical all over the world. In contrast, products based on an international concept afford more scope for variations in the advertising and presentation of the brands in different countries, provided that the overall basic positioning and consumer promise are the same everywhere.[4] This view is also held by Sir David Orr, past chairman of Unilever Ltd.:

> The transfer of products and associated know-how between countries is a key source of economies for a multinational marketing company. There is a whole spectrum of degrees of feasibility of transfer. At one extreme, the product, its positioning, and its presentation, including its name, can all be used in a number of countries – Colgate Toothpaste is an example. In most cases, there will be a degree of tailoring, so that it might be the product concept – for example, instant soup or low-fat spreads – that is transferred and presented with a variety of names. At the other end of the spectrum, there are relatively few products for which there is no scope to learn from experience elsewhere.[5]

Lux Toilet Soap meets the definition of an international brand because its name, its packaging, its basic consumer promise and the expression of this promise in terms of advertising are virtually the same all over the world.

THE POSITIONING OF LUX TOILET SOAP

The advertising positioning for this product runs as follows:

> Lux is the classic skin care soap, made from pure, natural ingredients which give the lather its creaminess. This special creaminess is your assurance of the care Lux is taking care of your skin, leaving it softer and smoother, and this is the reason why international (film) stars have consistently trusted their skin to Lux, and recommended it for use by other women.[6]

Not only is the product's positioning the same throughout the world, so is its brand name. The tablet and wrapper are also designed for international use, but they need not always be identical in all countries at any one time. Perfumes may differ too, as can the varieties of Lux Toilet Soap for special types of skin. However, these small divergences do not affect the overall policy that Unilever's Detergents Co-ordination wishes to pursue with regard to this important international contributor to the company profits.

From an advertising point of view, there again are no divergences from the basic policy: Lux Toilet Soap advertising will always feature a film star, explaining why she is using the product and recommending it to other women because of its perfect care for the skin.

ORIGIN AND DEVELOPMENT

Interestingly, the name Lux was not originally the name of a toilet soap. Before the soap was developed Lever Brothers in the USA had been marketing Lux Flakes for washing delicate textiles, a field in which they were the market-leader. Consumers were so satisfied with this product that they also used it for washing their hands, for bathing babies and as a shampoo, and this evident demand for a Lux product in tablet form resulted in the introduction of Lux Toilet Form, as the soap was initially called. Incidentally, it is interesting to note that little is known of the origin of the brand name; a situation that we have encountered on other occasions in this book. One would like to know who had the imaginative notion of calling the product Lux, a name that still carries the same connotations of luxury or luxuriousness as it did at the beginning of this century.

Once the decision had been taken to launch Lux as a toilet soap, the bar and wrapper had to be designed, and in spring 1923 J. Walter Thompson, the advertising agency for Lux products ever since Lux Flakes had been introduced, produced what parents or grandparents of readers of this book may still remember as the 'sampler' design: 'it was felt that such a wrapper, with its touch of culture and quality, would make a strong appeal through its historic background and the then present interest Americans had in sampler and cross stitch work.'[7]

The product was test-launched in October 1924 in Framingham, Massachusetts, and it began its roll-out in New England, in March of the following year. The product was launched in Lever's home country, the UK, in September 1928 and is now an international brand sold in about 79 countries all over the world, including the Soviet Union and China.[8]

Unfortunately, the two countries in which Lux Toilet Soap started its triumphant process of expansion, the United States and the United Kingdom, now produce disappointing levels of sales. In the USA, advertising for the brand ceased in the late 1960s, for various reasons – severe competition from new (deodorant) soaps, falling cinema audiences and the fact that film stars were losing much of their glamour. Today, the product is still on sale, but enjoys limited popularity. In the UK, the company encountered problems in signing up top personalities to endorse the product, and serious doubts arose, anyway, as to the current appeal of film stars. The traditional Lux advertising was replaced by a campaign claiming that Lux 'was the soap of the world's most beautiful women'. It failed, and the brand has never recovered.

The main development of the brand is now taking place in continental Europe (which accounts for 20 per cent of total Lux sales), and in Brazil and the Far East. However, it is to be hoped that one day the two countries that originated this highly successful concept will find commercially acceptable ways to conform with the policy pursued by Unilever's Detergents Co-ordination and once again make a significant contribution to the success of this international brand.

THE CHRONOLOGICAL DEVELOPMENT OF LUX

To return to the visual presentation of the product – which is of particular importance because it should reinforce the product's promise of a beautiful skin – it is interesting to see how, over the years, the bar and wrapper of Lux Toilet Soap have continually been adapted to changing tastes and life-styles. The soap's history provides another piece of evidence that 'life-cycle' theories have no real validity as long as a brand and its image are nurtured with infinite care and kept up-to-date in the eyes of consumers. Consider what would have happened if the 'sampler' design of the wrapper, attractive as it was at the time, had not been adapted to the styles and tastes of later generations.

To underline this point, let us briefly review the development of the Lux Toilet Soap tablet and wrapper since the introduction of the brand, in the USA in 1924:[9]

---

1. In 1924, a 'rectangular' shape of tablet and the 'sampler' design of wrapper were used for the launch of the product; and these remained unchanged over a number of years. In this connection, it is interesting to note that, whilst the 'sampler' wrapper conformed perfectly well to the first advertising for Lux, in later years this wrapper was not entirely in keeping with the prevailing image of film stars and their lives of beauty and glamour, as expressed in the slogan 'Pure mild Lux Toilet Soap is the beauty care of nine out of ten film stars'!

2. A first step towards creating a closer association between the product's advertising and its packaging was taken in the late 1950s and early 1960s, when gold and coloured foil wrappers were introduced, giving the product a more glamorous presentation, more in line with the image of the film stars.

3. The tablet also underwent changes. In 1964, the 'full cushion' shape, with flattened and rounded edges, to make the soap easier to handle, was introduced in the UK.

4. In 1970, the 'stadium'-shaped tablet was introduced in Italy – later followed by a few other countries. It was thicker and more rounded and had more planes than the 'full cushion' and remained in use until 1985.

5. The international launch in the early 1970s of a superfatted product resulted in the introduction of a wrapper design still closer to the concept of the product itself. Its new elements – a woman looking in a mirror adorned by a rose-underwent several refinements in the late 1970s and early 1980s. It is of interest to note that, although the woman was very beautiful, she was not a recognizable film star, as might have been expected; technical and contractual problems apparently prevented the company from using a film star's face.

6. In 1985, Lux was relaunched with a new formula, promising a richer, creamier lather and a firmer bar; the new formula was supported by yet another tablet design – with a 'moon scoop' shape – first introduced in Germany. The tablet's shape is supposed to evoke associations with a pot of face-cream, suggesting soft and gentle care for the complexion. In 1986, all other European countries followed the German design, dropping the previously used 'full cushion' and 'stadium' bars.

This survey of the development of Lux packaging shows that new designs of tablets and wrappers were not always introduced simultaneously, so that there was not always one uniform design in all European markets. Apart from being attributable to technical and distributional problems, this was also a reflection of the way in which Unilever was organized at that time; the managements of the national companies had considerable authority in those days. Since the mid-1950s, much has changed in this respect, as we shall see later. Following the introduction, in the early 1970s, of the 'mirror' wrapper design, greater uniformity has gradually been achieved throughout Europe; similarly the tablet's 'moon scoop' design, associating the emotional and functional properties of the product, is now practically identical all over the Continent. Having reviewed the most significant developments involving the actual product and its packaging, it seems opportune to recall the advertising used at the time of its launch.

EARLY LUX ADVERTISING

J. Walter Thompson had recommended that, both because of the prevailing popularity in the USA of French toiletry products and in order to differentiate clearly between advertising for Lux Flakes and for Lux Toilet Soap, the headline of the launch campaign for the new product should run:

'Made as France makes her finest toilet soaps, but it costs only 10c.'

This was soon followed by:

96% of the lovely complexions you see on the screen are cared for by
Lux Toilet Soap . . . There are in Hollywood 433 actresses doing
important work, including all stars. 417 of these use Lux Toilet Soap.
White, delicately fragrant, luxurious!

The slogan that followed and became famous was, of course:

'9 out of 10 screen stars use Lux Toilet Soap.'

It ran for almost forty years but had finally to be abandoned because of legal quibbles. At present, the headline in magazine advertisements runs, 'Let your skin be the star', the body-copy concentrating on the rich, creamy lather and the soothing natural oils, which leave the skin soft and attractive; the pay-off is 'The beauty soap of international stars'.

As in the case of the wrapper and tablet, the content and presentation of the film-star testimonial had to be adapted constantly to changing tastes and styles and to consumers' attitudes towards the stars themselves. This was the only way for Lux advertising to remain credible and convincing to the buying public.

CHANGING PROFILE OF LUX USERS

Because of the importance of this factor, Unilever Detergents Co-ordination closely monitors changes in the attitudes and behaviour of women over a period of time. The trends that emerge help the company and the advertising agency to match the film-star presentation with the current views and opinions of women on the role and value of these artists in the world of today. For example, between 1925 and 1945, women saw the care of their husbands and children as their main task in life. They had little self-confidence and depended heavily on their spouses. Advertising to women in those days was informative, with an emphasis on women's chores, and, at the same time, rather patronizing. During the first decade after 1945, women gained in confidence but were, in the main, still trying to please their husbands – though, they were also beginning to want to project an aura of beauty and glamour to the world at large by coming as close as possible to the image of airline stewardesses and screen idols. Lux advertising in those days emphasized beauty and a lovely skin with the words, 'Lux gives you a special complexion for the man in your life'.

After 1955, women became much more self-confident, and subjects such as sanitary protection were no longer taboo. Women had their own opinions and started to participate in public life, and their passive role changed into a more active attitude towards their existence. The film stars in Lux advertising became 'friends', sharing beauty secrets or being shown in more private situations at home or in their spare time. Later, with the development of international feminism during the 1970s, women took part in democratic movements and wished to be seen as the equals of men, able to talk about various matters with conviction and knowledge. This attitude was reflected in Lux advertising, which assumed a new aura of naturalness; the film-star aspect of the campaign was treated with greater subtlety, and the stars were no longer depicted as screen goddesses but were shown in the normal situations of daily life.

By the 1980s, the 'new woman' had become an individual, who wanted to be treated as such. The modern woman is self-confident, independent, active and assertive. Her use of beauty care products is no longer motivated by a desire to please others but by a desire for inner satisfaction. Lux advertising is again trying to take all this into account. Glamour alone is no longer good enough, and naturalness with an emphasis on personality and individuality are the characteristics of recent campaigns, though they never lose the touch of glamour and sex-appeal that has always characterized Lux advertising.[10]

LUX ADVERTISING NOW

The importance of the above review of trends in women's attitudes over the years becomes even clearer in the light of the positioning statement for Lux referred to earlier in this chapter and the way in which this statement has been translated into strategy and execution. In fact, positioning, strategy and execution are so interwoven – the incentives for using Lux (pure, natural ingredients that will make your skin softer and smoother) and the method of presenting them (international stars recommending the product) so inseparable and, above all, so permanent and timeless – that the continuing success of Lux advertising depends almost entirely upon the extent to which its creators are able to maintain a contemporary, socially acceptable and consumer oriented presentation. It could be argued that the need to study the consumer continuously applies to all brand advertising, but, in the case of Lux Toilet Soap, the importance of the presentational nuances, all relating to women's mysterious ways of attracting the opposite sex, is probably more decisive than in the case of many other advertised products.

THE PROFILE OF THE FILM STAR

The presentational nuances mentioned in the previous paragraph all centre around the film star, who should evidently be portrayed in such a way that women will wish at all times to identify with what they see as her life-style and expectations. Today, stars represent much more than just beauty or glamour. The real female star possesses a number of qualities that are rarely found in one person and that can be expressed visually as follows:[11]

If the qualities of the product itself can be successfully matched with the beneficial effects attributed to them by stars who have 'got it all', and if the selected social situation and the setting for the commercial suggest the same high quality, the total impression left on consumers should result in the acceptance and repeated purchase of the product by a large part of the audience to whom the advertising is addressed.

THE STARS

Over the years, a number of well-known film stars have featured in the Lux commercials, and while a few countries have preferred to use local stars to recommend the brand, there have been many stars under international contract. A dozen of the most famous names are:

Brigitte Bardot	Sophia Loren
Joan Collins	Shirley MacLaine
Marlene Dietrich	Victoria Principal
Jane Fonda	Ginger Rogers
Rita Hayworth	Elizabeth Taylor
Audrey Hepburn	Raquel Welch

The decision of certain countries to use local stars requires some comment. One could argue that an international product should only be recommended by internationally known stars, but there are cases when a local star has made at least as much impact on the public as a lesser known international star might have done.

The contract signed by J. Walter Thompson, representing the advertiser, and by the artist or her agent or representative usually covers a period of three years, during which Unilever is entitled to use the star's testimonial in advertisements for Lux toilet soap or for extensions to this line of products in any country that it wishes. The amount of time needed for the shooting of the commercial(s), for taking still photographs for magazines and for synchronization are all laid down, and so are the fee and the travel expenses that the star will receive. An important clause in the contract requires:

> the artist to confirm that she has used the Product regularly and that
> all the remarks either made by her or attributed to her for the purpose
> of exploiting the Product by means of the Commercials or the Artist's
> Image represent her true opinions of the Product which were held
> before any approach was made to her by the Company to endorse
> the same.[12]

Here, a point made in other chapters needs to be repeated: the centralized production of advertising for international use will not only offer considerable economies of scale but will enable the best available creative talent to be concentrated on the project, thereby producing optimum results. The production of Lux Toilet Soap commercials, with their famous stars and equally famous directors, is an expensive exercise, so local Unilever detergents companies who use the material bear a proportionate share of the costs, which are still considerably lower than those that they would incur by producing their own commercials.

ROLE OF INTERNATIONAL ADVERTISING AGENCY

It seems almost superfluous to emphasize that a special relationship exists between Unilever and J. Walter Thompson as regards the advertising of Lux products. After all, it was the wife of the agency's founder who produced one of the most successful advertising ideas ever developed, and the relationship between the two organizations has existed, not only at head-office level but also at all the national levels, for well over 65 years; the only comparable bond is that between Philip Morris and Leo Burnett for the advertising of Marlboro cigarettes, also described in this book.

An interesting aspect of JWT's handling of the Lux brands has been the setting up of an International Unilever Unit at JWT's offices in London. This unit supervises all the stages in the preparation and production of Lux commercials or cinema-films, including, as we have seen, the signing up of the stars. Once the unit has finished producing a commercial, it draws up a folder for all JWT's offices around the world. This contains precise information about the material available and copies of the script. It also informs the agency's offices about the availability of commercials on tape with different packshots for those countries not yet using the 'scoop' bar. The film-star testimonial, in different languages, is available as recorded synchronized lines; while other material includes colour photographs, as well as notes on the English text (explaining, for example, the meaning of the words 'star treatment' that are used in the commercial; or elaborating on a reference to a 'firm' bar, meaning an improvement in the soap's composition intended to ensure that it will not soften when left briefly in water). Finally, in addition to this, the folder also includes an order form to be sent to JWT in London for processing.

Unilever, of course, pays for the production of the films, but it enlists the assistance of JWT's London co-ordinating unit to obtain a 'contribution fee' from each country using the material. The fee is charged to the local detergents company, and this procedure is also followed with respect to the cost of the actual materials ordered; the local JWT office is billed for these costs and collects the money from its local client. For its important co-ordinating role, the London agency receives a fee from Detergents Co-ordination, while the local JWT offices in the various countries involved work on the basis of the commission system, the details of which are arranged separately in each case.

THE MEDIA SITUATION

During the late 1920s and early 1930s, magazines were the sole medium for advertising. Radio advertising started in 1930, and in 1934 the Lux Radio Theatre was introduced, a full hour-long show with popular stage and screen plays featuring well-known stars; this programme lasted for more than 21 years. Clearly, when commercials for Lux began to be shown on television, in 1950, this became the main medium for the brand's advertising, but cinema films played an almost equally important role, particularly since some countries were still without television; and as a supporting medium, magazines, with their excellent colour reproductions, have always retained their significance. To this day, the combination of these three media provides the most crucial advertising support for Lux Toilet Soap.

LINE EXTENSIONS

When, after the Second World War and the times of austerity that followed, a greater selection of products was once more available to the public, resulting in strong competition, Detergents Co-ordination responded with a series of changes in, and additions to, the existing product. These included the introduction of a new superfatted formula, of new perfumes and new colours. The original product had always been white, supporting its claim to be made from natural ingredients, but a wider choice of colours was felt to be in line with prevailing fashions and tastes. In addition, some time ago, the company went further and experimented with the production of different formulations of soap for different types of skin, and in some countries this was successful. Some people, however, have doubts that women in the more sophisticated markets find it entirely credible that an ordinary bar of toilet soap can have the same beneficial effects on their skin as they expect from a specialized skin cream.

It was a different matter when alternatives to toilet soap became increasingly popular, and personal washing habits became more sophisticated. The importance of these changes in the 'personal wash' market in Europe can best be illustrated by the following market indices.[13]

Personal Wash Market Europe
(Index 1987–1989)

	1987	1989
P W generally	100	103
P W toilet bars	100	93
P W liquid soaps	100	108
P W shower gels	100	132
P W bath additives	100	103
P W others	100	98

These figures clearly indicate that toilet soaps are losing ground to shower gels and bath additives. Lux had thus to respond by offering a wider variety of products for personal washing, so that the Lux range now includes both gels and additives, which also have to be advertised. The Ornella Muti commercials therefore include a testimonial for either the toilet soap or for the shower gel, but as this could leave doubt in consumers' minds as to which of these two products Ornella Muti really prefers, it is stipulated in the contract that: 'the Company will not be entitled to broadcast the Commercials featuring both of the Products within 1 (one) week of one another in any country'.[14] Finally, in addition to the line extensions just described, Lux is now also available in Japan as a shampoo – another indication that Detergents Co-ordination is firmly bent on developing the brand further, in accordance with new opportunities in the market-place.

1993 AND BEYOND

In the discussion of Unilever's successful range of frozen products elsewhere in this book, much attention was paid to the organizational steps that the company has taken to exploit new opportunities in the important food market as efficiently and effectively as possible.[15] Unilever's Detergents Co-ordination has taken comparable action, though its approach is rather different. It has gone a step further in making certain that its European interests, accounting for approximately 45 per cent of Unilever's worldwide detergents business, will be safeguarded and expanded. It has set up the Lever Europe organization, based in Brussels and responsible to the detergents co-ordinator for Unilever's European detergents business. The management of the new organization represents many nationalities, and in order to produce, market and distribute products on a European basis rather than on a national one, European Brand Groups have been formed, responsible to the management of Lever Europe for the key brands, which are grouped together in categories such as household cleaning, dishwashing, fabrics and personal wash. Each of these European Brand Groups (EBG) consists of representatives from Unilever's various detergents companies in Europe with a special interest or expertise in its particular category of product; and each EBG is based in the offices of one of the detergents companies concerned. It is also of interest to note that the function of the advertising specialist, who, in the past, supervised all detergents' advertising from the company's central office, has been discontinued. This responsibility has now been taken over by the marketing member of the relevant EBG.

The reorganization has meant a significant reshuffling of people and their responsibilities that will not have been welcomed equally by all the executives concerned, but the importance of these changes for the future of the business is generally understood. It will enable Lever Europe confidently to pursue the following objectives: (a) to internationalize existing brands; (b) to introduce new brands on a European scale; (c) to react more quickly to steps taken by competitors; and (d) to find the proper response to the increase in central buying by large supermarket chains and the like, a problem of great concern to practically all companies operating internationally. If all works out as expected, the result should be a marked increase in profits. Thus, Unilever has taken two significant initiatives in relation to its most important categories of products in order to be prepared for the years to come, indicating foresight, and confidence in the future of the company.

As regards the future of Lux Toilet Soap and its offshoots, there can be no doubt that the very successful film-star concept will be continued, albeit in a different manner. The personality in the commercials will always remain a star, but the image of Hollywood glitter and glamour will make way for the woman who is a 'Venus in her own way', referred to by Brigitte Bardot in the quotation at the beginning of this chapter. The stars will descend from the sky and will present themselves as ordinary human beings, albeit hard-working and famous ones admired for the enjoyment that they give to others by vast audiences all round the world. The audiences of the commercials will wish to choose a particular item for the care of their skins from a wide variety of Lux products, ranging from a bar of toilet soap or a bath foam to a shower gel or maybe even a skin cleanser, all available in different colours to match the bathrooms of today's sophisticated women. One can be confident that Unilever's Detergents Co-ordination and its European Brand Group for the personal wash market, made up of representatives from France, Germany, Italy and the UK, will succeed in finding the right formula for the continuation of one of the most successful advertising ideas of all. A simple idea, of everlasting value.

Notes

1. Green, Jonathan (1982) (ed.), *A Dictionary of Contemporary Quotations*. London: David & Charles, p. 55.
2. Jones, John Philip (1989), *Does It Pay to Advertise?* Lexington, KY; Lexington Books, p. 87.
3. See chapter 3 on Unilever's 'Captain' range of frozen products.
4. *Ibid.*
5. Jones, p. xx.
6. *Lux Toilet Soap, an International Brand History* (undated), compiled by the 'Personal Wash' European Brand Group of Detergents Co-ordination, Hamburg, Appendix 5.1.
7. Personal letter to the author from Eliza Oxley, J. Walter Thompson Company, London, 30 November 1989.
8. *Lux Toilet Soap*, point 1.
9. *Ibid.*, points 2 and 4.
10. *Ibid.*, Appendices 5.3.3.–5.3.8.
11. Personal letter to the author from Margret Dixon, Lever GmbH, Hamburg, Germany, 17 August 1990.
12. Agreement for the Services of Ornella Muti (1986), between the J. Walter Thompson Company Ltd. and Reteitalia S.P.A., 28 November, point 8.8.
13. See note 11.
14. See note 12, point 6.3.
15. See Chapter 3.

MARLBORO

'Come to the Flavour of Marlboro Country'

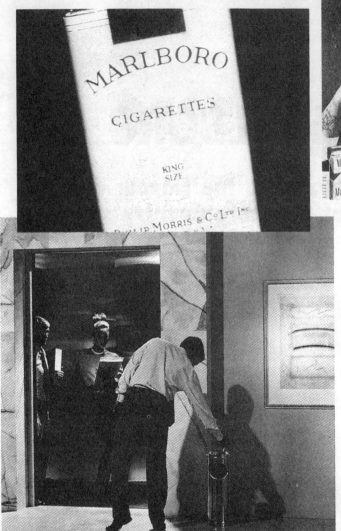

New from Philip Morris

Marlboro
FILTER CIGARETTES

The new easy-drawing filter cigarette that delivers
the goods on flavor. Long size. Popular filter price.
Light up a Marlboro and be glad you've changed to it!

CONSIDERATE SMOKING IS IMPORTANT.

Smoking needn't mean friction, even in confined spaces.

Non-smokers will appreciate simple acts of courtesy, like being asked if they mind you lighting up a cigarette.

Managers can help by ensuring that office ventilation works properly. And there is an important contribution everyone can make: being tolerant of individual likes and dislikes.

In short, both smokers and non-smokers should try to see things from one another's point of view.

Smoking doesn't have to be a burning issue in the workplace.

Consideration on one side, and a little tolerance on the other, may be all that's needed to take the heat out of the argument.

COURTESY. IT CAN TURN YOUR CIGARETTE INTO A PEACEPIPE.

Brought to you by Philip Morris in the interest of courteous smoking.

For a free booklet on promoting courteous smoking in your workplace, complete and return this coupon to: Corporate Affairs Department, Philip Morris (EEC), Brillancourt 4, Case Postale, Lausanne 1001, Switzerland.

Name _____ Position _____
Company _____
Address _____

Come to where the flavor is. Come to Marlboro.

TRY ARISTOCRATIC SMOKING

Spend a few extra pennies just to find out how much pleasure choicer, richer, milder tobaccos can bring you. Today — for a treat — try Marlboro!

Ivory Tip, Plain Ends, or Beauty Tips (red)

Now only 20¢

MARLBORO America's Luxury Cigarette

MARLBORO
'Come to the Flavour of Marlboro Country'

Writing of a visit to the Arents Collection in the New York Public Library, Bernard Levin, the well-known British art critic and author, recalls that: 'carved over the fireplace in the Arents Room was a rubric that would now lead to a lynching, or at least a tarring and feathering: "The man who smokes, thinks like a sage and acts like a Samaritan."[1] There are still a few people around who might agree with these sentiments and who not only accept the risk of being tarred or feathered but ignore the grave health warnings that are now obligatory on virtually all cigarette packs and in most cigarette advertising.

Among the brands that appear to satisfy their cravings, Marlboro is undoubtedly the market-leader: not only is it the top-selling cigarette in the world, it is the world's best-selling consumer packaged product. Of the 580 billion cigarettes that Philip Morris sold in 1989, representing a market share of almost 11 per cent[2], Marlboro accounted for by far the greatest portion. Thus, one can safely assume that throughout the world, every minute of every day of every year, one million Marlboro's go up in smoke, to the obvious enjoyment of their users!

TOTAL CIGARETTE CONSUMPTION

World consumption of cigarettes is ten times greater than Marlboro's share of the market, so even the most fanatical opponent of smoking will have to admit that cigarette smoking is not an obsolescent habit! This is confirmed by industry sources and independently available statistical data. Looking at the figures for Europe alone (Table 1), it is of interest to see how consumption differs from country to country.

Table 1

Country	Percentage of smokers in adult population	Number of cigarette smokers (millions)	Consumption of cigarettes per capita per day		
			1982	1984	1987
W. Germany	34	17 760	5.0	5.3	5.3
Italy	33.8	15 835	4.9	5.0	4.7
UK	33	14 740	5.0	4.8	4.6
France	38	15 941	4.4	4.5	4.7
Spain	39.5	10 555	5.0	5.3	5.6
Greece	76.6	5 970	7.2	7.8	8.1
Belg. Luxemb.	32	2 510	5.8	5.6	4.8
Netherlands	40.3	4 795	4.2	3.0	3.0
Portugal	25.6	1 970	3.7	3.7	3.8
Denmark	38	1 605	4.0	4.1	3.9
Ireland	43	—	5.3	4.9	4.3
Norway	—	—	1.2	1.3	1.8
Sweden	—	—	4.0	3.8	3.6

Forecasts of total cigarette consumption between 1987 and 1998 indicate that in the countries listed above it will decline by 12.2 per cent, i.e. from 629 457 million cigarettes in 1987 to 552 593 million in 1998.[3] These figures confirm the well-known fact that cigarette consumption is indeed already decreasing; the negative publicity about the ill effects of smoking on one's health have prompted many people to give it up, or not to start at all. Against this trend, Third World countries that have gained independence from European colonial powers still see smoking as a status symbol, so in these parts of the world smoking is not decreasing. In addition, more and more women perceive smoking as an additional confirmation of their independence. Young people, however, follow the general trend and are smoking less. The EC Commission confirms the industry figures and states that on average 33 per cent of Europeans are cigarette smokers, 3 per cent smoke cigars or a pipe, 19 per cent have stopped smoking and 45 per cent have never even started smoking.[4]

Turning to advertising, one thing is certain: all available research and evidence suggests that it has little to no effect on total consumption, particularly among the young 'advertising plays a negligible role, if any, in the initiation of smoking by the young, compared with that of personal and social factors, and irrespective of the presence or absence of strict restrictions on tobacco advertising.'[5] Indeed, it is a sign of the inherent strength of this habit that when the Berlin Wall was demolished, Philip Morris in Germany could hardly deliver enough cartons of Marlboro cigarettes to satisfy the demands of the East Germans streaming into the West . . .

HISTORY AND GROWTH

In 1990, Philip Morris produced an operating revenue of $51 billion, of which 40 per cent was from tobacco, 50 per cent from foods and 8 per cent from beer and other interests; its operating income amounted to $8.730 billion and its earnings before income tax were $6.3 billion. The company currently employs 168 000 people worldwide. (See also the company's Annual Report for 1990.)

The business started in 1847 as a small tobacconist's shop in Bond Street, London. It was owned by Philip Morris Esq., who, in 1854, produced tobacco in a new form called 'cigarettes'.[6] Subsequent highlights in the company's history were as follows:

1872	Philip Morris begins exporting cigarettes to the USA.
1902	Philip Morris & Co. Ltd. is incorporated in New York.
1919	A new firm, owned by American stockholders, acquires the Philip Morris company in the USA and incorporates it in Virginia under the name of Philip Morris Co. Ltd. Inc.
1954	Benson & Hedges merges with Philip Morris and Philip Morris (Australia) Ltd. becomes the company's first major subsidiary outside the USA.
1961	Philip Morris International is set up in Lausanne, Switzerland. (This will be discussed separately.)
1965	In January, a self-imposed cigarette advertising code comes into effect in the USA, under which companies voluntarily and individually agree not to promote cigarettes to young people and to avoid implying that smoking has health benefits or is essential to social prominence.
1970	Philip Morris obtains whole ownership of the Miller brewing company.
1978	Philip Morris acquires the Seven-Up company and also buys the international cigarette business of the Liggett Group Inc., acquiring foreign rights to Lark and Chesterfield.

1985	Philip Morris acquires General Foods, which owns Maxwell House coffee etc.
1988	Kraft joins the concern, with its natural and processed cheese, mayonnaise, dressings etc.
1989	Kraft General Foods Inc. is formed.
1990	Philip Morris acquires Jacobs Suchard A.G., the makers of Toblerone and Milka chocolate products.

The above facts and figures only serve as a background to the story of Marlboro, which is still Philip Morris' most profitable product. As we have seen, the company is trying to diversify, and the acquisition of Kraft may well reduce the importance of Marlboro to the company as a whole, but in 1989, tobacco – mainly represented by Marlboro – still accounted for 64 per cent of the total operating income of the Philip Morris companies, as against only 40 per cent of their total operating revenues. The Marlboro brand seems simply to be irreplaceable, and Stratford P. Sherman may, after all, have been right when he wrote some time ago: 'Getting Philip Morris off cigarettes has seemed as hopeless as offering an inner-city crack dealer a job flipping burgers at McDonald's.'[7]

MARLBOROUGH OR MARLBORO?

Philip Morris Esq. began exporting cigarettes to the USA in 1872, but it is difficult to trace the precise origin of the brand name Marlboro. An executive at the company's headquarters in New York assumes that the location of a Philip Morris office in Marlborough Street in London inspired the owners, in 1894, to use this name for one of their varieties of cigarettes, then, indeed, called Marlborough.[8] However, the company's vice-president for corporate affairs in New York writes that '. . . the brand was named after a county in England and first appeared in the United States in 1885 as "Marlborough" with the slogan "The Ladies Favorite" . . .'[9] As there is no county of such a name in England, the origin of the name may forever remain a secret, but be this as it may, in 1908 the trademark was registered in the USA as Marlboro, which has, of course, been the spelling ever since.

MARLBORO LANDMARKS

1940	In the early 1940s, Philip Morris launched Marlboro in the USA in a white pack, as a cigarette for women; there were three varieties: plain, white filter-tips and red filter-tips, the last variety advertised as the cigarette 'To match your lips and fingertip'.
1954	The breakthrough occurred when Philip Morris introduced a new flip-top box, in the now familiar red design, and appointed Leo Burnett as its advertising agency, which, in turn, recommended changing Marlboro's image as a women's cigarette into one as a cigarette for men, by featuring 'rugged men' in its new advertising.
1955–1960	The 'rugged men' were initially cowboys, pilots, deep-sea divers or successful businessmen. Their hands were tattooed, and they all represented successful character types, whom the male user would aspire to emulate: the 'Marlboro man' was born.

1962   Of all the types used for Marlboro advertising, the cowboy, with his background and origin in the American West, proved to have widest appeal to a male audience. The 'Marlboro man', coming from 'Marlboro country' and always accompanied by the striking music from the film 'The Magnificent Seven', became one of the most successful advertising concepts ever produced.

MARLBORO AS A PRODUCT

There are, of course, several varieties of cigarettes now sold under the Marlboro umbrella; in addition to the main product, Marlboro Red, these include Marlboro 100 and, more recently, also Marlboro Lights and Marlboro Menthol. These line-extensions have all been integrated into the core brand's advertising; this will be discussed later.

As regards the products themselves, the company discloses little about the choice of tobacco leaves and other ingredients. The composition is basically the same everywhere, but the influences of water and air at the different production sites cannot be totally avoided, so small variations in the flavour of the final product may always occur, though they will be hardly noticeable to the public. Of course, one of the highest priorities is to ensure that the product is of top quality at all times. A former chairman and chief executive officer of the company, Hamish Maxwell, puts it as follows:

'We check Marlboro cigarettes worldwide to make sure they meet objective standards for moisture content, tobacco density and filter draw, and we regularly run blind tests against the competition to make sure the Marlboro taste keeps giving smokers the satisfaction they have come to associate with the product name . . .'[10]

PHILIP MORRIS INTERNATIONAL

Before we review the policy and execution of Marlboro's advertising and the relationship between the company and Burnett, its international advertising agency, the international, and particularly the European, organization of the company should be briefly discussed. In 1990, Philip Morris International, which is responsible for tobacco sales outside the USA, accounted for 21 per cent of the company's total operating revenues, or $10.7 billion, as compared with 20 per cent, or $10.3 billion, from domestic US tobacco sales. Within Philip Morris International, there are five regional groups, covering Australia, Asia, Latin America, the EEC and the so-called EEMA (the EFTA countries, Eastern Europe, the Middle East and Africa), the organizations responsible for the last two regions being based in Lausanne, Switzerland. Of all these regions, the EEC is by far the most important, accounting for 75 per cent of total international revenues. The UK is not included in this region, because, in 1989, an agreement was made between Philip Morris and Rothman in the UK, under which the latter company took over the distribution and selling of the Philip Morris brands. Apart from Marlboro, the main brands of Philip Morris International are Chesterfield, Philip Morris, Merit, Lark, L&M and Virginia Slims.

In view of developments in Europe, Philip Morris International may one day expand its activities beyond the tobacco trade and embrace the concern's other interests, such as foods, outside the USA. At the moment, however, a simplified chart of the total organization looks as follows:

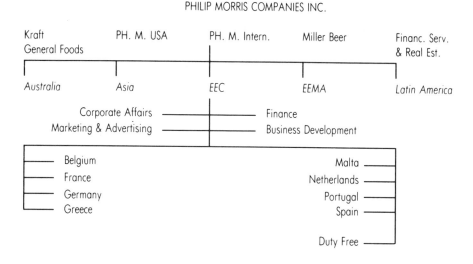

PHILIP MORRIS COMPANIES INC.

AUTHORITIES

The Philip Morris offices are all fully owned subsidiaries, but once plans have been agreed and approved, the execution of these plans is very much in the hands of the managements of the national offices. As far as the EEC is concerned, each September the offices in its countries produce what is called an 'original budget', including sales estimates and advertising expenditures for the coming year. This budget is discussed with, and approved by, the management of Philip Morris in Lausanne. During the month of January, a revised marketing plan is again reviewed and approved, and in the following June there is a final round of discussions concerning the latest estimates.

MARLBORO AND ITS ADVERTISING

The role and responsibilities of all involved in the advertising of Marlboro, be it at company or at advertising agency level, are quite unique. Ever since 'old man Burnett' created the 'Marlboro man', over 35 years ago, this brilliant advertising idea has been developed and nurtured by company and agency alike, working as one team to make the product into one of those very rare international or, as some people prefer to call them, 'global' brands. The appeal of the cowboy image does, indeed, seem to have been universal. Just as Unilever successfully used a very European-looking sea-captain in its advertisements in Japan, of all places, Philip Morris used the cowboy in its advertisements in Switzerland where it soon found that his attraction was as strong in Zürich as it was in El Paso, USA. This simply confirms that as long as an idea will successfully convey a uniform message to an agreed target audience in a number of countries, it can be used internationally with advantage. Marlboro's cowboy represented a life-style, and an image with sexual overtones, with which many men wished to identify. It thus became one of those rare advertising ideas that work equally well everywhere and established Marlboro among the extremely small group of real international or 'global' brands.

THE ROLE OF THE INTERNATIONAL ADVERTISING AGENCY

The advertising for Marlboro is developed by Philip Morris and Leo Burnett in Chicago. The material for commercials, films, outdoor hoardings, printed advertisements etc. is made available to all Philip Morris offices free of charge; the only exception is when one has a special request. Normally, however, offices will select from existing material whatever will best suit their local requirements. The question of alternative advertising does not arise, and the 'Not Invented Here' syndrome gets no chance. The product and its advertising together form one indivisible concept, and the only variations in the advertising for the brand between one country and another will consist of different emphases on the various elements of the campaign, such as the close-up of the cowboy, who may or may not have a cigarette, a match or a lighter in his hand, the country scene or the pack, of which the basic design has not changed since its introduction, in 1954.

THE MARLBORO COWBOY

This section represents a slight digression aimed at correcting a popular misconception: that the Marlboro cowboys are not real cowboys from Texas, but hired Hollywood actors. This is not true. The cowboys are genuine and are selected with infinite care. In practice, it is difficult to find men who exude masculinity, look their part on camera and are excellent riders; while those that do possess these qualities have to be available for the shooting of the commercials at very specific periods. Over the years, there have only been a small number of cowboys who have met these criteria and passed the stringent screening process, but those who were put under contract have used the money that they have earned to improve the farms from which they make their living.

MARLBORO ADVERTISING STRATEGY

Since 1954, when Marlboro was positioned as a brand for 18-year-old to 25-year-old men who preferred a fully flavoured filter cigarette, the advertising strategy has been to convey the distinctive characteristics of masculinity, outdoor life and the 'Texas look', as personified by the 'Marlboro man' from 'Marlboro country', with his attraction for the opposite sex. In more recent years, when new varieties were developed and advertised, becoming genuine line-extensions, the link between them and the original Marlboro Red was maintained. Thus, in advertising for Marlboro Lights, although the cowboy from the Marlboro Red advertisements was dropped because he did not suit the image of a light product, the famous landscapes were retained, albeit in a lighter colour. The presentation of the original Marlboro advertising proved to be so strong that consumers had no difficulty in identifying Marlboro Lights with the family of products from which it had originated.

The strength of the Marlboro Red campaign also became apparent in 1971, when cigarette advertising on television was forbidden in the USA and the moving scenes of cowboys in action had to be replaced by still photographs for print advertisements and posters. This transition was completely successful; a combination of strong close-ups, wide and varied vistas, and action shots of cowboys and horses provided a suitable alternative and produced excellent results. As a consequence, in those countries where tobacco advertising is still allowed in cinemas. Similar advertisements are also extensively used.

CRITERIA AND STANDARDS

It is, of course, of the utmost importance that all parties involved in the creation and adaptation of a campaign should apply similar criteria and standards. In the case of Marlboro, these are as follows:[11]

1. The cowboy is the hero; he controls the world around him.
2. The cowboy must be credible; the authenticity of every detail must never be questioned.
3. Marlboro pictures are candid; they should never be artificial or mannered.
4. Marlboro advertisements must be executed to the highest standards to ensure optimum impact.
5. There must be great variety in Marlboro advertisements with regard to both subject and lay-out; there still is so much to discover in 'Marlboro country'.
6. Marlboro country is grand; the beauty of its scenery and its impressive size should always be emphasized.

The application of these standards has resulted in advertising that is never boring but that always explores new angles, thereby maintaining its freshness and originality.

SPONSORSHIP

As is generally known, Philip Morris has always been heavily involved in sports sponsorship, and particularly in that of Formula 1 motor racing, which is the most prestigious of all. This sponsorship programme is one of the most important activities of its kind and Philip Morris Lausanne centrally co-ordinates and controls it on a world-wide scale. The Formula 1 drivers were seen to be the best modern equivalent of cowboys in the popular mind: rugged, virile, honest, adventurous, hard-working, conscientious people – who like a full-flavoured smoke! Hence, Marlboro has maintained its support of Formula 1 motor racing for more than eighteen years. The company does not take this responsibility lightly. It realizes full well that if the reputation and performance of Formula 1 racing teams were to decline, so would its own. Thus, the public manifestations of Marlboro's sponsorship seen at Formula 1 races, for which a separate budget is allocated annually, represent only a fraction of the company's involvement. Behind the scenes, it only takes a considerable interest in all aspects of these races but also helps to finance the training of promising young drivers to prepare them for the day when they too will take part in the top events. The company is also closely involved in all the safety aspects of racing and the precautions that are taken to prevent races from becoming accident spectaculars that people attend 'to see something happen'; this would not be in the interest either of the organizers or the sponsors.

Apart from Formula 1 racing, the company takes an interest in many other sports events, such as cart racing, rallies, motorbike racing, skiing, horse racing and cycle racing. Sometimes these events have a purely local character and, again, the company has laid down a number of criteria that have to be met, such as (a) the event must be related to an activity of interest to a particular target group; (b) the event must generate good press coverage; (c) the event must be a prestigious occasion with which the company wishes to be associated; and (d) the publicity for such an event must be in line with the standing of a market-leader.[12] In summary, it is fair to say that the company would like to be seen as recognizing and encouraging the efforts of others to become the 'number one' performers in their particular fields, as Marlboro is in its field of operation.

MARLBORO'S ADVERTISING BUDGET

According to published information, Philip Morris spends approximately $300 million per annum in Europe on advertising for all its brands, of which Marlboro, of course, takes the largest share.[13] *Media International* reports that in 1987 Marlboro's print advertising in European media accounted for 9.6 per cent of a total 'ad spend' in these media of $225 million, giving a figure of $21.5 million. Of this expenditure of $21.5 million, roughly 10 per cent is spent in the 'international' print media, the remaining 90 per cent in print media in 13 individual European countries.[14] The size of each local budget depends, of course, on a number of factors, and Marlboro certainly is not the biggest spender everywhere. In fact, it is often argued that being the market-leader in a given market need not entail the brand also being 'number one' in terms of advertising expenditure. Finally, when reviewing advertising expenditures on cigarettes, one must, of course, bear in mind that up to 75 per cent of the consumer price for a packet of Marlboro represents excise duties, the remaining 25 per cent being available to cover manufacturing, distribution, marketing and advertising costs and – ideally – to provide a profit!

Readers hardly need reminding that in most European countries the broadcast media cannot be used for cigarette advertising. As remarked earlier, an alternative scheme for presenting Marlboro in other media has been developed in the USA, so, in most countries, the Philip Morris offices simply have to choose between cinema advertising, magazine advertising, outdoor advertising, sponsorship and promotions; product sampling is unfortunately also prohibited in most countries. The authority of the national subsidiaries includes making the necessary arrangements with the local Burnett offices as regards agency compensation. Bearing in mind that the Chicago headquarters of Philip Morris makes advertising material for campaigns available free of charge and carries the total cost for the production of Marlboro cowboy and 'Marlboro country' advertising, local remuneration for the Burnett offices will usually be below the customary 15 per cent commission.

LEGAL RESTRICTIONS

This section deals with an aspect of international communications that is complex and extremely worrying to both advertisers and advertising agencies alike. It concerns the legal restraints imposed upon industries by governments, severely curbing the role of advertising. As these restraints are of particular importance to the tobacco industry, they merit particular attention in this chapter; the case for the freedom of advertising has to be argued somewhere, and this can best be done in relation to the industry that is affected worst of all. For many reasons, public opinion is against smoking, and it has been influenced, at least in part, by people who combine an undeniable concern for the welfare of the public with an equally undeniable concern for their own interests, be they political or otherwise. There is little point in discussing when and how this situation arose. The fact of the matter is that the influence of those against smoking caught both the tobacco industry and governments off their guard; the industry did too little too late to be able to reverse the trend, while governments could not very well ignore medical opinion and statistical evidence for the health risks involved, resulting in considerable pressure on them to take appropriate steps. However, governments were disinclined to forego '. . . more than $30 billion per year in excise taxes and VAT from the sale of tobacco products – roughly equivalent to the whole EC annual budget . . .' [15] Consequently, they took the easy option and decided, or are in the process of deciding, to restrict the advertising of cigarettes practically to the point of no return.

The feeling against smoking may even tempt official government representatives to make intemperate and irresponsible statements. For example, in the USA the Surgeon-General, Antonia Novello, has said, 'Five million of today's children in the United States will die of smoking-related illnesses if the rate of tobacco use by young people continues.' [16] In Europe, the EC Commission joined the chorus of hostility by submitting, on 7 April 1989, a 'Proposal for a Council Directive on the advertising of tobacco products in the press and by means of bills and posters'. This would permit tobacco advertisements to show only cigarette cartons or packages and would also forbid the use of tobacco brand trade-marks or logos on other commercial items, even ones totally unrelated to tobacco or a tobacco company. [17] Whilst the wording of this particular directive was not accepted by the Council of Ministers, one must expect that a modified version will one day be approved. The directive also illustrates the serious threat posed by such measures to the freedom of speech, the general concern being that, once tobacco advertising has been 'regulated', other product categories seen as directly or indirectly affecting people's health will be controlled too. For the tobacco industry, the particular difficulty is that it cannot categorically disprove the assertion that smoking will affect one's health. If it were possible to establish which ingredient(s) in cigarettes cause cancer, this would come as a considerable relief to the entire industry, but despite the many millions of dollars spent on research, the answer has not yet been found.

THE PHILIP MORRIS POINT OF VIEW

The company has issued an official statement entitled 'Consumer Issues', in which it says that the basis for the accusation that smoking is the principal cause of serious illnesses, such as lung cancer and heart diseases, 'is primarily statistical'. Philip Morris and the industry 'have contributed nearly $130 million to fund independent research on smoking and health . . . the results of scientific investigations to date fail to demonstrate a cause-and-effect relationship between smoking and chronic diseases.'

On advertising, the statement continues:

> Our advertising is intended to convert consumers who smoke to our brands, not to encourage smoking. . . . Research over the years has confirmed that brandswitching is the only effect advertising has. . . . The United States Supreme Court has ruled that commercial free speech – advertising in particular – is protected by the Constitution. We believe that if products are legal, society is best served by the freest possible flow of information about them.[18]

In Europe, the company will defend its interests in co-operation with various trade associations, such as the European Advertising Tripartite, representing the entire advertising industry at a European level. This body evolved from informal co-operation between advertisers and advertising agencies in the early 1970s when the first wave of 'consumer protection' legislation was at its peak. It became an official organization in 1980, when advertisers, advertising agencies and the media founded the EAT to defend common interests at international level.[19] Today it operates as an entirely independent community of interests.

European Convention on Human Rights

In the context of controls on tobacco advertising, readers should be reminded of the European Convention on Human Rights, signed in 1953 by the members of the Council of Europe. The Convention explicitly states, in Article 10, that, 'Everyone has the right to freedom of expression'. It is generally argued that 'commercial speech' is covered by the Article, as in the United States it is covered by the Constitution. Nonetheless, there still are governments that interpret freedom of expression more narrowly,[20] despite a recent UNESCO report stating that:

> La Commission et la Cour européennes des droits de l'homme ont établi une jurisprudence selon laquelle la publicité commerciale peut être protégée en vertu de l'article 10 de la Convention européenne de sauvegarde des droits de l'homme et des libertés fondamentales. Dans sa décision en date du 1er mars 1983, la Commission européenne des droits de l'homme a rappelé qu'elle avait précédemment émis l'opinion que les publicités commerciales et les campagnes de promotion sont, en tant que telles, protégées par l'article 10-1 de la Convention (requête no. 9664/82).[21]

Although it would be tempting to bring the restrictions on tobacco advertising – and for that matter on advertising of alcoholic and pharmaceutical products – before the Council of Europe's Court of Justice, such steps have not yet been taken. It is generally felt that such action would cause considerable public uproar and might do more harm than good, but, more importantly, industry prefers to try to come to terms with individual governments and the Commission of the EC in Brussels before bringing things to a head by appealing to the highest court. One, nevertheless, sometimes wonders how much longer industry will be prepared to accept governmental interference of this kind before forcing the issue, despite the risks involved.

'Considerate Smoking'

Leaving aside these legal skirmishes, it is remarkable how obligingly smokers have accepted restrictions that treat them almost as if they are indulging in a criminal act. Some initiatives have, however, been taken on their behalf; for example, since May 1990, the Information Office Cigarettes and Shag in the Netherlands has been running a campaign in a number of newspapers and magazines, in defence of those four out of ten adult Dutchmen who like to smoke; the campaign tries to achieve greater understanding and acceptance of the points of view of both smokers and non-smokers, resulting in more mutual tolerance. Similarly, the Philip Morris EEC region ran a campaign in a number of international magazines with the heading 'Considerate Smoking Is Important'. The advertising created by Gold Greenless Trott in the UK argued that 'Consideration on one side, and a little tolerance on the other, may be all that's needed to take the heat out of the argument'. The advertisements included a coupon enabling the reader to obtain two brochures: the first, entitled 'Fresh Air in the Workplace', dealt with indoor air quality in general, explaining that smoking may just be one of the factors causing discomfort among people at work; the second, called 'Smoking in the Workplace', examined the practical aspects of the smoking issue and made recommendations on how to develop a policy or guidelines that will satisfy both smokers and non-smokers.[22] All these efforts are commendable. They try to bring back some perspective into what is increasingly becoming an issue on which there would appear to be only one point of view and one answer.

PHILIP MORRIS AND ITS CORPORATE PROGRAMMES

The Philip Morris Public Affairs Department is not just heavily involved in defending the company's interests; fortunately, it also engages in more positive activities. The company runs a number of 'corporate citizen programs', which are described in one of its publications: the Philip Morris Companies contributed money and in-kind services valued at more than $40 million to groups working in the areas of health and welfare, conservation and environment, education, nutrition and the arts.[23]

In 1989, over half the company's contributions were devoted to education, but the fund also financed totally different projects; for example, it enabled the exhibition 'Picasso and Braque: Pioneering Cubism' to be mounted in New York's Museum of Modern Art.[24]

1993 AND BEYOND

In its 1988 annual report, the company stated that in 1989 it would 'face yet another round of challenges on excise taxes, advertising bans, and restrictions on smoking'. The company's point of view on these and on other relevant subjects is now also presented in the *Philip Morris Magazine*, which reaches more than 13 million households six times a year.[25] The 1989 annual report does not make any special reference to these important issues. However, as this chapter does not deal with the company as such but with its most important single brand, Marlboro, it should suffice to say that this top-quality product, marketed and advertised on the basis of a consistent long-term international policy, managed by a team that pursues its objectives with an almost single-minded conviction, has now maintained its position as the 'number one' brand in the world over many decades and that there is no reason why its success should not continue. Single European Market or not, competition or not, legal restraints or not, many of the 33 per cent of adults in Europe who continue to smoke will still aspire to the freedom represented by the Marlboro cowboy and his country – a place 'where the flavor is', where the land stretches out for ever and where man can be the master of his own destiny.

Notes

1. Levin, Bernard (1989), *A Walk up Fifth Avenue*. London: Jonathan Cape, p. 80.
2. *Annual Report 1989*, Philip Morris Companies Inc., New York, p. 7.
3. *The 1988 International Survey of the World Cigarette Market*. Newmarket, UK: E.R.C. Statistics International.
4. *Eurobarometer*, Brussels: Commission of the European Communities, No. 31, June 1989.
5. Boddewyn, J.J. (1989), *Juvenile Smoking Initiation & Advertising*. New York: International Advertising Association.
6. Brochure (undated), Philip Morris Companies Inc., New York, p. 1.
7. Sherman, Stratford P. (1989), 'How Philip Morris diversified right,' *Fortune*, 23 October, p. 82.
8. Personal letter to the author from Richard Camisa, Brand Manager, Marlboro, Philip Morris Companies Inc., New York, 7 June 1990.
9. Personal letter to the author from Guy L. Smith IV, Vice-President, Corporate Affairs, Philip Morris Companies Inc., New York, 13 June 1990.
10. Maxwell, Hamish (1989), 'Harnessing the power of global brands,' *International Advertiser* (New York), May–June, pp. 12–17.
11. 'The Marlboro Story' (undated), a slide presentation by Noordervliet & Winninghof/Leo Burnett, Amsterdam.
12. *Ibid.*
13. *Tobacco Reporter* (1989), 'Legendary marketing skills,' September, p. 24.
14. *Media International*, 'Tobacco makers fight for market share,' December 1989.
15. *Tobacco Reporter.*
16. *Straits Times* (Singapore), '5m kids in US may die from smoking,' 2 June 1990.
17. *Official Journal of the European Communities* (1989), 'Proposal for a Council Directive on the advertising of tobacco products in the press and by means of bills and posters,' COM (89) 163 final/2-SYN 194, Brussels, 19 May, No C 124/5. See also: EAT's 'Submission on the Proposal for a Council Directive on the Advertising of Tobacco Products in the Press and by Means of Bills and Posters' (undated).
18. 'Consumer Issues' (undated), included in the Philip Morris brochure (note 6 above).
19. For detailed analysis, see Rijkens, Rein, and Miracle, G.E. (1986), *European Regulation of Advertising*. Amsterdam: Elsevier, pp. 88–91.
20. *Ibid.*, pp. 185–90.
21. *Rapport sur la communication dans le monde* (1990). Paris: UNESCO, p. 193.
22. *Fresh Air in the Workplace – the Tobacco Smoke Myth* and *Smoking in the Workplace*. brochures prepared by Burston-Marsteller, London, and published by Philip Morris, EEC Region, Lausanne, Switzerland.
23. *In the Public Interest* (1988), Philip Morris Companies Inc., New York, p. 1.
24. *Annual Report 1989*, Philip Morris Companies Inc., New York, p. 56.
25. *Annual Report 1988*, Philip Morris Companies Inc., New York, p. 8.

MARTINI & ROSSI

'Making Life Exceptional'

MARTINI & ROSSI
'Making Life Exceptional'

'Please, don't call Martini a vermouth, it is a drink,'[1] said Dino Aiassa, a director on the International Martini Committee of the parent company, in his office in Paris, the city from which the company that produces Martini controls its worldwide marketing and advertising operation.

The firm was established more than 100 years ago, when, in 1863, Alessandro Martini, Teofilo Sola and Luigi Rossi took over a vermouth-producing firm in Turin, which had been founded in the eighteenth century. In 1879, the business was moved to Pessione and renamed Martini & Rossi. Today the official name of the company is the General Beverage Corporation and it has its general domicile in Luxembourg, though it is run by General Beverage Management, which has its administrative base in Geneva. The chief executive officer of General Beverage Management, also referred to as the 'International Management Committee', is Count Gregorio Rossi, and the managing director is Marquis Gianluca Spinola. In addition to these two gentlemen, this International Committee has three central directors: Mr Maurizio Cibrario's main responsibility is corporate structure and strategic operations; Mr Fernando Pique is mainly involved in finance and management; and Mr Dino Aiassa, mentioned earlier, has the day-to-day responsibility for the marketing and advertising of the concern's products throughout the world.[2]

The total turnover of this family business amounts to $1.5 billion, and grows at an annual rate of 5 per cent in volume and 10 per cent in value; of this turnover, approximately 75 per cent is derived from Europe, while North America accounts for 10 per cent, South America for 10 per cent and the rest of the world for about 5 per cent. The company invests at a rate of $150 million per annum in advertising and public relations for the range of alcoholic drinks that it produces. This is manufactured and sold by 140 fully owned subsidiaries and affiliates in 30 countries, employing a total of more than 4 000 people, of whom 1 250 belong to the group's sales force. The name of the General Beverage Corporation is indeed an appropriate one for a company producing and distributing such a wide variety of alcoholic beverages, of which the most important are the following:

Martini (in four well-known varieties: Rosso, Bianco, Dry and Rosé)

William Lawson (a Scotch with one of the fastest sales growth rates in Europe)

Glen Deveron (a twelve-year-old single malt whisky, produced at Banff in eastern Scotland)

Offley (the second most popular port wine in the world, from Vilanova de Gaia, near Porto in Portugal)

Eristoff (a vodka, which has belonged to Martini & Rossi since 1956)

Noilly Prat (a dry vermouth, often used by connoisseurs for preparing a Dry Martini cocktail, and produced in Marseillan on the Mediterranean coast of France)

Asti Spumante (a fruity sparkling wine)

Gaston de Lagrange (a cognac, taken over by Martini & Rossi in
1962)
Bénédictine (a liqueur)
Boulard (a calvados)
Duquesne (rum, punch, daiquiri)

Other drinks that may not have the same international significance also belong to the list of 300 products that are produced and/or distributed by Martini & Rossi; for example the well-known Saint-Raphael apéritif, Veuve Amiot sparkling wine or Bosford gin. Several prestigious brands not owned by the group are also distributed by the General Beverage Corporation's companies in different markets. These include Laurent Perrier, Pommery, Long John, and Bell's. However, of all these brands, Martini itself is by far the most important and accounts for approximately 50 per cent of the firm's total turnover; it is also the second most popular drink in the world, Bacardi rum being the first. It is interesting to note that the companies that produce both these most popular drinks are privately owned; and there is co-operation between the two giants in the field of distribution in the USA, the UK and Denmark.

THIS PRODUCT CALLED MARTINI

Martini's vermouths are 'wines which employ aromatic herbal blends to obtain their distinctive taste. Vermouth was invented, according to legend by Hippocrates over 2 000 years ago, when he blended almonds, herbs and gray amber with wine to create "Hippocras" '.[3] Production and bottling of the Martini & Rossi beverages takes place in France, Italy, Spain, Portugal and South America, and bottling alone in Germany and in the UK, at a total of about 25 sites. The largest of these sites is, as one would expect, in Pessione, close to Turin, where 300 employees produce four million cases of different beverages every year, 50 per cent of which is shipped to countries outside Italy. Whilst research will never be ignored by any serious and professional marketer, in the case of Martini & Rossi, given the long-standing reputation of its products, research is mainly used to ensure that the quality of its drinks remains constant.

MARTINI & ROSSI'S RANKING

Impressive as the concern's sales figures are, the business has formidable competitors, of which the most important are shown in Table 2.[4]

In recent years, the total market for alcoholic beverages has been levelling off slightly, the 'apéritif habit' tending to become a habit of drinking wine before a meal, as well as with it. Martini & Rossi admit that people, particularly the young, may be drinking less, but emphasize that they are also becoming more selective, preferring quality to quantity; a point that will again be discussed when the company's advertising policy is reviewed.

Table 2

Company	Sales (million cases)	Major brands
1. International Distillers & Vintners/Heublein	85	Smirnoff vodka, J&B Scotch, Gilbey's gin
2. Seagram	76	Seagram's VO, Chivas Regal Scotch, Sanderman's port & sherries
3. Pernod Ricard	57	Pernod, Ricard, Biscuit cognac, Pastis 51, Dubonnet
4. Allied-Lyons/Hiram Walker	51	Teacher's Scotch, Ballantines Scotch, Harvey's Sherry, Courvoisier Cognac, Canadian Club whisky, Tia Maria
5. United Distillers Group & Schenley	47	Johnnie Walker, Haig, White Horse, Dimple, Bells and other whiskies; Gordon's, Tanqueray and Booth's gins
6. Martini & Rossi	33.5	As already indicated, and representing 400 million bottles, of which 30 per cent is sold in France
:	:	:
9. Bacardi	23	Bacardi rum, Don Emilio tequilla etc.

MARTINI & ROSSI AND ITS COMMUNICATION POLICY

Alongside his many other responsibilities, Count Gregorio Rossi takes a special interest in the company's advertising and public relations, a task in which he is assisted by an international marketing and advertising department, under the leadership of central director Dino Aiassa, who has served the company for more than 20 years. Martini & Rossi has, for understandable reasons, always attached great importance to the role of advertising, spending half of its $150 million per annum advertising budget on the Martini brand alone. Thus, it is hardly surprising that its chief executive officer, who combines the required managerial skills to run a company of this size with great creative flair and good advertising judgement, should devote much of his time to every aspect of the way in which Martini & Rossi presents itself to the outside world. The international advertising and marketing department that assists him consists of a small team of four international marketing managers, each of whom is responsible for the advertising of some of the Martini & Rossi beverages or for more general activities, such as the sponsoring of sports events, the handling of the related Martini Racing Sportline products (shirts, jackets, shorts, bags, etc.) or the provision of support in the important duty-free market.

MARTINI & ROSSI'S PUBLIC RELATIONS ACTIVITIES

The public relations activities of the Martini & Rossi business have been intensified since 1987, when it was decided that Martini & Rossi should increase general awareness among 'opinion moulders' of what the business stands for and the values that it wishes to represent. For example, Martini & Rossi owns and runs the 'Terrace Martini' on the ninth floor of a building in the Champs-Elysées, offering a panoramic view of France's famous monuments, such as the Eiffel Tower, the Arc de Triomphe and the Sacré Coeur. This operation started as far back as 1950, but the 'Terrace' was completely redecorated in 1987, when it was turned into an audiovisual and communications centre, where well-known personalities from stage, screen, the arts, politics and business, are entertained in luxurious and elegant surroundings in line with the high-class image that the company wishes to establish for its products. There are other 'Terraces' in London, Milan and Barcelona.

Other initiatives have also been taken. On 7 October 1987, the *International Herald Tribune* included a four-page, full-colour insert featuring Martini & Rossi International, which, in an unusually open and interesting way, gave much information about the group's business, its history, products, advertising, long-term ambitions etc. Three years later, on 14 May 1990, *Time Magazine* included another four-page insert, reminding readers of what Martini International stands for, its association with the world of sports, and the high-class products that it sells.

SPONSORSHIP

On the subject of Martini & Rossi's association with well-known sports events, the group used to sponsor the Formula 1 Grand Prix races, but now provides backing for a Martini-Lancia racing team, which takes part in rallies throughout Europe, such as the Monte Carlo Rally World Championship. There is also a Martini offshore speedboat racing event and the Martini Pilatus Civil Acrobatic flying team, both of which also associate Martini & Rossi as a 'winner' in its field with winners in the world of sports. This involvement in sports started in the 1970s and is still an important element in the company's programme of communications with consumers. However, the company also sponsors exhibitions and fashion shows, and wishes to be seen as a business that supports any activity that adds a little 'spice' to life; or, as Dino Aiassa once put it, 'The link between these sponsored events and our products is that they make life a little exceptional'.[5] However, important as these public relations and sponsorship activities are, they are, of course, only supporting elements in the total communications-mix, in which long-term media advertising plays the most significant role.

MARTINI & ROSSI'S INTERNATIONAL ADVERTISING

There can be no doubt that Martini & Rossi belongs to the small group of pioneering companies that decided long ago that considerable advantages could be obtained by running uniform advertising on a global scale. The first international advertising campaign for the Martini brand, employing McCann-Erickson as the international advertising agency, was, in fact, started by Count Vittorio Rossi (died May 1990) who was much involved in the company's advertising in the early 1960s.

Today, as Mr Aiassa explains, all offices take the international approach to the advertising of most Martini & Rossi brands for granted and will often themselves point out further opportunities to internationalize the company's advertising. This is a classic illustration of the theory that international advertising is, in essence, a managerial challenge. Assuming that a product has universal acceptance, it depends almost entirely upon the managerial skills of the advertiser and its advertising agency whether or not the available resources and manpower can be used in such a manner as to achieve optimum communications with consumers on an international scale.

A company that succeeds in establishing the necessary understanding of its international policy and reaches agreement with all concerned on the strategies to be adopted and the way in which they are to be executed benefits in two respects. Not only does the firm itself obtain considerable economies of scale; more importantly, the actual advertising will often be of a quality that could hardly be expected if the same scheme were implemented on a country-by-country basis. Although the economies of scale may not be the most significant factor, it is interesting to read Martini & Rossi's views on the subject:

Global advertisements give Martini & Rossi better control over its message and image while resulting in a more cost-effective production process. Analysts estimate it would cost three times as much to create the same amount of advertising on a nation-by-nation basis.[6]

The co-operation and understanding needed to produce 'global' advertisements are not acquired overnight. It requires patience and a receptive attitude to suggestions from all concerned, at national and international levels, to achieve, over the years, the kind of team spirit that no longer depends on rigid controls and extensive documentation but will produce the best results because everybody thinks and acts along the same lines. The management of people and resources is the key to successful international advertising, and, in this respect, Martini & Rossi set a splendid example to other firms.

THE ROLE OF THE INTERNATIONAL ADVERTISING AGENCY

Whilst the company fully accepts its duty to protect its brands and their market positions, the role of the advertising agency in giving creative expression to agreed advertising strategies and overseeing their implementation in various markets is, of course, of decisive importance. Although the company will occasionally appoint local agencies to support regional activities, important brands such as Martini, William Lawson's Scotch, and Offley port, are all handled by McCann's on a worldwide basis. The centre of the agency's activities is in London, where a senior executive is employed full-time on overseeing, approving and co-ordinating all creative work, wherever produced, before it is presented to the client – in this case, the formidable duo, Messrs Rossi and Aiassa. As McCann's local offices handle the Martini & Rossi account in all countries in which the company operates, their co-ordination from London is a major undertaking.

FORMER POSITIONING OF THE MARTINI & ROSSI BRANDS

One of the preconditions for advertising on an international scale, is, of course, that the brand itself should be uniformly positioned in all the markets concerned. Until a few years ago, this applied to all the Martini products; they were not advertised separately. The advertising concentrated on the Martini brand and often projected an alluring life-style that became known internationally as 'the Martini world'; its pay-off was the statement that Martini was the right drink 'any time, any place, anywhere'. Whilst the actual consumption of any one of the Martini varieties varied within Europe (the red wine culture of southern Europe, for example, explaining the great popularity of Martini Rosso in Spain), the overall patterns of usage, were sufficiently similar to justify uniform international positioning and uniformity in advertising strategy and execution.

PRESENT STRATEGIES . . . AND THEIR EXECUTION

More recently, the company has decided that the most important Martini varieties should be advertised separately and targeted at clearly and carefully defined audiences. Thus, Martini Rosso, a straight long drink that is by far the most popular variety, is aimed at a broad sector of the market; Martini Bianco, popular among people in their early twenties, with their preference for light alcoholic drinks, is targeted at a younger market; whilst Martini Extra Dry is aimed at the sophisticated drinker.

The execution of these different strategies makes high demands on the international advertising agency, which has to find the right locations, actors, directors and production units to do justice to each of the three varieties. Martini Rosso will always be shown being enjoyed either by an attractive couple – with the slogan, 'Our Martini is Rosso' – or by a small group of smart, and evidently chic people who are depicted in a relaxed mood, with glass in hand, in elegant surroundings, experiencing 'the bitter sweet sensation', as it says in one of its advertisements. Martini Bianco, on the other hand, is depicted being consumed by the young, sporty, somewhat boisterous set, at the seaside or on a tennis-court, and often is shown being drunk with ice to make it into the sort of light wine preferred by the young people who like to enjoy 'the sunny side of life'. Finally, Martini Dry advertising concentrates on the bottle and the product, presenting it in an atmosphere of cool sophistication as the dry drink with character preferred by the experienced and selective user who knows the world.

McCann has produced separate advertising for all three varieties, and, although the company tends to favour television and cinema as the ideal media to convey the message and create the right kind of quality image for the product, magazines and posters are also used, not simply as alternatives, but also because the company feels that addressing the various audiences from different directions at different moments will help to increase the campaign's total impact.

Apart from advertising in the classic media, the company spends about 15 per cent of its total advertising budget on promotional activities, which are mainly the responsibility of its various national offices. A typical example of a national marketing plan can be found in the sales brochure for 1989 of the firm's Dutch affiliate. It describes, in relation to each brand or variety, which media will be used and which consumer or trade promotions will take place in which month(s) of the year, the trade promotions being broken down into type of trade channel, such as grocers, licensed retailers, the restaurant business etc. The aim is to avoid as far as possible, any overlap between these advertising cycles.[7] In this connection, it is perhaps of interest to note that Martini & Rossi belongs to the growing number of companies that do not believe in the often debated product life-cycle theories; the company takes the view that, provided the particular brand and its advertising are continuously updated and kept in line with changing tastes and life-styles, there is no reason why a brand should gradually fade away. There might be occasional fluctuations in its popularity over the years, but if the brand is nurtured with care, there will rarely be major disasters. Martini & Rossi's current position provides clear confirmation of this point of view; with a slightly stagnant total market, it is the company's policy to present its products to consumers as high-quality drinks, savoured on special occasions or to add a little extra zest to a great party.

Advertising the Martini & Rossi brands is not made any easier by the involvement of governments and supranational bodies in regulating how manufacturers of alcoholic beverages should, or should not, communicate with consumers; this in spite of the fact that Martini is a naturally based wine, with added herbs and spices, of low alcohol content.

CONCERNS OF THE INDUSTRY

After a brief period of euphoria when the 'Internal Market' plans of the EC in Brussels had been unfolded and accepted, renewed regulatory activity, including that of some particularly interventionist governments intent on curbing the advertising of certain products and services, is of considerable concern, not only to the manufacturers of alcoholic beverages, but to industry as a whole. A UK trade magazine expressed the concern of advertising businesses as follows: 'There is an increasing tendency towards restrictive legislation in more and more products. We fear a sort of domino effect as the European Commission and the Council of Europe feed off one another.'[8] As advertising is a very important part of the marketing mix for Martini & Rossi's international products, its management is, of course, worried by any measures that could adversely affect its advertising campaigns. Such concern is particularly great in the context of the beverage industry, because there is so little evidence that advertising for alcoholic products increases consumption. In fact, when looking at published figures for the entire industry, one notices that, for example, in a country such as Finland, where no advertising for alcoholic products is allowed at all, alcohol consumption has gone up by 11 per cent between 1980 and 1987; whereas in countries such as Germany, Italy and Austria, where advertising *is* allowed, subject to certain ethical codes, total consumption of alcoholic products has decreased over the same period. However, this has not stopped governments or supragovernmental bodies from pressing for severe restrictions in the use of advertising for alcoholic drinks, on the grounds that they are assumed to affect people's health.

Leaving aside the often-heard general argument that 'as long as it is legal to produce and sell products and services, it should in principle also be legal to advertise them'[9], there clearly is no justification for controlling advertising of alcoholic products for fear that it might increase consumption. Martini & Rossi's position on this subject is as follows:

1. Advertising does not stimulate an increase in total consumption, its task is to convince consumers of the benefits of a given brand; advertising will therefore only affect the market shares of brands within a product category.
2. Martini & Rossi's advertising will highlight the nature of its

products, which are intended to be used on special occasions; it
will therefore contribute to people's quality of life, and not
encourage abundant consumption.

3. Advertising is an essential tool for informing consumers about
existing and new products, enabling them to exercise
well-considered freedom of choice.

Martini & Rossi is represented in several federations that speak out on behalf of the entire industry on all matters regarding the activities of public authorities, at both national and international levels. These federations take a positive stance by publicizing as widely as possible the view that moderate consumption of alcoholic beverages is part of a person's normal and healthy nutrition. Their publications are properly documented and endorsed by professional sources of unquestionable integrity, objectivity and authority.

An interesting and unprecedented initiative was taken in France in September, 1990, when eight well-known producers of alcoholic beverages, including, of course, Martini & Rossi, formed a 'Groupe de réflexions et d'initiatives de producteurs de boissons'. This group has published the first of a number of documents, openly stating its responsibility towards consumers and advising them about the proper use of alcoholic products, with strong warnings against their abuse. 'Nous sommes des adversaires de l'exces,' said the president of one of the participating companies and the spokesman for this group.[10] Fortunately, such excellent initiatives get the full support of all trade associations, not only those in the field of alcoholic beverages but also those representing advertisers, advertising agencies and the media in a more general way. As mentioned in the previous chapter, one of the latter is the European Advertising Tripartite, based in Brussels, in which the whole communications business is represented, and which speaks with one voice, for example in negotiations with the Commission of the EC in Brussels, on all matters regarding restrictions on advertising.

1993 AND BEYOND

In general terms, the Martini & Rossi management is firmly convinced that it owes its long-standing success to three main factors: the consistent and superior quality of its products; the long-term character and sustained execution of its policies; and the high quality of all its communications with the public. The small, but devoted, central management therefore sees as its first and foremost objective for the years to come the continuation of policies that have proved to be successful and that, in a stagnant market, will become even more critically important. An improvement in the general image of the company, the upgrading of its brands by differentiating them from the mass of generic products, and the use of socially responsible and relevant advertising of high quality and style will all be among the prime objectives for the future. In the context of advertising, bearing in mind the greater diversification of the range of Martini & Rossi brands, the use of satellite communications will not have top priority. Indeed, in view of restrictions on the use of the advertising classic media, public relations and sponsoring activities may well gain importance.

Most importantly, in line with similar actions by other manufacturers discussed in this book, Martini & Rossi is taking vigorous steps to expand its business in Eastern Europe and in the Far East. Martini & Rossi International has already distributed six million bottles of its drinks throughout eastern Germany,

Czechoslovakia, Hungary and Yugoslavia; and in Hungary and Yugoslavia the group has also established a joint venture. Until recently, Martini & Rossi's presence in Eastern Europe was limited because of the restricted buying power of the region's population. But, in view of the recent exciting developments and the considerable prestige of the Martini brands, rapid expansion should be possible. In the Far East, the Martini & Rossi group is already fairly well established – thanks to Bénédictine, Noilly Prat, Martini and Gaston de la Grange cognac. 'We are working on getting Martini better known in the Far East, and the response so far has been very favourable,' commented Count Gregorio. The General Beverage Corporation has recently acquired 52.5 per cent of Otard cognac, one of the leading brands in the Far East, which will reinforce the presence of the group in this part of the world. Looking at the company's track record and its consistent marketing and advertising policies, there is no reason why, during the next decades, present and future generations of owners of this remarkable family business should not be able to maintain and further develop its high reputation throughout the world.

Notes

1. Personal discussions with Dino Aiassa, Central Director of the General Beverage Management S.A., Paris, 31 July 1989 and 2 March 1990.
2. See also special insert in the advertising section of the *International Herald Tribune*, 7 October 1987, p. 1.
3. *Ibid.*, p. 11.
4. *International Drinks Bulletin* (1987), Vol. 2, No. 22, 11 December.
5. See note 1, above.
6. *International Herald Tribune*, 7 October 1987, p. 11.
7. *Vier Seizoenen Martini & Rossi 1989* (Four Seasons Martini & Rossi 1989), sales brochure produced by Martini & Rossi Nederland N.V.
8. *Campaign*, 'AA prepares to take on Euro attempts to ban alcohol ads,' 3 August 1990.
9. Rijkens, Rein, and Miracle, G.E. (1986), *European Regulation of Advertising*. Amsterdam: Elsevier, p. 123.
10. *La Lettre* (1990), a publication of Entreprise et Prévention, Paris.

MERCEDES-BENZ

COMMERCIAL VEHICLES
'Committed to Your Success'

In 1955 was het in feite al een topprestatie als een zware bedrijfswagen 100.000 km op de teller had. Vandaag de dag is een

De verkiezing tot »Truck of the Year 1990« bevestigt nogmaals ons streven naar kwaliteit en transport-rendement.

miljoen kilometer een aardig gemiddelde. Bovendien rijdt onze Eurogeneratie tussen twee servicebeurten de hele wereld rond. Een grote stap voorwaarts dankzij onze ruim 100 jaar ervaring in de auto-industrie. Vooruitstrevende technologie en uitstekende materiaalkeuze vormen het geheim van ons succes. Dit resulteert in betrouwbare, verkeersveilige en duurzame bedrijfswagens die - jaar in, jaar uit - een hoog rendement bieden. En wanneer u uw Mercedes ver-

vangt, profiteert u van zijn bekende hoge restwaarde. Wij geloven in onze produkten en geven 12 maanden garantie ongeacht het aantal kilometers en 24 maanden garantie of 200.000 km op de aandrijflijn. Vervoerders in de hele wereld delen het geloof in ons produkt. Het is dan ook geen toeval dat wereldwijd de meeste vrachtwagens onze ster dragen. Evenmin is het toevallig dat een internationale jury van vakjournalisten onze nieuwe serie zware bedrijfswagens, de Eurogeneratie, tot »Truck of the Year 1990« heeft uitgeroepen. Al met al kwaliteitsbewijzen die staan voor een groot merk.

RIJDEND RENDEMENT

Mercedes-Benz maakt ernst met het milieu.

Als belangrijkste fabrikant van bedrijfswagens is Mercedes-Benz zich bewust van zijn milieuverantwoordelijkheid. Daarom hebben wij ons tot taak gesteld met behulp van innovatieve research hoogwaardige vervoersconcepten te ontwikkelen, waarin een schone toekomst voor onze bedrijfswagens centraal staat.

Mercedes-Benz
Bedrijfswagens

MERCEDES-BENZ
COMMERCIAL VEHICLES
'Committed to Your Success'

The very first motor car worthy of the name was built in 1885 by Carl Benz, then aged 41, who, in 1886, drove it through the streets of Mannheim in Germany at the reckless speed of 13 km per hour. Benz, however, had serious competition; in 1887, Gottfried Daimler, then 43 years old, built an experimental car in Cannstadt, also in Germany, followed, in 1891, by the very first van.[1] Wisely, in 1926, the two businesses, Benz & Co. and the Daimler Motoren Gesellschaft merged, under the name Daimler-Benz A.G.[2]

The Daimler-Benz concern, as we know it today, is rather different from what it was then. In 1990, the Daimler-Benz holding company had a worldwide turnover of DM.85.5 billion, employing 377 000 people and making a profit before tax etc. of DM.7.8 billion.[3] The holding company covers Mercedes-Benz, selling private and commercial vehicles, AEG with its electronic business, the German aerospace company and a separate service company. Of the concern's total revenues, about DM.55.6 billion come from Europe, including DM.37 billion from Germany alone, the remaining DM.30 billion being derived from other parts of the world. With more than 55 per cent of its revenue foreign trade, the company can certainly be classed as an international business, a point to which we shall return later.

In 1990, Mercedes-Benz accounted for 68 per cent of the concern's total business; of this, 40 per cent represented sales of cars and 28 per cent sales of commercial vehicles, giving production figures in 1990 of 574 000 cars and 259 000 commercial vehicles.[4] Daimler-Benz's worldwide share of the commercial vehicle market is estimated at 20 per cent, making it the largest manufacturer of such products in the world, despite competition from companies such as Fiat, DAF-Leyland and Volvo.

Not only do Mercedes-Benz passenger cars represent 40 per cent of the concern's total turnover, clearly making the most important contribution, these well-known and elegant vehicles also represent the more glamorous aspect of Daimler-Benz's operations. However, with a turnover of DM.24 billion and as world-leaders in their particular market, the less elegant heavy trucks and large buses should not be ignored; on the contrary, they deserve a place in this book alongside the other market-leading products that it discusses, particularly as they represent a totally different type of business. Consequently, in this chapter it will be the luxurious Mercedes cars that will be neglected and the trucks, vans, buses and coaches that will receive our full attention. Nonetheless, the story of Mercedes-Benz commercial vehicles must start with a brief review of a more general topic: the origin of one of the best known trade-marks and emblems in the entire world – the name Mercedes and its equally well-known star emblem, which are exclusively used for both the passenger and commercial vehicles of the Daimler-Benz concern.

WHAT'S IN A NAME?

Emil Jellinek certainly was a most unusual man. Born in Leipzig, Germany, on 6 April 1853, he was a poor student at all the schools that he attended. However, he was always fascinated by engines and, in 1893, he managed single-handedly to persuade the Daimler motor company, from whom he had bought a car, to make certain improvements to their engines that he considered necessary – and that were actually approved by Daimler's famous engineer Wilhelm Maybach. Jellinek, who had meanwhile established himself as a car dealer in Nice, in France, ordered another four motor cars from Daimler in 1896 and sold them rapidly. In 1899, he took part in the Nice–Maganon–Nice rally and made further recommendations for improving the performance of Daimler engines. By then convinced that he could make a commercial success out of selling Daimler cars, he ordered 36 more to a total value of 550 000 gold Marks, on the condition that he would get the sole agency rights for Austria – Hungary, France and America. His ambition did not stop there. In 1903, a firm consisting of the Daimler motor company, a number of banks and Jellinek himself was set up in Paris, with Jellinek on the board of directors.

Jellinek died in 1918 in Geneva, at the age of 65, and will always be remembered as someone who, despite never having had a technical training, exerted considerable influence on the early development of the motor car. However, he was also responsible for another event in the history of motoring. When he placed the order for 36 Daimler cars mentioned above, he not only acquired important agency rights but also made it a condition that these cars should be named after the daughter from his first marriage, born in 1889. The Daimler motor company agreed and that is how the name Mercedes was given both to the cars that the girl's father had ordered and to the many millions of other cars that the firm has produced since! The name Mercedes was officially registered in 1908, when the Mercedes era really started.[5]

The now equally well-known and distinctive brand emblem, consisting of a three-pointed star inside a circle, symbolizing motorization on land, on water and in the air, that adorns the radiators of all Mercedes-Benz vehicles was originally designed in 1909. It was modified several times but in 1923 it was entered in the register of legally protected designs. Few such emblems, without an accompanying name or trade-mark, will be immediately recognized all over the world; the Mercedes-Benz sign is.[6]

THE DAIMLER-BENZ CONCERN AND ADVERTISING

Before we deal with the commercial vehicles of Mercedes-Benz in more detail, it is as well to put the subject in a proper perspective by looking at one or two general aspects of the concern and its advertising. Throughout this book it has become clear that the nature of the advertising function and its place in an organization depend upon a number of factors, such as: (a) the type of product or service concerned; (b) the importance of the advertising function for the success of the product or service in the market-place; and (c) the business background of those at senior levels who ran the company in the past and of those who are doing so at present.

It is not unusual for top advertising executives to report directly to the chief executive officer of, for example, a mass consumer goods company, in which advertising is vital to the firm's results. The situation is, of course, quite different with a business such as Mercedes-Benz. Advertising will only be one of the factors affecting the buying decision; design and engineering will be at least as important to the future buyer, who will have to make a significant financial sacrifice to purchase such a car. It follows that the percentage of sales revenue spent on advertising a Mercedes car will only be a fraction of that needed to advertise a mass consumer product.

For all these reasons advertising may be considered by some to be of subordinate importance to a manufacturer of motor vehicles. Yet, one cannot but wonder whether the advertising function – which, in the case of Mercedes-Benz, receives funds equivalent to less than 0.5 per cent of the company's turnover (though even this represents a figure in the order of DM.115 million per annum for its Commercial Vehicles Division alone) – is not of much greater significance to the success of the business than its share of turnover would appear to indicate. In the long run, even a Mercedes could not be sold without advertising.

Another example of the low priority that Mercedes-Benz appears to give to advertising is found in the company's annual report. In this otherwise excellent and detailed review of the concern's activities, there is not a single reference to the role that advertising has played in enabling the firm to achieve its desired financial results. It is the report of a company that is still very much production oriented.

It is also interesting to note that, in spite of the large proportion of its revenue that Mercedes-Benz derives from foreign business, there do not appear to be many non-Germans with executive authority in the company; the management is centralized in Germany, and very few employees from abroad work in any of its offices. As we shall see later, the marketing communication department of the Commercial Vehicles Division has made a commendable effort to internationalize its advertising by involving some of the important foreign subsidiaries in devising and implementing the company's advertising strategy. However, this development seems rather uncharacteristic, and, despite the fact that English is the generally accepted language in the advertising world, the 'lingua franca' in the Daimler-Benz concern is still German.

THE POSITION OF THE ADVERTISING FUNCTION

From an organizational point of view, the marketing communication department just mentioned is rather far-removed from the top echelons of the Mercedes-Benz company. The company has two divisions: one for passenger cars and one for commercial vehicles. The board of the Commercial Vehicles Division has responsibilities for: research and development; production; sales; and finance and administration. Contrary to the situation that one often finds in consumer goods companies, the marketing and advertising functions are subordinate to the company's sales management and are not on a par with the sales function. The marketing communication department, which executes agreed advertising policies, is not only responsible for advertising strategies but, as we shall see, also controls or gives advice on advertising planning, advertising research, sales promotions and choice of advertising media, both in Germany and outside. It is interesting to observe that not only the fully owned subsidiaries, but virtually all the agents and other representatives involved in the marketing and selling of the commercial vehicles, follow, in the main, the recommendations regarding basic advertising strategies issued from the company's headquarters in Stuttgart – though the execution of these strategies is, of course, the responsibility of local managements.

As well as having subsidiaries and selling agents in Germany itself, Mercedes-Benz AG produces and sells its vehicles in a number of countries outside Germany, mainly through fully owned subsidiaries. In some countries, the company has a minority share in a number of businesses that also produce and sell its commercial vehicles, whilst there are countries too where the company operates through independent selling agents. In fact, there is hardly a country in the world where the Mercedes-Benz company is not represented in some form or other.[7] Before dealing with the advertising aspects of the company's operation in more detail, it will probably be helpful if we review briefly the types of vehicles that the company is selling, and their main characteristics.

WHAT ARE MERCEDES-BENZ COMMERCIAL VEHICLES?

Only a few people are aware of the importance of commercial vehicles to any country's economy. Those with immediate business interests in them are likely to be alone in sharing the following view, expressed in a Mercedes-Benz brochure: 'It can be said without exaggeration that the truck has been as important a driving force for industrial developments in the twentieth century, as the train was in the nineteenth century.'[8] In another of the company's publications, Mr Werner Lechner, a member of the board of the Commercial Vehicles Division of Mercedes-Benz, said:

The restrictions to trade which still exist within the 12 country European community will be abolished as from 31.12.1992. The increasing flow of goods means that commercial vehicles will win more importance, as will the customer back up services offered by vehicle manufacturers. The demands made on computerised management instruments will increase further, particularly in the field of logistics, in order to provide truck fleets with an even more efficient work distribution and organisation system.[9]

If one realizes that more than 50 per cent of all the transportation of goods in Europe takes place on an international network of roads, the significance of the trucks and vans that carry these goods is obvious. In this respect, it is interesting to note the view of the Dutch Prime Minister that 'without a "Europe of transportation" the Single Market, as well as a Europe without frontiers would be ridiculous'.[10]

How can one classify the vehicles involved? What is the difference between a small truck and a large van? Mercedes-Benz gives the following breakdown, allowing for some overlap between the categories concerned:

1. Light, economically run vans with a loading capacity of up to 5 tons.
2. Light trucks, giving good value for money and convenient use, with a 'Gross Vehicle Weight' of up to 15 tons.
3. Heavy trucks with a GVW of more than 16 tons; probably the most important category for transportation of goods throughout Europe after 1992. (Mercedes-Benz gained considerable acclaim for its new 'Eurogeneration', a truck which was selected by an independent jury as the 'Truck of the Year 1990'.)
4. A heavy-duty, so-called Unimog range of versatile four-wheel-drive working machines, to which a whole variety of different implements can be attached; it is ideally suited for road construction firms, motorway works units etc.
5. Tailor-made special-purpose vehicles, such as those required by fire-brigades, police forces and rescue services.
6. Buses and coaches – these constitute a relatively small category with a total production to-date of 30000 vehicles; but as the company produced the first bus in the world, from the point of view of its overall prestige, they fulfil an important function.

Whilst the vehicles in these six categories represent a wide variety of commercial uses and will be sold and advertised to many different target groups, they have two elements in common: they are all called Mercedes-Benz, and they all carry the three-pointed-star emblem. These two elements make an important contribution to the image of the commercial vehicles, emphasizing that they come from the same stable as the fashionable and popular Mercedes-Benz passenger cars. Perhaps this family relationship accounts for the excellent image of the light trucks and vans – almost as good as that of the cars themselves. On the other hand, drivers of heavier trucks sometimes feel happier in the square, large, solid products of Mercedes' competitors – maybe because they find it difficult to reconcile the ruggedness of the Mercedes truck with the elegance of the new Mercedes Roadster.

ADVERTISING COMMERCIAL VEHICLES

The sale and advertising of trucks, vans and buses require a set of communications skills that in many ways differ considerably from more conventional communications methods. It is of crucial importance to define most thoroughly the various target audiences and the means by which they are to be reached. For example, advertising for the different vehicles must not only take into account the specific qualities and characteristics of each of them, but also the fact that the purchase of many commercial vehicles does not always depend upon the decision of one person. In fact, there are three different groups to be taken into consideration: (a) fleet-owners; (b) – most importantly – drivers; and (c) individual buyers. Advertising for commercial vehicles will therefore not only require a clear definition of the needs of the future owner but, in many cases, a clear definition of the particular wishes of the future drivers(s) as well. On the whole the owners will be mostly interested in the relevant logistics, whereas the drivers will attach more importance to driving qualities and comfort. Advertising will have to explain to both groups why Mercedes-Benz trucks meet their needs best. Elaborating briefly on this point and on the factors that will influence the decision of these groups to buy a vehicle that, after all, represents a considerable capital outlay, the following selection of arguments illustrates the complexities of this particular communications problem:

1. As already mentioned, the logistics of such a purchase, not only in terms of capital investment, but perhaps even more in terms of the running expenses (fuel, oil, tyres, repairs, servicing, road tax, insurance etc.) are of the utmost importance to the future owner of such a vehicle. The company therefore has a Mercedes-Benz transport consultancy service to provide the customer with solutions tailored to his requirements.

2. As with practically every product or service on sale in European markets, the quality of the back-up arrangements that a company can offer is becoming of increasing importance. Since the intrinsic properties of products differ so little today, these arrangements are the sort of additional advantages that will often make the difference between a successful and an unsuccessful operation. This point certainly applies to a business selling capital goods, such as commercial vehicles. Mercedes-Benz has a service network in Europe comprising 2700 customer service centres; in addition there are another 400 centres offering a round-the-clock emergency repair service.

3. It has become easier to control a fleet of trucks from its base thanks to a computerized system installed on board the trucks themselves, as well as at the base.

4. There are a number of other factors about which a future truck owner will wish to be informed, ranging from the spare-parts service and available accessories to the comfort of the driver's cab and his sleeping compartment. In the case of a bus or coach, the quality of the exterior and interior finishes, the quality and comfort of the passenger seats, the provision of convenient access for children, parents with prams, senior citizens and handicapped people, the type of air conditioning or ventilation systems, and many other features will also have to be described.[11]

As these points illustrate, the production and sale of commercial vehicles and the communication of their advantages make special demands on the skills of those involved in these activities; how Mercedes-Benz has tried to tackle the problem is described below.

A HANDBOOK: COMMUNICATION GUIDELINES

In its introduction to a recently published folder intended for the company's European subsidiaries and sales agents and called 'Marketing Communication for Mercedes-Benz Commercial Vehicles – a Handbook for our Communication Partners', the firm makes the following statement (translated from the original German text):

In view of the development of European communications and the integration of the creative potential of our partners, we intend to complete the move from co-ordination to co-operation. In this edition of the handbook we take the first step towards establishing the most important principles of our European co-operation.[12]

The handbook goes on to describe the objectives for the advertising of Mercedes-Benz commercial vehicles and how the company would like these vehicles to be perceived by present and future users. From this positioning statement, there follows an explanation of the overall strategy for Mercedes-Benz commercial vehicles in general, and of strategies for the specific advertising of the many different types of vehicles and their target groups. After a discussion of the media to be used for reaching these groups, there comes an analysis of the execution of agreed strategies and additional explanatory notes about the visual presentation of the campaign. Finally, and very importantly, the handbook explains the advertising roles of the Stuttgart head-office and of the company's subsidiaries – and their interrelationship – with special reference both to the firm's international campaign and to additional advertising on a national basis. Most of this information is summarized below.

Positioning

The company would like Mercedes-Benz commercial vehicles to be perceived by their present and future users as vehicles that offer long-term reliability because they are produced by the largest manufacturer of commercial vehicles in the world. It would also like to be seen as contributing to the solution of all transportation problems in an effective and efficient manner, while attaching great importance to the environment.

Strategy

Such a positioning statement can be used as the basis for an advertising strategy, which will usually involve 'the formulation of an advertising message that communicates the benefit or problem-solution characteristics of the product or service to the market'.[13] In spite of the many different types of Mercedes-Benz vehicles, each designed to solve a different transportation problem, it has been possible to define one overall strategy that, in essence, is applicable to the complete range; this can be supplemented, on either a national or an international basis, by emphasis on the special advantages of each individual variety of vehicle. The overall strategy can be defined as follows:

Mercedes-Benz offers solutions for transportation problems of any kind because of its innovative research and development, its integrated programme involving high-quality vehicles and their spare parts, its effective and efficient before and after-sales services, and its competent and motivated management and staff, who are totally committed to the success of their customers and fully accept their environmental responsibilities.

It is a very 'rational' strategy and is likely to differ from the strategy developed for Mercedes-Benz cars, which will have stronger emotional overtones and use rational arguments mainly in a supporting role. It is also interesting to observe how much importance the company attaches to environmental factors, which are, of course, of particular relevance to those involved in public transport. Since these have long been a topic of public debate, it is no wonder that they have high priority in the marketing and advertising of Mercedes-Benz commercial vehicles. In future, these vehicles will have to be as competitive as possible from an environmental point of view, as well as in more traditional areas.

Execution

In the execution of agreed strategies for European countries, the company differentiates between local advertising based upon the special requirements of individual countries, which are responsible for achieving their own particular sales targets, and advertising aimed at creating one uniform image for all Mercedes-Benz commercial vehicles throughout Europe. 'All business is local,' says the handbook, but this does not mean that an 'international' campaign will not add additional weight to advertising carried out on a national scale, provided that it enables a local fleet-owner to identify with it.

With regard to the international campaign, the handbook describes in detail the format, visual treatment and type of photography to be used, and the print to be employed for headlines and body-copy, as well as supplying the pay-off – 'Committed to your success' – which is followed by the Mercedes-Benz logo and the added words 'Commercial Vehicles'. The reader is attracted with a strong pictorial image of the commercial vehicle against a background supporting the advertisements' basic message; while themes such as efficiency, environment, experience, research, a unified Europe and service, are all expressed in turn as headlines in each of the international advertisements and further amplified in the body-copy. In addition, for the benefit of those who like to skim, two separate text blocks contain the essence of the advertisements' content and highlight the importance that the company attaches to environmental aspects. It is only to be hoped that this abundance of information does not distract readers' attention from the advertisement's main message.

Fortunately, unlike certain industries operating in the field of mass consumer goods, there are no legal or voluntary restrictions of any importance that could create serious complications in conveying the right message to buyers of commercial vehicles, nor is the EC Commission active in this field.

MEDIA

It is clear that the Mercedes-Benz company, with so much information to convey about so many different products to so many different target groups, attaches the greatest importance to defining each target group and choosing the media for its advertisements as effectively and efficiently as possible; this again is the responsibility of the subsidiaries and their advertising agencies. Apart from newspapers, trade publications and magazines, direct marketing is of considerable importance, and on average about 50 per cent of the Mercedes-Benz budget is used for this activity, which is mainly directed from Stuttgart, where most of the impressive and well-designed brochures are produced and printed.

In this connection it is of interest to note that the company naturally attaches great importance to informing its subsidiaries and agents of any new developments or launches. For example, when the 'Eurogeneration' truck mentioned earlier was introduced, a twenty-minute video cassette was produced for the benefit of subsidiaries, agents and potential customers to highlight the special advantages of this new vehicle, such as its greater power, its greater efficiency, its reduced servicing requirements, the greater comfort offered to the driver, the availability of 2750 service stations throughout Europe etc.

OPTIMIZING COMMUNICATIONS IN EUROPE

With a staff of about 30 people, the marketing communication department is responsible for developing worldwide strategies for the advertising of Mercedes-Benz commercial vehicles and also has executive responsibility for the advertising of these vehicles in Germany itself. In addition, it fulfils an advisory role with regard to the implementation of agreed advertising strategies in countries outside Germany. As has already been explained, the company wished to achieve greater co-operation, at least in the field of advertising, between its headquarters and its subsidiaries. This was not only because of general trends in this direction, it was also in line with the recommendations of a special concern study-group, appointed by the board of the company, which, in anticipation of a much more homogeneous Europe, had concerned itself with all aspects of the future operations of the Mercedes-Benz Commercial Vehicles Division in the region. Consequently, the marketing communication department reviewed its entire organizational structure with a view to achieving greater efficiency and effectiveness of commercial vehicle advertising throughout Europe. It appointed a co-ordination team, chaired by the director of the department and including the advertising executives of the most important European subsidiaries. This co-ordination team now operates as follows:

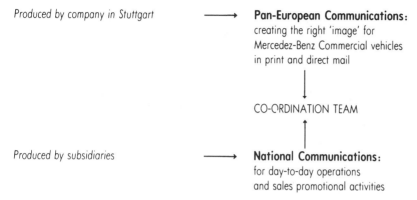

Produced by company in Stuttgart ⟶ **Pan-European Communications:**
creating the right 'image' for
Mercedez-Benz Commercial vehicles
in print and direct mail

CO-ORDINATION TEAM

Produced by subsidiaries ⟶ **National Communications:**
for day-to-day operations
and sales promotional activities

The idea behind the co-ordination team is clearly to encourage greater co-operation between all parties concerned in the communications process, to achieve a better and more frequent exchange of information, and to encourage cross-fertilization between the work done in individual countries and in the Stuttgart headquarters. This is aimed at obtaining greater coherence and uniformity in all the advertising for commercial vehicles in Europe, without in any way upsetting the fundamental policy of the company of leaving final responsibility for local advertising to the subsidiaries in the various countries concerned. The company calls this its 'European parallel strategy' and what this amounts to in practice can be summarized as follows:

1. Headquarters in Stuttgart develops and pays for the creation of the 'image' campaign for all Mercedes-Benz commercial vehicles, to be used on an international scale.
2. Local subsidiaries implement this campaign with a minimum of adaptations, dictated by the market conditions in the countries concerned.
3. Local subsidiaries are permitted to develop and place any additional advertising, as deemed necessary.
4. In consultation with headquarters in Stuttgart, and subject to its final approval, the subsidiaries can appoint their own advertising agencies to make the necessary adaptations to the international campaign and to create and place any national advertising.
5. Frequent contacts between all concerned with the advertising of commercial vehicles at national and international levels should produce a cross-fertilization of ideas calculated to ensure the optimal quality of all advertising throughout Europe.

The company's efforts, described above, should be seen as a first step towards producing greater uniformity of advertising throughout Europe. However, there will undoubtedly be a number of questions that will only be resolved with time. For example: how far can individual countries go in adapting or deviating from international recommendations to suit their circumstances?

ROLE OF ADVERTISING AGENCIES

There is clear distinction between work done for the international campaigns and for the national campaigns of this division. As has already been indicated, the company's subsidiaries are free to appoint their own advertising agencies; but the international campaign is created by the Schellenberg advertising agency, in Stuttgart, so that the locally appointed agencies will have to make any necessary adaptations to the international campaign as it has been developed in Germany.

A question raised in other chapters of this book also rises with regard to Mercedes-Benz: should the company not employ one international advertising agency to be responsible for creating and co-ordinating all advertising done on an international and on a national scale? The director of the marketing communication department states quite emphatically that he is not in favour of using one advertising agency internationally, mainly because the advertising of commercial vehicles makes very special demands on an agency's skills, which can rarely be met in all the offices of one international network. In his opinion, the local subsidiaries are in the best position to select an agency on the spot that will meet these very special requirements. The long-standing experience and know-how of the Schellenberg advertising agency in Stuttgart in this particular field of business was one of the main reasons for selecting it to create the international campaign.

There are, of course, companies that take the totally opposite point of view and have, over long periods of time, built up exclusive relationships with a single advertising agency that have often resulted in remarkable success. The managements of these companies clearly feel that, by delegating some of their responsibilities to one international agency, they will not only achieve optimum creative solutions everywhere but, if successful, they will also enhance their own reputation as a result.

1993 AND BEYOND

We have already referred to the study-group that has made recommendations about the future in Europe of the Mercedes-Benz Commercial Vehicles Division; a similar study-group was appointed for the Passenger Vehicles Division of the company. Both appointments illustrate the great importance that the company attaches to developments within Europe in the years to come. Concentration of production may well be one aim, as well as concentration of the costly storage of vehicles and spare parts, which at present takes place in practically every European country. Fleet-owners with international operations, who are growing in size and importance, may well wish to make their purchases centrally, which, in turn, raises the subject of harmonization of prices, of concern to many manufacturers.

As far as the advertising function is concerned, the first steps towards greater concentration of advertising planning and execution have already been taken. However, if the concern wishes to obtain the same kind of total integration of national and international advertising policies that has been achieved by some of the successful consumer goods companies it may have to give more weight, at all managerial levels, to views and suggestions from non-German countries during the decision-making process. Such steps might well help to bring about the kind of total integration that the management of the Mercedes-Benz Commercial Vehicles Division must have had in mind when it set out on the course towards greater centralization of its communications in Europe.

In any case, Emil Jellinek and his little daughter Mercedes certainly set momentous developments in motion at the turn of the twentieth century, when the Daimler motor company not only benefited from Jellinek's enthusiasm and authority, but also gained wide recognition for its Mercedes cars. Since 1926, when the two manufacturing giants Daimler and Benz merged and wisely decided to incorporate 'Mercedes' in the name of the new company, with the three-pointed star as its emblem, Mercedes-Benz has become a household name throughout the world, evoking a pioneering spirit and a great tradition in the building of high-quality luxury cars and commercial vehicles. Its products should continue for many decades to satisfy the needs of those who prefer road transport to other means of moving goods and people.

Notes

1. *Grote Winkler Prins* (encyclopaedia) (1956). Amsterdam: Elsevier, Part 2, p. 706.
2. Oswald, Werner (1986), *Mercedes-Benz Lastwagen und Omnibusse 1886–1986*. Stuttgart: Motorbuch Verlag, p. 134.
3. *Das Geschäftsjahr 1990*, (annual report 1990), Daimler-Benz A.G., Stuttgart, inside cover.
4. *Ibid.*, p. 11f.
5. For more details, see: Max Gerrit von Pein (1986) (ed.), *Mercedes – Where the Name Came from*. Daimler-Benz A.G., Stuttgart.
6. *Ibid.*
7. *Das Geschäftsjahr 1988* (annual report 1988), Daimler-Benz A.G., Stuttgart, p. 26f.
8. *Werk Wörth* (Wörth Factory) (undated), Daimler-Benz A.G., Stuttgart, p. 4.
9. *The Mercedes-Benz Commercial Vehicle Magazine* (1989), Daimler-Benz A.G., Stuttgart, p. 3.
10. Lubbers, R.F.M. (1990), 'Europa's Akkers liggen open' (Europe's fields lie open), *NRC Handelsblad*, Rotterdam, 2 August.
11. *Mercedes-Benz Commercial Vehicle Magazine*, pp. 17–35.
12. *Marketing Kommunikation für Mercedes-Benz Nutzfahrzeuge – ein Handbuch für unsere Kommunikationspartner* (Marketing Communication for Mercedes-Benz Commercial Vehicles – a Handbook for our Communication Partners), Mercedes-Benz, Stuttgart, June 1990.
13. Schultz, Don E. (1981), *Essentials of Advertising Strategy*. Chicago: Crain Books, p. 9.

MIELE

'Anything Else Is a Compromise'

Unsere schmalste Antwort auf die Frage, wer heute abwäscht.

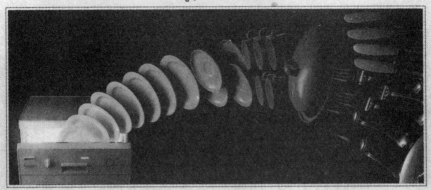

Domnes lingua, institutis, legibus inter se differunt omnis ab Aquitanis Garumna flumen, a Belgis Matrona et Sequana dividit. Horum omnium altissimi Hi omnes lingua, institutis, legibus inter se differunt vergla ad.

Aquitanis Garumna flumen, a Belgis Matrona et Sequana dividit. Horum omnium fortissimi sunt Belgae, propterea quod a cultu atque humo cives effeminandos animos pertinent, important proximique sunt Germanosrion.

Rhenum incolunt, quibuscum continenter bellum gerunt.

Helvetii quoque reliquos Gallos virtute praecedunt, quod fere coti dianis proeliis cumer manis contentalot dichem.

Finibus bellami geniat. Eorum una pars, quam Gol obtiere dictum est, initium capit a flumine Rhodano, continetur flumine Oceano, finibus Belgarum, attingit etiamnbs anis et Helvetii flama.

In septhentrionem siolam orientem solem, Aquitaniad. zruno

Miele
Die Entscheidung fürs Leben

WASHING
MACHINE
OR
TIME
MACHINE?

Miele

Miele, Miele
sagte Tante, die alle
Waschmaschinen
kannte

Nur **Miele Miele**
sagte Tante,
die alle Waschmaschinen kannte

Mielewerke A.G.
Größte Waschmaschinenfabrik Deutschlands
Gütersloh/Westfalen
Über 2000 Beamte und Arbeiter.

MIELE
'Anything Else Is a Compromise'

'Please write in your book,' said Rudolf Miele, part-owner and executive director of the Miele company, 'that in my opinion there are no international advertising agency networks that function equally well everywhere; they all want to do their own thing and they will not always fall in line with the strategies that we have laid down.'[1] Mr Miele feels strongly on this point, which he also raised, at the beginning of 1988, when addressing a meeting of the company's employees on the subject of the European Internal Market. On that occasion he said:

> Back in the fifties I was already endeavouring to arrive at completely
> integrated European advertising. I must honestly admit that so far I
> have not succeeded, because the views on the visual and textual
> creation of advertising are as abundant as the number of advertising
> agencies in Europe.[2]

A look at some of the company's advertising for its dishwashers and washing machines, introduced in May 1988, corroborates Mr Miele's point of view. The pay-off lines in Miele's advertising vary considerably: 'Miele – a decision for life', is used in Germany, and also in Spain and Switzerland, but in neighbouring Austria the pay-off runs, 'Reliability for many years'; and in Holland and Belgium, it says, 'Miele – there is no better one', a pay-off that is also used in the USA and in Canada. However, it would be unfair and unjustified to conclude from Mr Miele's remarks and from the different pay-off's in Miele's advertising that there is little uniformity in Miele's policies, or that control over what is happening around the world in the advertising context is hardly noticeable.[3] On the contrary, the company is strongly committed to a uniform policy for its marketing and advertising in the countries in which it operates, and the fact that this is not yet apparent from all forms of visual communication should not be interpreted as a lack of determination on the part of Miele's management to achieve such uniformity. The following passage from the speech quoted earlier makes this clear:

> If we want to arrive at a uniform marketing policy, a uniform
> customer service in accordance with a uniform philosophy and quality,
> then a uniform advertising message in all European countries should
> unquestionably be part of it.[4]

This point of view is confirmed and reinforced by a statement in one of the company's more recent publications, saying that an international brand such as Miele increasingly requires to communicate its messages across borders, both in the context of its advertising and in that of its sales promotions.[5]

Before discussing in greater detail how Miele is trying to put its European policy into operation, the history of this German family business should be briefly reviewed; in doing so, the progress, development and present character of what started nearly 100 years ago as a small local manufacturer of milk-separators for the production of butter, will become clear and should serve as useful background information.

MIELE's HISTORY AND DEVELOPMENT

In 1899, in the small town of Herzebrock in Westphalia, Carl Miele and Reinhard Zinkann founded the Miele company, which soon extended its production of milk-separators to include washing machines. At that time, these appliances consisted of oak-wood barrels with a swivelling iron cross to produce the suds needed to clean the laundry. In 1907, Miele moved its 60 employees to nearby Gütersloh, now a thriving, well-preserved and charming town with approximately 90000 inhabitants, which has several well-known firms, such as Oetker, Melitta, Nixdorf and Bertelsmann, in its vicinity. The firm grew apace, surviving both world wars, and now has seven factories throughout Germany, which employ some 14000 people and achieved a turnover of about DM.2.8 billion in 1989, of which more than 60 per cent represented foreign sales.[6]

Total turnover 1925–1989

		Foreign Sales
1925	RM.12 million	7 per cent
1950	DM.47 million	10 per cent
1960	DM.200 million	21 per cent
1970	DM.620 million	38 per cent
1980	DM.1 415 million	40 per cent
1988	DM.2 400 million	54 per cent
1989	DM.2 800 million	59 per cent

Today, Miele is run by Mr Rudolf Miele, the firm's commercial head, and Dr Peter Zinkann, who is responsible for the technical side of the business, both members of the third generation of the Miele family to own the firm. They are directly supported by about 30 managers and their staffs. Among them is Mr Peer Hilbig, Miele's advertising manager, who reports directly to Mr Rudolf Miele, an indication of the importance that the business attaches to the role of advertising. Contact between directors and their managers is friendly and informal; directors drop into their managers' offices to discuss and resolve day-to-day problems, and everyone has a direct telephone link with everyone else – there is no prestigious secretarial network. The loyalty of Miele's employees to the business is exemplary; there hardly is any staff turnover.

MIELE's SUBSIDIARIES

As well as exporting to countries where it does not have affiliates, Miele sells its products in Germany and in the following countries exclusively through fully-owned subsidiaries, which act as profit centres, reporting directly to headquarters in Gütersloh:

Europe		Outside Europe
Austria	Luxembourg	Australia
Belgium	Netherlands	Canada
Denmark	Norway	USA
Finland	Portugal	Japan
France	Sweden	
Greece	Switzerland	
Ireland	Spain	
Italy	United Kingdom	

Once annual business plans have been approved, the local subsidiaries have the final decision regarding the implementation of agreed policies. The same applies to matters regarding advertising, but this does not mean that advertising is a kind of 'free-for-all'. As we shall see later, Miele's central advertising department has an important role to play, but there is a distinction between its executive responsibilities for advertising in Germany itself and its more advisory role as regards Miele's advertising in other countries around the world.

MIELE PRODUCTS

Miele has adopted the wise policy of the cobbler who sticks to his last; the company mainly markets products for use in private kitchens, or in the larger kitchens of hotels, restaurants, hospitals etc., a field in which it has considerable experience and expertise. However, this was not always the case; the repertoire once included motor cars, motorbikes and bicycles, but production of these extravagances has long been discontinued. The current range of products includes: washing machines, dryers and ironing machines, dishwashers, built-in kitchens, fridges, ovens, microwave ovens and extractors; the one anomalous item is the Miele vacuum cleaner, introduced in 1927 and still enjoying considerable success.

Miele considers itself to be in the forefront of technical innovation; the fifteen new developments for which it was responsible between 1901 and 1988[7], including the introduction, in 1929, of the dishwasher, the incorporation, in 1978, of microcomputer technology in washing machines and dishwashers and the launch, in 1988, of a dishwasher with a separate box for cutlery, all provide evidence of Miele's firm intention to be the leader in its field.

. . . AND THEIR REPUTATION

'Better all the time' has always been Miele's catchphrase, and although this slogan had, in later years, to be dropped from its advertising for legal reasons, the policy of ensuring the top quality and high-class presentation of its products still prevails. Miele's excellent reputation is confirmed by research. At the beginning of 1989, a report by the Gesellschaft für Konsumgüterforschung – a German consumer research institute that interviews 2000 consumers annually about the brands in which they have greatest confidence – put Miele in third place, with its main competitors low down on the list, which ran as follows[8]:

1.	Daimler-Benz	6.	W.M.F.
2.	B.M.W.	7.	Blaupunkt
3.	Miele	8.	Bosch
4.	Porsche	9.	Siemens
5.	Volkswagen	10.	A.E.G.

Miele does equally well in other countries; research carried out by independent institutes in Austria, France, Portugal, Switzerland, the UK, Australia, Belgium, Holland and the USA, shows the excellent reputation for quality and performance gained by the more than two million units that left Miele factories in 1988.[9]

POSITIONING MIELE PRODUCTS

Miele's policy has always been to sell top-quality products at a premium; all its products are substantially more expensive than those of the company's main competitors. Such a policy does, of course, require the highest technical standards and a rigid quality-control system at all production levels, but it also necessitates optimum service to trade and consumers, an aspect of the company's operation to which headquarters and subsidiaries pay considerable attention. Advertising must also reflect company policy in this respect, convincing trade and consumers alike that, whilst Miele products require a greater financial outlay than those of Miele's competitors, they are undoubtedly worth it.

In short, Miele would like its products to be seen by consumers as offering the best value for money and as being supported by an excellent before-sales and after-sales service. This positioning naturally applies all over the world; as we have seen, this privately owned German company does 59 per cent of its total business outside Germany. Thus, the following paragraph from the second issue of the Miele advertising magazine refers to the need for a uniform marketing and advertising policy in the years to come:

Better corporate identity produces European profile – and it saves money.
Of approximately 320 million Europeans, about 30 million are travelling continuously on business to other countries. About 100 million Europeans spend their holidays abroad.

If Miele positions itself in its advertising as unmistakably European, every European, whether on a business trip or on holiday, will receive confirmation through advertising that Miele stands for a highly appreciated European product. And making Miele advertising truly European also means saving costs.[10]

The above statement served as an introduction to the presentation of Miele's international advertising plans to all its subsidiaries, explaining its future advertising strategy and its execution in considerable detail to all concerned.

MIELE's ADVERTISING STRATEGY

As one would expect, Miele's international advertising strategy aims at convincing consumers of the superior quality and specific advantages of each of the Miele products. It tries to do so with a presentation combining relevance, uniqueness and style; the advertising should be striking, memorable and competitive, as well as helping to improve still further the high-quality image enjoyed by Miele products in all countries.

If we compare this strategy with Miele's past advertising, we discover that the company has come a long way since the days when Miele's fame and popularity were established with the help of a German rhyme: 'Nur Miele, Miele sagte Tante, die alle Waschmachinen kannte'. (This is impossible to translate literally, but means: 'only buy, Miele', said Auntie, who knew all the makes of washing machines!)

Interestingly enough, 'Auntie's' message has remained basically unchanged; Miele's advertising is still designed to convey the superior quality of all its products. Thus, in Miele's present advertisements, the product itself, shot from a special angle and always represented with a burst of light coming from within it, is the 'star of the show' and holds pride of place. Similarly, the headline always highlights its unique advantages, though the pay-off, as we pointed out at the beginning of this chapter, still varies somewhat from country to country.

ADVERTISING RESEARCH

Before presenting its latest advertising to its subsidiaries, the company wisely decided that the new proposals should first be tested. The advertisements for the dishwasher, drier and vacuum cleaner were subjected to attitude-shift research, carried out by the German consumer research institute, mentioned earlier. It employed the so-called 'Ad★vantage Print' method, developed in the USA for testing the expected effectiveness of advertisements. The results showed that in all three cases Miele's advertising scored better and obtained higher brand awareness among respondents than that of its main competitors.[11]

Table 3.   Attitude shift of competitive brands and the Miele vacuum cleaner after exposure to advertisements

	Miele	Siemens	AEG	Progress	Rowenta
Before ad. exposure	5.86	5.93	6.09	4.90	4.50
After ad. exposure	6.51	6.09	6.12	5.10	4.34
Difference	0.65	0.16	0.03	0.20	−0.16
Attitude shift	21 per cent	5 per cent	1 per cent	5 per cent	–

Average values: 1 = would never buy; 9 = would like to buy.

THE ROLE OF THE MIELE SUBSIDIARIES

Although fully owned by the company, the subsidiaries exercise considerable influence on company policy, including the advertising of Miele products; much freedom is given to their staff, because of their expert knowledge of local conditions and the local competitive scene. However, as Mr Miele has said, the long-term objectives of the company certainly include establishing a great deal of uniformity in the advertising of Miele products throughout Europe, indeed throughout the world, and much progress has already been made in this respect; the majority of Miele subsidiaries now accept recommendations from head-office, which they adapt in accordance with local circumstances. During a discussion of this point with staff of the Dutch Miele subsidiary (one of the oldest and most important), its advertising & sales promotion manager said that: 'there are no basic differences of opinion between Gütersloh and ourselves, we all understand the need to become more international, it is simply a process of growing closer and closer together.'[12]

There is of course the important factor of the economies of scale that can be achieved by centralizing advertising production in one place, a point that will be discussed later. Suffice it to say, at the moment, that the co-operation between headquarters and its subsidiaries leaves little to be desired, an essential prerequisite for optimum results in the implementation of agreed policies.

MIELE's MEDIA POLICY

Approximately 65 per cent of Miele's total advertising expenditure is spent on the international campaign, the final choice of media being left to the local offices and their advertising agencies. Television is, of course, one of the media employed in some countries, but the question of advertising by satellite has not yet acquired acute importance. Naturally, developments are monitored closely, but until there is a satisfactory solution to the problem of language, satellite TV will not appear on the company's media schedules.

The remaining one-third of Miele's advertising budget is almost entirely devoted to its very important trade-promotions and consumer-promotions campaigns, many of which are designed by the advertising department at Gütersloh, not only for use in Germany, but also for adoption and adaptation by the subsidiaries. The vast amount of brochures – about 1000 per year – and trade literature, in 11 different languages, is mainly produced by the company in Gemany; it is not surprising, therefore, that the central advertising department comprises some 35 people. In this connection it is of interest to note that the staff on the advertising department includes hardly any non-Germans. One would have assumed that, in spite of the excellent relationship between Miele's head-office and its subsidiaries, the significance of Miele's foreign trade would also be reflected in the composition of its head-office staff, to the benefit of all concerned. Perhaps this kind of cross-fertilization will one day be introduced.

MIELE AND ITS ADVERTISING AGENCIES

As we have seen, neither Mr Miele nor Mr Hilbig has great confidence in international advertising agency networks. Miele worked with one some time ago, but the experiment did not produce the desired results, so the company now uses the German advertising agency Springer & Jacoby for its centrally produced creative work. The responsibility for the adaptation of the agreed basic advertising idea to local requirements, and for appointing a local advertising agency to help in doing this, rests entirely with the managements of the Miele offices around the world. The company employs 19 different agencies for the handling of its business in different countries. This way of operating is explained by Miele's advertising manager as follows:

> As Miele advertising is in all countries the responsibility of the boss,
> we also expect that the boss of the agency will be available for
> discussions. Experience has also taught us that advertising is
> extremely sensitive, so if the relationship between the partners in this
> discussion does not work properly, the advertising itself will not work
> either. Nor would there be any point to appoint centrally an agency
> network whose individual representatives in the countries concerned
> are unknown to us. [13]

One can only hope that the 'boss' will indeed always be available for discussions, but let us, at this stage, merely observe that Miele's main competitors in Germany – Siemens, Bosch, AEG and Bauknecht – have either nominated, or are about to nominate, an international agency network to handle their advertising. [14] Miele, as we have seen, takes the opposite view, to the point that, in Germany, Springer & Jacoby do not even place Miele advertising; this is done through a separate media-buying agency.

REMUNERATION OF MIELE's ADVERTISING AGENCIES

As Miele requires its German agency only to handle the creative aspects of its advertising, the usual 15 per cent agency commission arrangement does not apply. Instead, the company discusses annually with Springer & Jacoby the nature and scope of the services that the agency will provide, for which a fee is then agreed. Miele will make all artwork produced by the Germany agency available to its office free of charge. These offices will, in turn, negotiate special terms with their local agencies for the services that these agencies are to provide, arguing that the company itself will supply an important part of the necessary artwork.

This way of remunerating advertising agencies is, of course, used by many multinational advertisers, who will often pay handsomely for high-quality creative work, since this can then be used by their regional offices, which could never afford to buy comparable material locally and save a lot of money by not even trying to. Naturally, the larger the number of subsidiaries willing to use centrally prepared material, the greater the economies of scale. In the case of Miele, optimum uniformity has been achieved in 18 markets and developments in this respect are promising. The importance of this point can best be illustrated by the fact that if all Miele's advertising production were indeed centralized, a saving of DM.2.5 million could be made. Although it is often argued that the primary reason for adopting an international advertising policy is not a financial one, but to have an opportunity to buy the best available creative talent, it is difficult to ignore the importance of saving this amount of money.

1993 AND BEYOND

As we have seen, from an advertising point of view, the company is already preparing itself fully for the years to come and for the more unified Europe that will exist from 1993 onwards. These activities are entirely in line with Miele's confidence in the future of Europe and in the company's opportunities for further expansion, including in Eastern Europe. As regards its opportunities in the West, Mr Miele observes that if his company's sales per head of population outside Germany were to equal those in Germany itself, the company's present total turnover of DM.2.8 billion would increase to DM.6.3 billion.[15]

Not only is Mr Miele optimistic about the future of his own business, he also shows himself to be among the optimists on the subject of Europe in general, when he says:

> The wheels of history cannot be reversed. The people of Europe have grown so close that the European Community has already become history, and I am certain that by the early nineties this will also be the case with the European Internal Market.[16]

Does this point of view indicate the personal involvement of Miele's directors in tackling the problems that the forthcoming European Internal Market is still facing, particularly the ones of importance to the industry in which Miele operates? Naturally, the company's senior management will be alert to all developments within the EC Commission that could possibly affect its business, but Mr Miele believes that, generally speaking, the handling of these industry-level matters is best left to the national and international trade associations representing the electrotechnical and metal industries. Is he worried about today's trends regarding mergers and take-overs and competition from outside Europe? No, he is not:

> Of course we follow all these developments carefully, but we are an independent business and we would like to keep it that way. . . . Yes, there is and there always will be competition from companies bigger than ourselves, but it has always been our policy to be satisfied with offering high quality products to that part of the population that can afford to buy them. . . . No, we are not unduly distracted by such developments beyond our control . . . we concentrate all our attention on running our business the way we believe it ought to be run.[17]

When asked which factors, in his opinion, have contributed most to the success of his company over such a long period, Mr Miele's spontaneous answer is: the quality of its products and the consistent emphasis on innovation; the established policy of trading only through fully owned subsidiaries and the considerable attention given to providing optimum services to consumers and trade customers; the support given to the products by high-quality advertising; and, finally, the special character of the family business, with its strong commitments to staff and to national managers, ensuring continuity of agreed policies, loyalty and high motivation. Independent, self-confident and single-minded, the owners of the company intend to preserve and to continue the policies that have made their business successful. One can only hope that members of the fourth and fifth generations of the Miele and Zinkann families will have the same dedication and will-power to continue the work of their predecessors, showing to the world at large that the opportunities for well-run family businesses are as great as ever!

Notes

1. Personal discussion with Rudolf Miele, a Director of Miele & Cie, Gütersloh, Germany, 9 June 1989.
2. Miele, Rudolf (1988), 'Miele auf dem Weg zum Europäischen Binnenmarkt 1992' (Miele on the way to the European Internal Market), a presentation to the staff of the company, Gütersloh, 28 September 1988, p. 18.
3. Hilbig, Peer (1990), *Das 3. Werbemagazin von Miele* (1990), Miele & Cie, Gütersloh, May, pp. 6–31.
4. Rudolf Miele 1988 presentation, p. 18.
5. *Ibid.*, p. 3.
6. *Miele, Qualität hat einen Namen* (undated), Miele & Cie, Gütersloh, p. 34f.
7. *Ibid.*, p. 14.
8. *Das 2. Werbemagazin von Miele* (1989), Miele & Cie, Gütersloh, May, p. 4.
9. *Miele Geräte im internationalen Test* (1989), Gütersloh, 1st Edition.
10. *Das 2. Werbemagazin von Miele*, p. 5.
11. *Ibid.*, p. 34.
12. Personal discussion with W. S. Roijers, Advertising & Sales Promotion Manager of Miele Nederland B. V., Vianen, Netherlands, 8 August 1989.
13. Written reply from Peer Hilbig to questions from the author, Gütersloh, 18 April 1989.
14. *Das 2. Werbemagazin von Miele*, p. 4.
15. Rudolf Miele 1988 presentation, p. 15.
16. *Ibid.*, p. 20.
17. See note 1.

NESCAFÉ

The World's Leading Brand of Soluble Coffee

Café grande, café puro, café especial, café superior. In het land van Cap Colombie heeft de taal prachtige woorden voor de nieuwste koffie van Nescafé. Cap Colombie is koffie van 100% Arabica-bonen, een kwaliteit die men zelfs op de beste koffieplantages ter wereld als uitzonderlijk betitelt. Dus proeft u koffie met een ongelooflijk aroma en een heel verfijnde, haast fruitige smaak. Cap Colombie, een ervaring die u zich niet moet onthouden als u echt van koffie houdt.

Cap Colombie.
Un nuevo café grande
de Nescafé.

NESCAFÉ®
1982

NESCAFÉ®
1988

NESCAFÉ
The World's Leading Brand
of Soluble Coffee

It is quite refreshing when, amidst all the turmoil about Europe after 1992 and the need for greater central control of European marketing operations, you suddenly hear one of the 'captains of industry' taking the opposite view. And that was precisely what Mr Helmut Maucher, chairman and chief executive officer of the Nestlé group did, when asked if his company would ever consider concentrating responsibility for the European marketing and advertising of the Nestlé products at the company's headquarters in Vevey, Switzerland:

> We will never erode the responsibilities of our national managers. . . .
> Yes, there is an important staff function, recommending strategies for
> a number of our products on a worldwide basis, but the final decision
> will always be taken at the national level.[1]

Mr Maucher feels strongly that the local Nestlé companies are best placed to analyse and judge how the firm's many different products, mostly in the food sector, should be marketed to suit local tastes, habits and preferences, taking into account national legislation, of which there is so much relating to food.

Though Nestlé has a minority interest in the cosmetics company l'Oréal and is involved in a few other activities, the dominant role of its food business is clearly apparent from the following breakdown of the firm's turnover, which amounted in 1990 to SFr. 46 billion[2]:

Drinks	23.6%	(e.g. Nescafé, Nesquik, Milo, fruit juices, mineral water)
Cereals, milks and dietetic products	20.0%	(e.g. Carnation 'Coffee-Mate', coffee-creamers, infant milks and cereals, baby foods)
Chocolate and confectionery	16.0%	(e.g. Smarties, After Eight, Nestlé Crunch)
Culinary products	12.7%	(e.g. Maggi bouillons and dishes for microwave ovens)
Frozen foods and ice cream	10.1%	(e.g. Stouffers 'Lean Cuisine' and 'Right Course' range of health-food dishes)
Refrigerated products	8.9%	(e.g. Chambourcy yogurt, Herta cold meats)
Petfoods	4.5%	(e.g. Friskies)
Pharmaceutical and cosmetic products	3.0%	
Other products and activities	1.1%	

Although approximately 24 per cent of the group's total turnover comes from drinks, a figure of SFr. 11 billion, it is clear from the above list that Nestlé is more than a producer of soluble coffee. However, Nescafé is the company's most important single brand, accounting for an estimated 15 per cent of the Group's turnover and being sold in more than 100 countries.

HISTORIC GROWTH AND PRESENT SIZE

As we mentioned earlier, Nestlé total sales in 1990 amounted to SFr. 46 billion, of which 48.7 per cent derived from Europe, followed by 24.2 per cent from North America. In the same year the concern achieved a total trading profit of SFr. 4.6 billion and employed close on 199 000 people. The company's growth over a period of more than 120 years can best be traced using the following list of important dates in its history:

1866	The Anglo-Swiss Condensed Milk Company opens the first European condensed milk factory in Cham, Switzerland.
1905	The Nestlé group proper results from the merger between this company and Farine Lactée Henri Nestlé.
1929	Peter–Cailler–Kohler Chocolats Suisses merges with Nestlé.
1938	Launch of Nescafé.
1960–1977	Nestlé acquires various companies, including Crosse & Blackwell (1960), Findus (1962) and Libby (1970), and obtains a minority interest in l'Oréal (1974).
1977	Nestlé Alimentana S. A. is renamed Nestlé S. A.
1978–1988	Nestlé acquires further companies, including Chambourcy (1978), Carnation (1985), Buitoni-Perugina (1988) and Rowntree Mackintosh (1988).

The manufacture of Nestlé's more than 300 products takes place in 421 factories spread over 61 countries. Very strict instructions are issued from Vevey with regard to recipes, brands, quality control and the main raw materials, such as the coffee beans used in Nescafé; but the final blend of each product is determined by the requirements of each country.

ORGANIZATION

As is clear from Mr Maucher's comments quoted at the beginning of this chapter, the executive authority over Nestlé products in the various countries in which they are sold, rests in the main with the managers of the national companies. Each head of market reports to a regional manager responsible for one of Nestlé's five 'zones': Europe; the USA and Canada; Latin America; Africa and the Middle East; and Asia and Oceania. The general managers or executive vice-presidents responsible for these zones operate from Vevey and are members of Nestlé's general management, which, in turn, reports to the board of the company. In addition to this regional management, there is a product management group, also at general management level, acting in a staff capacity and representing a number of important functions concerned with strategic planning for the worldwide development of the most important Nestlé products. Other departments, also at general management level, are responsible for areas such as research, finance and technical matters. Mr Helmut Maucher is both chairman of the Nestlé board and managing director of the company; in the latter capacity he also heads Nestlé's general management group. The Nestlé headquarters at Vevey has about 1 500 staff, of whom 50 per cent are non-Swiss. The large number of foreign employees is explained in part by the fact that only 2 per cent of the company's total turnover comes from Switzerland itself. The following chart represents the upper levels of the Nestlé organization:

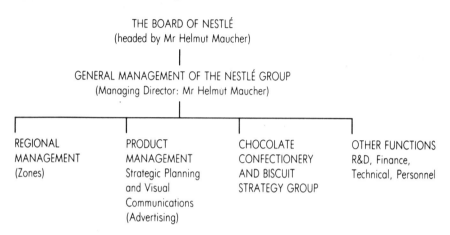

The visual communications department, with advisory responsibilities for packaging, advertising, promotions and corporate identity, is involved in counselling the national companies and the strategic planning groups at head-office on all aspects of the presentation of the company and its products to consumers and trade outlets; it employs a staff of approximately 30 people. However, before discussing the advertising of Nescafé in some detail, the history of the product – and, indeed, its raw material; coffee – should be briefly reviewed.

NESCAFÉ AND COFFEE

The word 'coffee' is derived from the Arabic word 'kahweh', meaning 'strength or vigour, although it could also be a transposition of "Kaffa", the name of a province in Ethiopia which is generally considered to be the country coffee originally came from.'[3] Because of its pleasant taste and stimulating effect, it is among the world's most popular drinks. One of the many publications on the origins of the coffee bean, which provides millions of people with so much satisfaction, says:

> The home of the coffee tree is the tropical forest, and the area in
> which it is grown today is a belt reaching to a latitude of about 24
> degrees to the north and south of the equator. The biggest producers
> are Brazil, Columbia, Indonesia, the Ivory Coast and Mexico, followed
> by about fifty other countries.[4]

Although there are more than 60 different varieties of coffee tree, the most popular and best-known are Arabica, which grows mainly in the Latin American countries, and Robusta, which grows primarily in Africa.

The habit of coffee drinking dates back to the early seventeenth century, and today, according to an estimate of the International Coffee Organisation, around 90 million 60-kg bags of coffee are consumed each year, by about 40 per cent of the world's population. As the most popular brand of coffee, Nescafé itself has a consumption rate of more than 170 million cups per year.[5]

IS NESCAFÉ REAL COFFEE?

It is still a popular misconception that Nescafé is an artificial substitute for real coffee, even though Nestlé celebrated the product's 50th anniversary in 1988, with justified pride and satisfaction. Nescafé was the invention of Dr Morgenthaler and his research team at Nestlé, who developed a spray-dried coffee powder that maintained its blend and taste thanks to the addition of carbohydrates, and released its aroma when water was added. When it was launched, in Switzerland on 1 April 1938, this real coffee product was the first soluble (instant) coffee ever made; and it was soon being sold in France, the USA, the UK and other countries. Its development represented a considerable technical breakthrough, because previously coffee beans had had to be ground by hand. Since machine-ground coffee only became popular in the 1970s, Nescafé was able to exploit the considerable advantage that it offered in terms of convenience for about 35 years. (As we shall see later, in the context of its advertising, there might have been a risk that its convenience would be over-emphasized, an argument that would easily have backfired, but Nescafé advertisements soon began to concentrate on the product's intrinsic properties, such as its purity, taste and aroma.) During the Second World War, American G.I.'s acted almost as an unpaid sales-force for Nescafé, helping to create awareness of the new way of making coffee that it represented.

The next important technical breakthrough occurred in the mid-1960s, when the technique of spray-drying was supplemented by a new freeze-drying method, creating a granulated product that was 'comparable to its fresh counterpart. It keeps the same appearance, texture, taste and aroma, the nutritional value is preserved to the maximum, and the content in essential fatty acids, proteins, vitamins, oligo elements, enzymes, etc. remains unchanged.'[6] This freeze-drying method requires costly technical equipment and considerable know-how and is a more elaborate process than spray-drying, so that the freeze-dried product must be sold at a premium – which is also justified by the use of higher quality beans in its manufacture.

THE MANY DIFFERENT VERSIONS OF NESCAFÉ

The above survey of Nescafé's development gives no real impression of the range of Nescafé products. Alongside the (spray-dried) standard and (freeze-dried) premium products, obtainable in light, medium and strong versions, there are, of course, also the decaffeinated varieties for those who wish to avoid the stimulating effects of caffeine or who worry about not being able to sleep after drinking coffee. The premium products include two top-of-the-range brands: Cap Colombie (a rather light, pure Colombian coffee) and Alta Rica (a somewhat stronger, pure Arabica coffee). These are produced in France and aimed at sophisticated consumers who are prepared to pay a substantial price for products that are of the same high quality wherever they are sold. In its advertising for these two brands, the company is able to concentrate entirely on the special qualities of the beans that are used in their production, thereby simultaneously upgrading the image of Nescafé in general.

Finally, in some countries, alongside its instant coffees, the company also markets under the name of Nescafé a small amount of roasted and ground coffee, to be prepared in the old-fashioned manner with a kettle of boiling water and a filter. Knowing that there are still those who like to smell their coffee when it is being prepared Nestlé saw no reason to cede this market to other producers. The entire gamut of Nescafé products can be simplified as follows:

freeze-dried	**Super Premium Brands** Nescafé Cap Colombie and Nescafé Alta Rica
freeze-dried	**Premium Brands** e.g. Nescafé Gold Blend (also available decaffeinated) Light Medium Strong
spray-dried	**Standard Brands** e.g. Nescafé Classic (also available decaffeinated) Light Medium Strong
	Roast and Ground

Although the proportions of the different categories that are sold differ from country to country, the bulk of Nescafé's business (over 50 per cent) is accounted for by the standard brands. Next come the premium brands; but while the top-of-the-range varieties only make a modest contribution in terms of volume, they contribute significantly to the quality image of Nescafé as a whole.

IS NESCAFÉ AN 'INTERNATIONAL' BRAND?

In reviewing the different varieties of the same basic Nescafé product, the question arises as to whether Nescafé is really an international brand. From a consumer's point of view, this would imply that travellers would find the same Nescafé products with the same blends and the same descriptions of their blends in every country. In fact, this is not the case. The brand name Nescafé will be the same everywhere and so, probably, will the graphics on the label, but the description of the product, and the product's actual blend and flavour, are likely to differ from country to country. For reasons already mentioned, there are more than 100 varieties of Nescafé, with their tastes adapted to the palates of the consumers in the countries in which they are sold. This makes it difficult for travellers to identify the product. With reference to the question of terminology discussed in an earlier chapter, it would, therefore, probably be more correct to refer to Nescafé as an international 'concept', rather than as an international 'brand', which will normally be uniform in all its basic elements. However, leaving definitions aside, with a more unified Europe in prospect, is the management taking any active steps to change its existing policy?

INTERNATIONALIZING NESTLÉ'S ADVERTISING

If only because of the nature of its products, Nestlé has quite understandably always followed a policy of decentralization. Foods, it has been argued – using coffee as a most convincing example – depend for their success so much on local tastes and preferences that it is not feasible to make them subject to a uniform international policy. The one exception is in the case of an entirely new product that has universal appeal and is unburdened by established habits and preferences – a point taken up by Ramon Masip, Nestlé's executive vice-president for Europe. He believes that to be a market-leader, you must be a 'low-cost producer', and that one of the ways to obtain such a position is to develop a new product for the whole of Europe, enabling the desired economies of scale to be achieved from the very outset: 'We are now starting a new project where the whole approach is to have not only one *product* but exactly the same package and the same label for all countries.'[7]

In addition to trying to achieve greater uniformity for new products, whilst accepting that local nuances in the composition and presentation of existing brands are likely to continue, a company should also be able to unify and simplify the ways in which it communicates messages about its products to consumers; in other words, to obtain greater efficiency in the areas of marketing and advertising. This is precisely what Nestlé management has decided to do and, in recent years, it has taken a number of steps to streamline the company's marketing and advertising. The main objectives of its long-term plan have been: (a) to lay down basic communication strategies for Nestlé's most important 'strategic' brands, such as Nescafé; (b) to produce guidelines for greater creative uniformity in the packaging and the labelling of these strategic brands; and (c) to improve the efficiency and effectiveness of communications with consumers, by reducing the number of advertising agencies working on each of these brands. Naturally, the resultant interplay between Nestlé's staff executives and, for example, those responsible for the company's various zones, requires to be handled with considerable managerial skill. The attainment of the dual aim of creating greater uniformity in a number of decisive areas, whilst still maintaining an overall policy of decentralization, will inevitably require a delicate balance that may easily be destroyed if all concerned are not thinking and acting along the same basic lines, with the same objective in mind.

INTERNATIONAL GUIDELINES

In order to implement its new policies appropriately and inform its affiliates of how to put them into effect, Nestlé has produced three important documents, covering the marketing strategy and product presentation details for its strategic brands.

The 'Labelling Standards' document is the only one that is mandatory; it gives precise specifications for the various elements that are to make up the design of the label, such as the Nescafé logo, the type-faces and colours to be used, and the proportionate emphasis to be given to the various details. The document includes examples of the labels for its many different varieties of product recommending that the affiliates should start using these labels at the earliest possible moment. The 'Package Design Manual' is a more flexible document, recommending various different ways of applying its standards to, for instance, the material or shape of the package concerned. The most important document is the 'Branding Strategy', containing details of Nestlé's marketing principles and the backgrounds and key attributes of its strategic brands. These key attributes include references to: (a) the brand characteristics; (b) the desired image; (c) the corporate association with the brand concerned; (d) the visual properties dealt with in the other two documents; and (e) developments in the usage of the brand.

The company's new policy with regard to advertising agencies will be discussed later, but, from the above, it will already be clear that Nestlé wishes to harmonize its operation where such harmonization is possible, without abandoning the basic principles of decentralization and without putting its products at any risk.

NESCAFÉ FRAPPÉ

In the context of Mr Masip's comments quoted earlier, and as an interesting example of the greater, though not yet complete, uniformity being introduced into the marketing of Nestlé's products, it is worth mentioning the case of Nescafé Frappé. The product was launched in Greece as far back as 1957, but it took a long time for Nestlé's central management in Vevey to be convinced of the international potential of this iced coffee concept, which now is on sale in a number of European markets. The basic marketing strategy is the same everywhere. The product is aimed at consumers aged between 13 and 24 everywhere, it is called Nescafé Frappé everywhere, the logo is the same everywhere, the blue and white colours of the packaging and the advertising material are the same everywhere – but that, unfortunately, is where the uniformity stops: the advertising is not the same everywhere. This seems to be a missed opportunity, and although the central management will now try to obtain as much uniformity in Frappé advertising as possible, this has not yet been fully achieved.

NESCAFÉ AND ITS ADVERTISING POLICY

Advertising expenditure on Nescafé is of the order of SFr. 350 million per annum worldwide, representing approximately 5 per cent of the product's net sales value[8]. Despite all efforts to increase the uniformity of the brand's advertising and make its budget go further, decisions on actual advertising presentation are still very much up to the national affiliates. However, it is difficult to dispute the logic of this policy. Not only does the company market different blends and varieties in most markets – though this in itself need not prevent the product's basic advertising promise from being the same everywhere – but attitudes to instant coffee and competitive conditions also differ significantly. As regards attitudes, in the UK instant coffee's share of the total coffee market amounts to more than 90 per cent, whereas in Germany it is only 10 per cent. Between these extremes one finds the USA, with 32 per cent, Canada, with 50 per cent, France, with 35 per cent, and Japan with 85 per cent.[9] This is graphic testimony to the wide variations between the various markets for coffee in terms of consumer preferences, habits and competition. It is not surprising, therefore, that the branding strategy document for Nescafé does not really contain a hard-and-fast branding strategy at all; it simply refers to brand 'attributes', leaving it up to the managements in the various countries in which Nescafé is sold to give them concrete expression through advertising.

CONTENT AND PRESENTATION

In general terms, the earliest Nescafé advertising can be described as having concentrated on the important proposition of 'convenience'. However, when it became apparent that convenience was being over-emphasized and also that this advantage was being eroded by time-saving and labour-saving appliances, the emphasis shifted toward the product's purity, good taste and rich aroma. As a result, Nestlé subsidiaries in many countries prefer to run product-oriented advertising, concentrating on the 'real coffee' aspect of Nescafé.

In the UK where instant coffee dominates the total coffee market, the company and its advertising agency, McCann-Erickson, decided to support the premium brand Nescafé Gold Blend with a series of advertisements in which it was shown performing the role of a catalyst in a romance between two people. The resulting seven commercials were so well written, acted and directed, that they received the 'Award for Creative Excellence' of the Marketing Society and *Marketing Week*. More importantly, '. . . since we started with them last year, consumption in the UK for Nestlé's Gold Blend has been one and a half million cups of Gold Blend more than previously.'[10] This 'slice-of-life' advertising is unusual for Nestlé. Most of the company's advertising is product-oriented, as in the case of its commercials for Cap Colombie broadcast in Europe in 1990 – though the actual presentation is very varied.

In discussing Nescafé advertising in Spain, John Philip Jones says, 'The Spanish advertising for Nescafé has always been written and produced in Spain, a result of Nestlé's belief that advertising should, subject to certain guidelines, be originated in local markets.'[11] It follows from this that the local Nestlé companies also decide on the media to be used, as well as on the advertising agencies that they wish to appoint. Their choice of agencies will be discussed in the next section, but here it is worth mentioning that it is standard procedure for the visual communications department to work closely with each product management group at head-office to ensure that appropriate advice is given to the companies in each market, not only regarding the selection of advertising agencies but also regarding all aspects of the content and presentation of the actual advertising.

NESTLÉ AND ITS ADVERTISING AGENCIES

As indicated earlier, the company decided some time ago to reduce considerably the number of advertising agencies that it employed around the world. It has now limited its agency commitments to five aligned international advertising agency networks for its main product categories, baby foods, chocolate and confectionery, drinks, petfoods, frozen foods and ice cream. The agencies concerned all belong to well-known, international networks and should be able to make the necessary talent available to produce high-quality advertising for all Nestlé's strategic brands, as well as to provide optimum co-ordinating services to Nestlé's head-office and Nestlé's affiliates around the world. These international agencies are:

McCann-Erickson
J. Walter Thompson
Publicis FCB
Ogilvy & Mather
Lintas

In order to leave the affiliates as much freedom as possible in selecting the agencies that they wish to appoint, Nestlé management has simply designated 'preferred' agencies for each strategic brand – three in the case of chocolate confectionery and two in the case of other product categories – from which the affiliates can make their own choice. In the case of Nescafé the preferred agencies are McCann and J. Walter Thompson. This scheme is certainly a step in the direction of a more centrally controlled advertising policy. Experience will show if it will work to the satisfaction of all concerned or if a further concentration of advertising services, for example by aligning each strategic brand to one international advertising agency alone, would be even more efficient and effective.

As regards the remuneration of the advertising agencies, it is largely left to the affiliates to negotiate the basis for this with the local office of the agency concerned, though, as in the case of all matters relating to advertising, this will be done in close consultation with Nestlé visual communications department in Vevey.

SPONSORSHIP

Nestlé has established that the younger generation is increasingly attracted towards soft drinks. This was the reason for the introduction of Nescafé Frappé, which, as we have seen, was mainly aimed at the youth market. However, the company felt that more should be done in all product categories to make them more popular with children. It has therefore signed a contract with the Walt Disney Group for a long-term association in Europe:

> On the one hand, Nestlé is to be the exclusive partner for food in
> Euro Disneyland's 'Magic Kingdom Park', which will open near Paris
> in 1992; our brands will be featured in the restaurants and shops of
> this park, where 11 million visitors are expected from the first year.
> Nestlé and Euro Disneyland will jointly develop marketing programmes
> extending throughout Europe, North America and the Middle East. On
> the other hand, from 1991 on, Nestlé will be the only company in
> Europe and in the Middle East authorized to sell food products using
> the Walt Disney characters in their shape, packaging or advertising.[12]

This agreement should serve the dual purpose of offering attractive promotions to consumers, whilst also strengthening the relationships between the company and its retailers.

In another effort to woo the younger generation, in 1988 Nestlé joined the Japanese makers of the well-known Yamaha keyboards in the sponsorship of a so-called 'Band Explosion'. This is an annual competition between amateur and professional bands from all over the world, with attractive prizes and considerable free publicity for the winners.

LEGAL RESTRICTIONS

Unlike the makers of tobacco products and alcoholic beverages, who are under constant attack from pressure groups and politicians because of the health risks attributed to their products, coffee companies are left to conduct their business relatively unhindered. However, because caffeine is of one of its major constituents, allegations that coffee is harmful continue to appear in the press, causing concern among its producers and the public at large. Although these allegations have not been shown to have any foundation, the coffee industry has wisely decided not to let matters rest, but to present to the media and to the consuming public the positive case for coffee and its beneficial effects.

At the beginning of 1989, a new bulletin appeared entitled 'Coffee and Science' and published by the International Coffee Organization (ICO), which has set up an Institute for Scientific Information on Coffee (ISIC), founded by six of the leading companies in this area, of course including Nestlé. Its first president is Serge Milhaud, a senior vice-president responsible for the strategic development of all Nestlé's drinks, who wrote of the new organization in the following terms:

ISIC personifies an industry-wide co-operation between coffee manufacturers, the International Coffee Organization (ICO) and the scientific community, working together on a project to enhance coffee's image by communicating the positive aspects of coffee drinking.[13]

The institute has a sub-committee, the 'Physiological Effects of Coffee Committee' (PEC), which is carrying out a research programme into the positive effects of coffee, the results of which will be published by the public relations committee of the new institute.

It is interesting to observe how, in comparison, for example, with the tobacco industry, which was late in taking active steps to protect its interests, coffee producers have realized early on that it is better to forestal criticism than to have to counter it and have been most timely in organizing their response. It has thus been able to make a strong case, supported by considerable medical evidence, for its contention that the consumption of coffee has no adverse effects on people, but, on the contrary, will improve their performance and general feeling of well-being. One wonders, nevertheless, if the ISIC will not go one step further and draw up, in consultation with the advertising industry, voluntary codes of conduct for marketing and advertising, to be underwritten by all coffee producers, thereby pre-empting any efforts, for example by the EC Commission in Brussels, to recommend that governments should introduce restrictive legislation. However, this particular subject has been covered in other publications[14], so it is sufficient here simply to point out that the precautions that the industry has taken should stand it in good stead if and when a move is made against it.

1993 AND BEYOND

Nestlé is ready for the years to come. Thanks to its acquisition policy it has established a strong position in almost all sectors of the food market, in which it is the world's dominant manufacturer. On the subject of Europe, Mr Maucher is quite convinced that 'the old continent still has growth potential . . . one has to look for new opportunities . . . health foods, foods for the elderly or the hospitalized, fast foods for the working woman.'[15]

As regards the future marketing and advertising of Nestlé products, some of the steps that the company has taken to optimize the efficiency and effectiveness of its communications have been described in this chapter and they may well represent the beginning of a new era in the advertising of this concern's brands. However, Nestlé's director of visual communications points out that, despite all efforts to bring about a unified Europe, national cultures, habits and languages will make it difficult for Nestlé to achieve uniform advertising for all its products. The company experimented with advertising via satellite, but he remarks, 'I still think that a key emphasis is going to be on the national linguistic area of the local media available'.[16]

The position of Nescafé as the number-one instant coffee is not likely to be challenged. However, competition from products such as Maxwell House and Jacobs (Kraft General Foods), Folgers (P & G – only sold in the USA), Brooke Bond (Unilever), and Moccona (Douwe Egberts) cannot be ignored; nor can one overlook the threat from the producers of tea or soft drinks. As Mr Milhaud has said, 'It just is a fight for a share of throat'.[17]

When Mr Maucher was asked which three factors had contributed most, in his opinion, to the continuing success of Nescafé, he promptly delegated the duty of answering this question to those directly responsible for the product. After some deliberations, they attributed its success to: (a) the fact that the product had been developed at the right moment and had benefited for a long time from the novelty of instant coffee; (b) Nescafé's consistent and superior quality – 'We have always been very good at taking water out of something'[18] – and (c) the quality of the communications used to support the product, and the scope of its geographical presence – as well, of course, as the dedication of all at Nestlé and their long familiarity with Nescafé, which have created what almost amounts to a Nescafé culture. One cannot but conclude that Nescafé is one of those enduring products that will continue to satisfy and stimulate millions of people all over the world for many years in the various different forms that have made it into a top-ranking international brand.

Notes

1. Personal discussion with Helmut Maucher, Managing Director of Nestlé S.A., Vevey, 5 October 1989.
2. *Annual Report 1990*, Nestlé S.A., Cham and Vevey, Switzerland, pp. 3 and 9.
3. *Coffee* (1977), published by the Marketing Services – Nestlé Products Technical Assistance Company Ltd., p. 2.
4. *Swissair Gazette* (1988), published by Verlag A. Vetter for Swissair, No. 1, p. 20.
5. Miéville, Madeleine (1988), 'Cinquante ans de Nescafé!' *Nestlé Gazette*, No. 2, April.
6. *Coffee*, p. 30.
7. Day, Barry (1989) (ed.), *Perspectives: Europe 1992*, interview with Ramon Masip, Executive Vice-President, Nestlé S.A., The Interpublic Group of Companies, New York, pp. 69–73.
8. Miéville.
9. Nestec: company estimates.
10. Wiel, Marcella van der, interview with Allan Allbeury, PR Manager of Nestlé, UK, in *De Telegraaf* (Amsterdam), 31 December 1988.
11. See also Jones, John Philip (1989), *Does It Pay to Advertise?* Lexington, KY: Lexington Books, pp. 101–14.
12. Nestlé, *Annual Report 1989*, p. 4.
13. Milhaud, Serge (1989), 'ISIC's role: giving coffee due credit,' *Coffee & Science*, No. 2, July.
14. See also Rijkens, Rein, and Miracle, G.E. (1986), *European Regulation of Advertising*. Amsterdam: Elsevier Science Publishers, p. 122 f.
15. See note 1.
16. Day, Barry (1989) (ed.), *Perspectives: Europe 1992*, an interview with

Michel Reinarz, Director of Visual Communications, Nestlé S.A., The Interpublic Group of Companies, New York, pp. 75–8.

17. Personal discussion with Serge Milhaud, Senior Vice-President of Nestec S.A., Vevey, 12 December, 1989.

18. *Ibid.*

PHILISHAVE

'The Perfect Performer'

PHILIPS

PHILI**S**HAVE

ELECTRISCH
DROOGSCHEERAPPARAAT

PHILISHAVE
'The Perfect Performer'

'I don't see much in a shaving product. After all, we're not barbers,' was the reaction of Dr Anton Philips, one of the founders of the Philips company, when the idea of an electric razor was presented to him![1] 50 years later, on 9 March 1989, 'more than 240 million (Philishaves) have found their way to users all over the world. At an average of 5 million a year. No mean number.'[2] No mean number indeed, so let us start this review of Philishave by putting the product and its financial record into the context of the Philips business as a whole.

In 1989, Philips' turnover amounted to Dfl.57 billion and its trading profit to Dfl.2.3 billion.[3] The 1989 annual report does not give separate figures for the turnover of each division within its various sectors (see organization chart below). However, an article in a leading Dutch newspaper reported that in 1988 the Domestic Appliance and Personal Care (DAP) Division, responsible for the Philishave throughout the world, as well as for many other products, produced sales of Dfl.2.5 billion, representing 5 per cent of the concern's total business, and showed a profit of Dfl.250 million or 10 per cent on its net return. This is double the average profit made by the Philips business as a whole.[4] As there is little reason to believe that this division's results were any different, in percentage terms, in 1989, the importance of the DAP Division is self-evident. This is confirmed in the 1990 annual report of the concern, a year in which the company went through an extremely difficult time, but when the DAP Division continued to do well.

Within the DAP Division, Philishave is by far the single most important product, accounting for about 40 per cent of the division's total sales. Thus, whilst in absolute terms its contribution to the fortunes of Philips as a whole may not be very substantial, there is no doubt that, considered from a turnover-to-profit ratio, its performance ranks among the best for any Philips product – as befits its status as a worldwide market leader.

HISTORY AND DEVELOPMENT

Though it is only fair to mention that the first dry shaver was introduced more than 60 years ago by a Colonel Shick, it was Philips that, in 1939, launched a dry shaver based upon an entirely new principle: the rotary action system.[5] As Jan Tollenaar, managing director of the Personal Care Business Group of the DAP Division remarked 'Up and down is an unnatural movement. It has two dead moments. That causes wear. A rotating movement is ideal.'[6] The idea of using a rotary action was developed by Professor Alexandre Horowitz, whose 150 or so inventions thus included the unique Philishave as we know it today. No wonder, then, that, to commemorate the sale of the 250-millionth electric razor, a statue of Professor Horowitz was unveiled in the Dutch town of Drachten, where the centralized production of the Philishave takes place.[7]

An unusual product deserved an unusual introduction – and, indeed, the Philishave received the sort of imaginative launch that one might have expected from a small and daring local manufacturer but that was surprising on the part of one of the world's largest and most prestigious producers of electric appliances. The first six Philishaves ever made were taken to the Spring Fair Exhibition in Utrecht, Holland, and the product was unveiled to the public. On 14 March 1939 it was described by one of the largest newspapers at that time, as:

> a black rod in the form of a lavatory chain handle which has to be pressed against the face, [after which] a circular thing, the size of a sixpence, shaves the face clean, thanks to the mysterious procedure of innumerable rotations.[8]

Shaving demonstrations, parades and fancy-dress events were organized. There was even a Philishave club, composed of people in Holland who had contributed in some special way to the success of the new product: they were taken to a deserted hall, lit only by a few candles, and tapped lightly on the shoulder with a Philishave to signify their acceptance as members.[9] Many years later a European Philishave conference agreed that:

> Gentlemen, there is work to be done. There are millions of men who don't shave electrically. Philishave, once a mere infant, has now reached adolescence. Let us unite to build a bright future for this promising creation.[10]

A new habit had to be inculcated and prejudices had to be overcome. Demonstrations in barber's shops were organized, and Philishaves were made available at checkpoints during car rallies; all sorts of orthodox and unorthodox methods were used to introduce the new way of obtaining a clean attractive shave. This activity was not confined to Holland. In 1947 the Philishave was introduced to France and demonstrations were again organized throughout the country in hotels and restaurants and even in specially equipped touring vans. In the UK, a man was put in a shop-window and started shaving with a Philishave whilst having his breakfast, reading the newspaper and drinking his tea. In 1948 the product was introduced to the USA under the name Norelco; dealers were invited to shaving breakfasts starting at 8 a.m., the only requirement being to arrive unshaven! Norelco now accounts for one-third of the worldwide sales of Philips' shavers.

The introduction of this product, using methods that were decidedly unorthodox even by communications standards of the time demonstrates an entrepreneurial spirit that one cannot help but admire, particularly in the light of continuing public criticism of Philips which is often represented as a slow, unwieldy, unimaginative, over-organized and over-staffed concern with too many diverse interests and an apparent incapacity to produce a decent profit. The very successful Philishave operation proves that a superior product, a consistent marketing and advertising policy and a dedicated team of people can produce remarkable results, even if they are part of a colossal business.

ORGANIZATION

Given the size and complexity of the Philips concern as a whole, the organization chart below only shows the most important functions and those most relevant to the subject of this chapter.

PHILISHAVE

SUPERVISORY BOARD

BOARD OF DIRECTORS

GROUP BOARD

| Sector Light | Sector Consumer Products | Sector Professional Products | Sector Components |

Consumer Electronics Division | Domestic Appliances and Personal Care Division

— Marketing Communication

| Business Group Personal Care | Business Group Kitchen Appliances | Business Group Home Comfort |

Including:
Philishave – Tracer
Ladyshave – Satinelle

The day-to-day running of the concern is the responsibility of the Group Board, which consists of members of the Board of Directors and top executives from the product divisions and central departments. The Group Board is advised by Philips International on the subject of international policies for the product divisions and for staff departments involved in the concern's international operations. The Group Board is responsible, amongst other things, for the four main sectors of the concern and their worldwide turnover; the light sector accounts for 13 per cent of this turnover, consumer products (consumer electronics, music, domestic appliances & personal care) for 39 per cent, professional products and systems (computer technology, information systems etc.) for 26 per cent and components (colour TV tubes etc.) for 20 per cent.

DAP Division is one of the six divisions that together account for practically the total turnover of the concern. Each of these divisions has a number of departments to assist the management in carrying out its tasks. In the case of the DAP Division, these departments include: (a) marketing communications; (b) marketing research; (c) corporate industrial design; (d) finance and accounting; (e) information; (f) laboratories; (g) product development; (h) patents & trademarks; (i) consumer affairs; (j) packaging and technical design; and (k) product application.[11] Most sizeable companies have similar departments to help to ensure that they are run efficiently and effectively. However, given that some of the tasks and responsibilities of the DAP Division – which employs 8 500 people worldwide – may, to a large extent, be duplicated by the other five divisions in relation to other product groups, and also bearing in mind the number of people who provide legal, financial, administrative, accounting and other services at the central head-office in Eindhoven, one may well wonder if there is not a considerable degree of overlap between the divisional support departments. This is not the view of the DAP Division itself, though; it is understandably proud of its exceptional performance and acts and operates as if it were completely independent. It is a compliment to the management of the division that, through adopting this attitude, it maintained such high morale among its staff in circumstances that were extremely worrying for the concern as a whole. Finally, as regards the advertising function for the DAP Division, the marketing communication services (which cover advertising) operate in a staff capacity and advise the separate business groups.

Although in the case of Philishave the company's organization appears to be working well, one cannot help but recall the comments on the organizational aspects of large multi-national corporations made by Peters and Waterman in their book *In Search of Excellence*: 'The underlying structural forms and systems in the excellent companies are elegantly simple. Top-level staffs are lean; it is not uncommon to find a corporate staff of fewer then 100 people running multi-billion dollar enterprises.'[12] However, the DAP people might well respond by saying, 'La critique est aisée mais l'art est difficile' or 'The proof of the pudding is in the eating', and they would be right on both counts!

THE PRODUCTS

Since Philishave was launched, much work has been done to maintain its lead over its competitors; the following landmarks in its development illustrate this point:

1939	Introduction of the first single-headed Philishave.
1951	The double-headed 'egg' model follows.
1952	The first battery-operated Philishave is introduced.
1959	The company launches the 'floating heads' model, which can follow the contours of the face.
1966	The first rechargeable and the first triple-headed Philishaves are introduced.
1980	The retraction, or 'lift-and-cut', blade is developed; the so-called 'double action' shaver is launched.
1987	The Philishave with the 'charge-level indicator', or 'power meter', is introduced, telling users when batteries have to be recharged.

At this stage reference should be made to extensions to the product line, such as the Ladyshave and the Tracer. The latter was introduced in 1985 to attract young people away from the habit of wet shaving and encourage them to start shaving with an electric shaver instead; the hope being that if they grew accustomed to dry shaving with the Tracer they might become Philishave users for life. Reflecting its targeting on young men, the product had an attractive design and modern style and presentation, and was also more affordable than the normal Philishave. More recently the introduction of the Satinelle epilator has completed the product range; the division has clearly adopted the wise policy of not leaving any gaps in the market that might be filled by competitors.

. . . AND THEIR DESIGNS

With respect to the design of the Philishave, DAP's Corporate Industrial Design Centre argues that 'there is a remarkable similarity between the design of shavers and that of cars. . . . As male status symbols both shavers and motorcars are continuously influenced by current fashion.'[13] The centre employs people such as Raymond Loewy to ensure an optimum combination of modernity and practicality; the technical performance of the shaver, its visual appearance, its weight and the way in which it fits into the hand are all given special attention as aspects of the total design that help to keep it ahead of its main competitors.

COMPETITION

We now come to the important subject of how consumers tackle the daily problem of looking clean and attractive, and who is competing in the market-place for consumers' preference in this respect. It is relatively easy to define the market for shavers: it comprises all adult males who do not wish to grow beards. Some men still wear beards for a number of reasons: because they believe that it makes them more attractive, or because they want to flout convention, or because they are just too lazy to shave. However, they generally form a small part of the population and tend to be obdurate, so that the makers of shaving equipment concentrate on the majority who wish to remove their facial hair. This can be done by using sand-paper, by wet shaving or by dry shaving.

Philips believes that its real competition does not come from other manufacturers of electric shavers, such as Braun or Remington, but from the popular image of the 'macho man', in the mould of the Marlboro cowboy, personifying adventure, courage, strength and sexuality. The 'Marlboro man' would not cut a credible figure in a commercial for Philishave any more than in one for sweets; he would shave with a steel blade sharpened on his leather boots! The main competition to Philishave is therefore from wet shaving, particularly in Southern Europe, where it is by far the dominant practice; in nothern Europe it is dry shaving that is more popular, so that Braun, for example, is a serious competitor there. Interestingly, unlike in the case of other Philips product categories, such as electronics, competition from Japan is not yet very strong. Philips has managed to seal off this market very effectively, firmly establishing itself as the market-leader. As Mr Tollenaar said, quoting an anonymous general, 'The easiest victories are in those places where there is no enemy'.[14]

PRODUCT AND CONSUMER RESEARCH

Philips has developed special methods for measuring the performance of Philishave. In its laboratories the reaction of the shaving head to the skin is tested under many different circumstances; while the Shaver Application Department users consumers directly in research conducted in its 'Marathon Shaving Salon', where 24 men simultaneously test the product's total performance against those of its competitors, again under various severe conditions. Many new ideas stem from this salon, though some never reach the production line.

Nor is research restricted to the product's performance or, indeed, to the product itself. The remarks of the design centre quoted above show how the appearance and shape of the shaver must be adapted to changes in current tastes, and so too must the design of its packaging. The models thus go through many stages of internal development and consumer research before they appear on the market. Philishave designers not only see a similarity between shavers and motor cars, but one of them has argued that:

> A shaver can be compared with clothing – both come into direct
> contact with the body but a shaver is in direct contact with the skin. It
> traces all the contours of the face. Shaving is a ritual, an expression
> of culture and the shaver has to reflect that.[15]

One cannot envy the consumer researcher who has to draw concrete conclusions from this multitude of intangible factors!

ADVERTISING POLICY

The fact that we have only now reached the subject of advertising may seem to be a reflection of the persisting view that Philips is a manufacturing-oriented company, rather than a consumer-oriented one. However, no advertising programme can be analysed and reviewed without some knowledge and understanding of the environment in which it takes place. This certainly applies to a complex business such as Philips, where the company's international organization has undergone some very fundamental changes in recent years, which have also impinged on its international advertising.

Until the early 1980s, the company's national organizations had total responsibility for all advertising in their respective countries. This included the appointment of local advertising agencies, with the result that the concern employed a vast number. However, even back in the late 1960s and early 1970s, those responsible for advising product divisions and central departments in Eindhoven on advertising matters, were already discussing a possible drastic cut in the number of agencies used. A system of aligned advertising agencies was proposed, with a number of international agencies responsible for the advertising of one or more of the Philips brands on an international scale. The outcome would be to simplify the existing relationships between the national organizations and their many advertising agencies. In addition, the scheme would allow creative talent to be concentrated on developing ideas to be used throughout the world, probably improving the quality of Philips' advertising and leading to significant economies of scale. However, conditions at Philips were not yet conducive to the implementation of the scheme. Although many welcomed the idea, a decision such as this could not be taken in isolation; it required a fundamental change in the concern's operations and in the relationships between Philips' headquarters and subsidiaries, particularly regarding the final responsibility for the national organizations' financial results. This responsibility had always been entirely local, but the situation could easily change if, in spite of mutual consultation, final decisions about a product's advertising were in future to be taken at head-office. The national organizations could argue that if they were no longer responsible for the advertising of their products, with its potential effects on sales, they could not remain responsible for their own sales figures and financial results.

Unlike Philips, other concerns, such as Unilever, were giving much thought to improving the efficiency and effectiveness of their decision-making by increasing centralization of their operations. However, at Philips, it was only in the mid-1980s that the decision was taken to implement a policy of greater centralization, including the adoption of an advertising-alignment scheme. Consequently, at the beginning of

1988 the DAP Division appointed D'Arcy Masius Benton & Bowles (DMB & B) to be responsible for practically all Philishave advertising around the world. Concentration of authority and centralization of a company's advertising require many abilities on the part of all concerned if the system is to work. Considerable goodwill, powers of persuasion, tact and infinite patience are needed to overcome inborn resistance to change. In the case of the DAP Division, the management feels that after some initial grumbles the system is, on the whole, functioning well.

PROCEDURES AND REMUNERATION

Although the final responsibility for all Philishave advertising now rests largely with the central management of the DAP Division in the Netherlands, this does not mean that advertising content and presentation are rigidly dictated from head-office; on the contrary, consultation and co-operation are paramount. The agreed procedures can be outlined as follows:

---

1. Divisional headquarters in the Netherlands and DMB & B develop an advertising strategy based upon agreed marketing objectives and the desired positioning of the brand in the eyes of consumers. This strategy is then forwarded to the national organizations concerned and discussed with them.
2. When agreement has been reached, headquarters briefs the advertising agency development of a campaign, which will be submitted for approval to central management in the Netherlands.
3. On the campaign's approval, the national organizations are again consulted and modifications may be made.
4. Once both the centre and the national organizations have given their approval, the campaign is formally accepted and distributed to all countries concerned.
5. It is then the responsibility of the local company and the local office of the advertising agency to make the necessary adaptations to suit national circumstances, and to select the appropriate media.

These procedures are clearly defined and strictly adhered to with the intention of avoiding any serious friction between the parties concerned – as is particularly important when an entirely new operating method is being implemented.

As regards agency remuneration, Philips does not adhere to the normal commission rate of 15 per cent. The DAP Division pays an agreed fee to its agency for development of the international campaign and then charges each of the national organizations a part of this fee proportionate to its budget. The national organizations, in turn, agree with the local DMB & B offices the terms on which the agency will work, taking into account the fact that the principal task of creating the basic advertising for the product has been done and paid for centrally. However, in employing these arrangements, Philips accepts that its advertising agencies must also make a profit, a consideration that applies to all countries where the DAP Division operates.

PHILISHAVE ADVERTISING

Earlier in this chapter, reference was made to the somewhat unorthodox ways in which the Philishave was introduced, as well as to the competitive environment in which it had later to be sold. Naturally, more conventional advertising methods also played an important part in its success. If we review the first decades of the Philishave's existence, we find that press advertisements, and later television, were extensively used, mainly to promote a Philishave as the ideal gift for a birthday or Christmas. Before the new dry shaving habit was firmly established, demonstrations, direct marketing, and consumer and trade promotions also remained important media for making Philishave known to the male population and convincing them that its use was preferable to wet shaving. In later years, when Philishave sales developed rapidly, the innovations mentioned above such as the 'double action' shaver, the cordless shaver and the 'power meter' could be used to project Philips as a technological pace-setter, keeping Philishave advertising up-to-date and exciting.

TODAY'S OBJECTIVES AND ADVERTISING STRATEGIES

Since advertising expenditure for Philishave currently represents approximately 12 per cent of the product's net sales value – which, in turn, is an estimated 40 per cent of the DAP Division's total turnover – worldwide advertising for the product must cost some Dfl.125 million per annum. This is a far cry from the era of demonstrations at fairs, so it is not surprising that the company and its international advertising agency pay considerable attention to precise definitions of objectives and strategies and the details of their execution. The company's main objectives are:

---

1. to attract new users, particularly among the younger generation; the lower priced Tracer has been introduced for this purpose and is advertised separately (see below).
2. to encourage those who are unsure about the relative merits of wet shaving and dry shaving to start using the Philishave; this applies especially to those countries where wet shaving is still the dominant practice, as in parts of Southern Europe.
3. to improve the product's leading position vis-à-vis its main competitor, Braun, in countries where the dry shaving habit is firmly established, for example some of the Nordic countries.

These objectives can be expressed in the following advertising strategy:

Philishave should be perceived by consumers as giving optimum shaving satisfaction because of its advanced technology and high quality, which make it superior to its competitors in every way. Its special benefits, such as the double action system and the charge-level indicator, enhance the products' performance, resulting in the closest possible shave, at any time, anywhere.

EXECUTION OF STRATEGY

It is, of course, true that, in essence, all males who are 16 years of age or more form the target group for the various Philishaves. However, in spite of the imminent Single European Market, considerable regional differences in taste, behaviour and social habits will persist for the time being and will have to be taken into account when advertising certain products. This certainly applies to shaving.

As we have already seen, shaving habits differ considerably from country to country. There are those countries where the dry-shaver market is well established and where Philishave commercials will mostly concentrate on the intrinsic qualities of the product and its advantages over its competitors. They will show elegant, modern businessmen using appropriately elegant, modern electric shavers; sexual associations will not dominate. In other countries, where wet shaving is still more popular than dry shaving, the product's special features will be of secondary importance; the commercial will concentrate on the message that a good-looking man will be even more attractive to a beautiful woman if he uses a Philishave, not least because his clean-shaven face will be so pleasant to caress! However, though the different shaving habits of these different countries result in different commercials, the basic strategy is the same.

Tracer advertising has another emphasis. It appeals to the young, modern male between 16 and 20 years of age, who wants to impress the girls with his dash and his daring, and even draws a parallel between a motorbike and Tracer's 'two wheels', to which he owes his good looks. Such young men are the same the world over; they dress, behave and act in the same fashion, irrespective of their country of origin, and they all want to have 'the looks of a winner' that the Tracer commercials promise them throughout Europe, north and south.

Advertising for Philishave encompasses more than television commercials and press advertisements. Consumer and trade promotions, effective point-of-sale material, direct marketing, outdoor advertising etc. are all necessary to maintain Philishave's image of uniqueness and of perfect performance. The selection of these media and the proper interpretation of the advertising strategy, is the responsibility of the national organizations of Philips and the local offices of DMB & B, working in close co-operation with the DAP Division's headquarters in the Netherlands.

1993 AND BEYOND

When the management of the DAP Division is asked to which three main factors it attributes the success of Philishave, it attaches greatest importance to the shaver's revolutionary rotary action system, which gave it an advantage over other shavers that it has always managed to maintain. The second most important factor, according to the DAP Division, is the continuous efforts made by Philips' management to maintain the company's leadership in this competitive market by keeping the quality, performance and presentation of its varying range of products at the highest possible level. The final element is the total commitment of the senior managers and all the other staff involved with Philishave to the success of what they see as *their* business. They see consistency in management and policy-making as one of the decisive factors behind the success of the product, a view that is shared by others.

In an advertising context, the DAP Division appears to have taken all necessary steps, both in terms of organization and content, to be well prepared for the future; with final authority firmly established in the division's headquarters and with the appointment of an international advertising agency, it is ready for the new European market of 1993 and beyond. However, in view of the different shaving habits prevalent in different regions, advertising media covering the whole of Europe are unlikely to receive high priority.

Fortunately, the division has few problems as regards legal or voluntary controls or restrictions on its communications with consumers. Nor does the Commission of the EC in Brussels appear to wish to extend its activities into this field of business. This does not mean, however, that the DAP Division is without problems; it has ones of both an external and an internal nature. Externally, the concentration of trade channels, so that more and more shavers are sold through fewer and fewer outlets, is a problem facing many manufacturers; although the DAP Division has concentrated the production of Philishaves at Drachten in the Netherlands, when all trade barriers are lifted within Europe, this could cause further concentration of trade channels damaging Philips' sales policies and creating severe difficulties. Internally, the Philips concern as a whole is, of course, going through troublesome times. But the highly profitable Philishave operation is one of which it can justly be proud. It is therefore to be hoped that the formidable success of this brand will continue and that it will get all the support that its exemplary performance deserves.

The management of the division is understandably optimistic:

Over the next fifty years Philishave's enormous success will be maintained – by sheer hard work! Of that there is no doubt – and Philishave will continue to triumph.[16]

Notes

1. Derks, Sergio (1989), *The Shaving Revolution*, Philips International B.V., Groningen, Netherlands, p. 10.
2. *Ibid.*, p. 7.
3. *Annual Report 1989*, NV. Philips Gloeilampenfabrieken, Eindhoven, Netherlands, p. 1.
4. Wittenberg, Dick, 'Philips, meer plus dan minus' (Philips, more plus than minus), *NRC – Handelsblad* (Rotterdam), 10 August 1989.
5. *Philishave – Rotary Action System* (undated), Philips, Netherlands.
6. Deltenre, Jaap, 'Monument voor een scheerapparaat' (Monument for a shaver), *De Telegraaf* (Amsterdam), 10 February 1990.
7. Krol, Ronald van de (1990), 'Cutting it fine,' *Holland Herald* (Amsterdam), May.
8. Derks, *The Shaving Revolution*, p. 16.
9. *Ibid.*, p. 55.
10. *Ibid.*, p. 56.
11. *Wegwijs in DAP* (Finding your way in DAP) (1988), Domestic Appliances and Personal Care Division, Philips, Netherlands.
12. Peters, Thomas J., and Waterman Jr., R.H. (1982), *In Search of Excellence*. New York: Harper & Row, p. 15.
13. Derks, p. 46.
14. Personal discussion with J.C. Tollenaar, Managing Director of the Personal Care Business Group of the DAP Division, Philips, Groningen, Netherlands, 24 November 1989.
15. Derks, p. 52.
16. *Ibid.*, p. 87.

SEIKO

'The World Leader in Watch Technology'

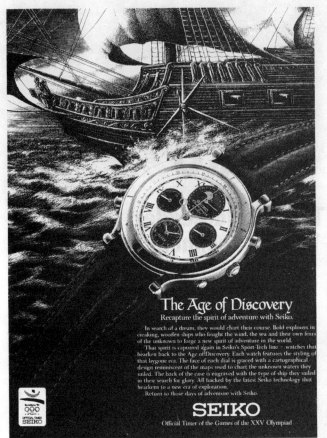

The Age of Discovery
Recapture the spirit of adventure with Seiko.

In search of a dream, they would chart their course. Bold explorers in creaking, wooden ships who fought the wind, the sea and their own fears of the unknown to forge a new spirit of adventure in the world.

That spirit is captured again in Seiko's Sport-Tech line — watches that hearken back to the Age of Discovery. Each watch features the styling of that bygone era. The face of each dial is graced with a cartographical design reminiscent of the maps used to chart the unknown waters they sailed. The back of the case is engraved with the type of ship they sailed in their search for glory. All backed by the latest Seiko technology that hearkens to a new era of exploration.

Return to those days of adventure with Seiko.

SEIKO
Official Timer of the Games of the XXV Olympiad

20 YEARS AGO
SEIKO STARTED A QUARTZ REVOLUTION.
TODAY, WE START A NEW ONE.

SEIKO

SEIKO
'The World Leader
in Watch Technology'

In the early 1960s, during a presentation to a large watch manufacturer in Switzerland, a senior executive of a London-based international advertising agency made a remark that he hoped would bring the long-drawn-out discussion about irrelevant details to a quick conclusion. What he said was, 'Well, when all is said and done, a person buys a watch because he wants to know the time, doesn't he?' After a long and somewhat ominous silence, the chairman of the company responded, 'Not really, a watch to most people is a nice ornament, a bracelet, a thing of beauty – its function in telling the time is of rather secondary importance.'

If this discussion had taken place in the early 1970s, shortly after the first precision timepiece, the quartz watch, had appeared on the market in 1969, the agency executive might well have been spared his embarrassment, but in the 1960s the decorative aspects of a watch were more important than the precision of its move-ment. Moreover, once the excitement surrounding the introduction of the quartz timepiece had died down, fashion again became an important consideration in watch manufacture. In 1989, the president of what was then called Hattori Seiko, expressed the situation as follows:

Our company's growth has centred around the watch and clock
business. Timepieces have an importance and a fascination that
extends far beyond their function of measuring and telling the time,
for while they use the very latest advances in mechatronics, they are
at the same time fashion goods, subject to tangible criteria of design
and aesthetics.[1]

In March 1990, the original name of the business – Hattori Seiko – was changed into the Seiko Corporation. It was argued that, outside Japan, the name Hattori was little known, whereas Seiko had become a household name in the context of watch-making all over the world. Today, the Seiko Corporation sells about 400 000 watches (as well as 100 000 clocks) throughout the world every day of the year, accounting for an annual turnover of more than $3 billion. This represents a remarkable growth in business since the company's foundation in 1881, when Kintaro Hattori started a small repair shop in Tokyo. In 1895, the first production plant for watches and clocks was established, called 'Seikosha', meaning 'precision manufacturer'. This name appeared on the clocks and watches, and in 1910 it was changed into Seiko, simply meaning 'precision'.[2]

THE TIMEPIECE INDUSTRY

Most people's knowledge of timepiece production is probably rather limited, so it may be of interest to point out that in 1988 the turnover of clocks and watches throughout the world amounted to approximately $20 billion, of which Hattori Seiko, as the largest single manufacturer, had a share of 15 per cent. Although it is not the function of this chapter to deal extensively with the many different types of watches and clocks, such as the quartz, digital or mechanical categories, the size of the market and the importance of the main producing countries, should be reviewed briefly (see Table 4).[3]

HISTORICAL PERSPECTIVE

In the timepiece market, the Seiko Corporation plays a leading role. A review of the company's development shows that its pioneering efforts, its expansion into many markets and its record as official timer at numerous sports events combined to give it an unequalled reputation in its field. During the period of over 100 years that has elapsed since the foundation of K. Hattori & Co. in 1881, the most important events are as follows:[4]

1881	Foundation of K. Hattori & Co.
1892	Wall clock production started.
1895	Pocket watch production started.
1913	Wrist watch production started.
1964	Seiko appointed Official Timer for Tokyo Olympic Games.
1969	World's first quartz watch marketed.
1970	Seiko Time Corporation (USA) and Seiko Time (UK) Ltd. established.
1972	Seiko appointed Official Timer at Winter Olympic Games in Sapporo.
1972	Seiko subsidiaries established in Germany, Brazil, Hong Kong, Canada.
1978	Seiko appointed Official Timer for Soccer World Cup in Argentina.
1982	Seiko subsidiaries established in Switzerland, Argentina, Australia, Sweden, Singapore, France, the Netherlands, etc.
1982	Seiko appointed Official Timer for soccer World Cup in Spain.
1982	World's first TV watches marketed.
1989	Introduction of the Seiko Sport-Tech wrist watch collection.
1990	Seiko introduces first 'automatic generating system' watch, generating its own power, responding to the wearer's every motion and converting it into energy.

On 27 April 1990, it was announced that Seiko would be the Official Timer for the 1992 Summer Olympic Games to be held in Barcelona, Spain. The Organizing Committee of the 1992 Games made clear that the timing services at the Games should be more complete and more sophisticated than at any previous Olympics and Seiko has promised to provide a level of technical support that will set new standards in sports timing.

Table 4. World Watch and Clock Production in millions (1988)

	Watches			Clocks
Hong Kong	350		Japan	85
Japan	265		Hong Kong	73
Switzerland	75		W. Germany	57
Others	160		Taiwan	31
			USSR	32
			China	25
			Others	32
Total	850			335

Those who wish to acquire a deeper insight into the history of the watch and clock industry in general, and Seiko in particular, should visit the Seiko Institute of Horology in Tokyo. It is an establishment for the study of the history and development of the watch industry in Japan and it has collected and classified valuable specimens and documents in this field. The institute began its activities in January 1977 and now possesses, through purchases, donations and loans, an impressive collection of watches, clocks, relevant literature and statistical information from all over the world.[5]

ORGANIZATION

The Seiko group consists of three manufacturing complexes and a trading company looking after the concern's commercial interests, all based in Japan. The Seiko trading company has three separate divisions, responsible for its business in the Far East, Europe and the USA. The company's organization chart looks as follows:

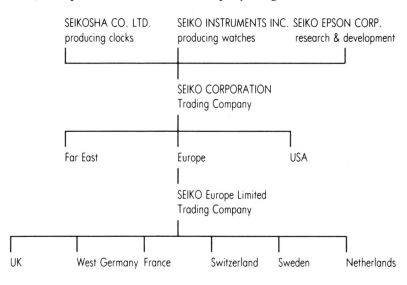

According to its brochure entitled 'In Motion', the company not only has interests in clocks, watches and related fields such as sports and sports events, but also in fashion, personal products and electronics.

In Japan, the company has a strong marketing department, supported by an extensive 'intelligence' operation, which, the president says, 'functions as the nerve centre for the acquisition, collation and analysis of the latest marketing information. A key objective is to use our electronic data processing expertise to enable real-time on-line control of the dynamics of today's worldwide business'.[6]

For many years, the Seiko Corporation has had a European office, based in the UK and accounting for approximately 25 per cent of the corporation's world sales. In response to developments in Europe, and particularly to the forthcoming Single European Market, a separate company called Seiko Europe Limited was established in October 1990. Its objectives were described as follows:

> While Seiko's member companies and distributors in Europe are carrying out marketing activities based on their own local perspectives, Seiko Europe will be primarily responsible for providing those companies with supporting services to strengthen their planning and marketing capacities and to improve the Seiko group's structure throughout the entire European market.[7]

The new company continues the marketing function of the earlier organization; it will co-ordinate the marketing activities of Seiko's subsidiaries and distributors in Europe, and it will continue to be responsible for the advertising strategies of Seiko's brands throughout Europe. However, in spite of a growing tendency towards the centralization of advertising decisions, it will still leave the final decisions on the execution of agreed strategies largely to the subsidiaries in the six countries mentioned on the organization chart. Before returning to this, we should look briefly at the range of products that the company markets on a worldwide basis.

THE SEIKO COLLECTION

Watches and clocks are, of course, Seiko's main products and account for over three-quarters of total sales. As already indicated at the beginning of this chapter, people's main motives for buying watches vary over time: after a period during which the decisive factor was the accuracy of the watch, trends in fashion and design again became important.

For Seiko, the real breakthrough was the introduction, in the late 1960s, of the first quartz watch, with a precision movement making for unequalled accuracy. The product's launch was supported by an advertising campaign created by the Ted Bates advertising agency, as it was then known, using the very successful slogan, 'Some day all watches will be made this way'. (It is interesting to note that, about 20 years after this excellent and intriguing slogan was used for the first time, it recently reappeared in a Seiko advertisement in the UK!) Accuracy was the principal requirement at this time, but the influence of fashion and the growing desire of consumers to express their personalities and their interests, through their choice of watches, means that today watches and their advertising are geared to specific tastes, life-styles and hobbies, such as sports. A case in point is the new Seiko Sport-Tech collection.

THE DESIGN ELEMENT

Following on from the growing use of watches to project an image, is the importance of design in today's watch marketing. Seiko draws on the expertise of designers in many different ways. Firstly, it employs its own specialists, most of whom are based in Japan and clearly concentrate mainly on Seiko's international collections. In addition, the subsidiaries are free to develop their own collections in accordance with local tastes and preferences; each, of course, also studies what the others are doing, and it will not come as a surprise to discover that the Italian subsidiary is often the leading innovator. In fact, the European influence on the more than 1 000 Seiko designs is quite marked and is noticeable even in the international collections. A good idea is a good idea, wherever it originates, and, with modern communications techniques, new designs can be transferred within seconds from one part of the world to another, and so processed for manufacture at very short notice.

RESEARCH

Interestingly, the appeal of the designs is rarely researched before they go into production; the speed with which they have to be introduced usually prohibits this. The research budget of $500 000 per annum is therefore almost exclusively used for attitude research concerning brands and watches in general. Electronic data processing and flexible manufacturing methods will, admittedly, enable the Seiko management to plan and control production lines with the speed and accuracy of their own watches, and 1 000 different designs does not mean 1 000 totally different products, but one does wonder how efficiency and profitability can be maintained with so many variant models. However, competition – for example from the Japanese Citizen watch and, of course, from the Swiss watch industry – forces the company to respond to the many changes of fashion and taste in various markets with the greatest alacrity.

POSITIONING THE SEIKO BRANDS

Although the Seiko brand itself is its most important single product, the company follows a multi-brand strategy with three other important brands: Lassale, Pulsar and Lorus. Each of these is positioned differently, as can be seen from the following outline:[8]

Lassale

Target Group:	Successful professional city-dwelling men and women, aged 30-45.
Profile:	An exclusive and limited collection of elegant watches, whose main common characteristics are thinness and sophistication.
Price Range:	$300–$900.
Positioning:	'The Modern Classic'.

Seiko

Target Group:	All men and women. (Specific groups of consumers are targeted with separate collections within the Seiko brand).
Profile:	The most complete watch collection in the world, featuring state-of-the-art technology expressed in both design and function, but with an image most sharply focused on sports products and usages.

Price Range:	$100–$600.
Positioning:	'The World Leader in Watch Technology'.
Pulsar	
Target Group:	All adults, with particular emphasis on women aged 25–35.
Profile:	A fashionable and up-to-date collection of dress watches.
Price Range:	$40–$200.
Positioning:	'A Statement in Style'.
Lorus	
Target Group:	Teenagers and adults, with particular emphasis on young males aged 15–30.
Profile:	An accessibly priced collection of functional (and often sporty) watches.
Price Range:	$20–$100.
Positioning:	'Watches for Winners'.

It is clear from their positioning statements that these four different watches should appeal to different consumers with different income levels. At the top of the pyramid is Lassale, modern yet classic and costing up to $900; it is followed by the more sporty Seiko, costing up to $600. Pulsar is clearly aimed at the fashionable female market, whilst Lorus is intended to attract young people who are just beginning to earn their own livings and will not be able to afford more than $100 for their first watch. This chapter deals specifically with Seiko itself.

SEIKO ADVERTISING POLICY

As already mentioned, at the time of the launch of the first quartz watch, Ted Bates was responsible for the worldwide advertising of the new brand. However, when, in the late 1970s, Seiko's management became more sensitive to local tastes and demands, subsidiaries were authorized to appoint their own advertising agencies and develop their own national advertising. Gradually a return to greater centralization is taking place, and Seiko's current overall advertising policy can best be described as mainly international in terms of strategy, but still national as regards the taking of the final decisions on the execution of agreed strategies. Even in the latter context, though, the management at Maidenhead, in the UK, is now actively pursuing greater uniformity of advertising expression throughout Europe, and most subsidiaries are happy to accept high-quality advertising produced in another country for use in their own areas. A good example is provided by the launch of Seiko's new range of Sport-Tech watches, for which the advertising has been centrally created by the Dentsu advertising agency in Japan. The new range is clearly aimed at sports enthusiasts who can afford to pay for the latest in watch technology. It comprises a number of different models for different uses and has been advertised in international magazines, such as *Time* and *Newsweek*, and also in certain well-known in-flight magazines. Unfortunately, information on the performance of new watches in general and of Seiko watches in particular is rarely available, and the advertisements' headline, 'Seiko Sport-Tech. The latest sports fashion statement', and their pay-off, 'Man invented time. Seiko perfected it', do little to rectify this. However, hidden in the body-copy of the international advertisements that appeared in the second half of 1989, is the news that the company has indeed introduced two innovative products: an Alarm Chronograph Timer and a World Time Alarm Watch. They both stem from the 'quartz revolution' that started 20 years ago, and, according to the company, 'Today we start a new one'.

The role of Seiko Europe's marketing department is thus largely a co-ordinating one. Except in the cases of advertising in the international media, the very important sports sponsorship programme and the production of sales promotional material for the launch of new products, the responsibility for Seiko advertising still rests to a large extent with the company's national subsidiaries.

In budget terms, national and international media advertising in Europe amounts to approximately $13 million. Sponsorship activities fall into a separate category of expenditure. Unlike the manufacturers of cigarettes and alcoholic drinks, whose products have little to do with the events that they sponsor, the producers of timepieces have a natural interest in sporting activities. No wonder that since

---

the 1964 Tokyo Olympic Games, Seiko has continued to boost
enjoyment for spectators and competitors alike as both official timer
and sponsor of an ever-growing range of sports events – wherever
people turn out to thrill to sports history in the making.[9]

ADVERTISING MANUAL

Like those of other companies discussed in this book, Seiko's central office for Europe at Maidenhead produces an advertising manual providing guidance for the company's subsidiaries and their advertising agencies. This explains creative and media strategies in considerable detail and also includes procedures for ordering artwork to be used in national campaigns. Earlier in this chapter reference was made to the positioning of the company's different brands. With regard to Seiko, this particular positioning has been translated into a strategy that the company presents in the following way:

Seiko Advertising Strategy

ELEGANCE   CLASSIC STYLE

SEIKO
The World Leader
in Technology

SPORTS   HIGH PERFORMANCE

A Distinctive Brand and World Leader in Time-keeping

In its advertising for Seiko, the company understandably wishes to concentrate on the brand's unique position as the worldwide market-leader; it therefore uses each of the product's four other characteristic qualities as alternative ways of introducing the advertisements' main message: Seiko's leadership in time-keeping.

EXECUTION OF STRATEGY

The execution of the international campaign, produced by Dentsu in Japan, and that of the individual national campaigns are, of course, both based upon the same strategy. Moreover, since, in both cases, the product itself is the central theme of the advertisement, the differences between the various approaches is unlikely to be very significant. A campaign produced in Germany in 1988 was considered to be so outstanding and in such conformity with present strategy that it was recommended for use throughout Europe. The campaign consisted of a number of advertisements, each with a well-produced photograph of one of the Seiko models as its central illustration and with a headline emphasizing one of the four main qualities of the product in support of the main theme of superior time-keeping. However, Seiko Europe does not concern itself only with the co-ordination of the creative aspects of its European advertising: 'We now employ Saatchi as media consultants with a brief to help our national offices understand the impact of international campaigns and sponsorships in terms of media reach and frequency and demographics.'[10]

THE ROLE OF THE ADVERTISING AGENCY

As the agency responsible for Seiko's international campaign, Dentsu places its advertisements in a few selected international magazines. However, one of the tasks of the local agencies that support the activities of Seiko's European subsidiaries is to advise the local companies on the media to be used for reaching each of the carefully selected target groups. This is particularly important because of the special character of the industry, which manufactures highly technical products, but ones that are profoundly affected by tastes and fashions. The appointment of these agencies is left to local managements. 'That is what we have local managers for', was the comment of Seiko's marketing manager in Maidenhead,[11] who prefers to run regular advertising workshops specifically for the company's national managers alone, so that they know precisely what is happening in other markets. In the context of the companies studied in this book, it is an exceptional point of view. The general consensus is that close co-operation between companies and agencies at all operational levels is of essential importance to the achievement of common objectives.

1993 AND BEYOND

Like so many other companies, the Seiko Corporation is torn between a desire to move towards greater centralization of its marketing efforts with all the built-in advantages in terms of economies of scale, and the need to satisfy consumers' tastes and demands, which differ from country to country and require mainly to be tackled at a national level. This would be easier if the company marketed a product such as Swatch, which has managed to get 'the best of both worlds'. However, its approach cannot be applied to the conditions faced by Seiko and well summarized in a trade magazine as follows:

> The post-1992 Europe will see, if anything, a hardening of national or
> regional tastes in fashion-oriented durables as consumers reject the
> concept of standardisation that is implied by much of the 'Single
> Market' rhetoric to which they are now subjected. At the same time,
> there will be considerable scope for achieving greater cost efficiency in
> marketing and advertising, especially in the early stages of the
> development of pan-European print and broadcast media.[12]

During the coming years one of the company's main preoccupations will probably be to find the proper answer to these conflicting interests. In any event, Seiko Europe has shown foresight by running a Seiko Sport-Tech commercial on Sky Channel, clearly believing that the target group for this watch is fairly uniform all over Europe. Consequently, if other TV stations using satellites to cover large parts of Europe can offer Seiko the right terms and the right audience, the company will probably be happy to make use of them as well. In this connection should be noted that the industry is not encumbered by the kinds of legal or voluntary restrictions on the advertising of its products that affect manufacturers in some other fields and hamper truly international operations and advertising.

As already mentioned, the Seiko marketing manager at Maidenhead, responsible for the company's European advertising, is not as convinced of the importance of advertising agencies as many of his colleagues in other international operations. In fact, he expressed doubts about the future of the advertising agency business altogether, questioning its role in today's communication process. For example, he did not think that help with media selection, marketing, or PR needed to be part of an advertising agency's package of services. These services could either be performed by specialized units or become part of the company's own in-house tasks. He certainly questioned the need for a full service capability in each national market, arguing that local managers had full access to central material anyway.[13] Whilst this last point will be accepted by many international advertisers, his general views about an agency's contribution to the success of an operation are not likely to be shared by those companies – including the ones surveyed in this book – that wish to optimize the contribution their advertising agencies can make. In any case, there is no doubt that discussions about the need for certain services that have traditionally been among the responsibilities of the advertising agency, continue to preoccupy many advertising executives and fill the editorial pages of trade journals. In this connection it is of interest to refer to some comments on the subject by Sir David Orr, a past chairman of Unilever, in the Foreword to a book by John Philip Jones:

In principle, advertising could be an in-house function, and for a long time Unilever owned an advertising agency. There are, however, a number of advantages to the advertising agency's being independent. The agency will accumulate a breadth of vision across a number of product fields. It can provide a pool of creativity, and it runs less risk of becoming stale or blinkered. It also, frankly, thrives on a very different culture, as John Philip Jones implies; the product company, whether in goods or services, is always more structured and hierarchical than the advertising agency should be. The producer will also be steeped in its product, whereas the agency is more sensitive to wider trends in the market. Both the producer and the advertising agent gain from being separate and specialized.[14]

Seiko can be proud of its position as market-leader in the watch industry, considering the formidable competition. Not only is this brand the world-leader in terms of sales, but in a survey of the most powerful corporate or consumer brand names in the US, Japan and Europe published in 1988 by Landor Associates, the world's leading image-management and strategic design consultants, Seiko was listed in the top ten worldwide, alongside brands such as Coca-Cola, IBM and McDonald's.[15]

When asked to which three main factors it attributed its continuing success, the company listed product quality as the first, followed immediately by its ability to keep ahead of competitors in terms of technology. As a third contributing factor, Seiko cited its presence in a large number of countries and its computer-controlled distribution system. There can be no doubt that these three qualities count among the company's outstanding achievements. The combination of the quality and elegance of design of Seiko's watches and the prestige conferred by the firm's time-keeping responsibilities at many important sports events should give the Seiko collection an almost universal appeal and an enduring reputation.

Notes

1. *In Motion* (1989), a brochure of Hattori-Seiko, Tokyo, containing 'A Message from the President', p. 1.
2. Notes from Rob Wilson, Marketing Manager, Seiko Europe, Maidenhead, UK, in answer to questions from the author, 3 March 1990.
3. *HS News Highlights* (1989), 'World timepiece production,' August, pp. 8–14.
4. *The World of Seiko Time* (undated), p. 3.
5. See also *The Seiko Institute of Horology* (undated), brochure, Tokyo.
6. *In Motion*, p. 2.
7. Press Release by the Seiko Corporation, Tokyo, 21 November 1990.
8. See note 2.
9. *The World of Seiko Time*, p. 21.
10. Personal letter from Rob Wilson, Marketing Manager, Seiko Europe, to the author, 14 December 1990.
11. Personal discussion with Rob Wilson, Maidenhead, 17 November 1989.
12. *Media International* (1989), 'Seiko sports new marketing model,' June.
13. See note 10.
14. Jones, John Philip (1989), *Does It Pay to Advertise?* Lexington, KY: Lexington Books, p. xxi.
15. *Hattori Seiko News* (1988), 'Seiko places in top ten – international image survey finds,' pp. 1–10.

CONCLUSION
Excitement of thoughts prevent decay
Saul Bellow[1]

In this concluding chapter I have drawn together some of the main findings from the 15 case studies in international advertising discussed in this book. In addition, I have included a few personal thoughts on the subject, based upon my own experience with international operations of this kind at both company and advertising agency levels. However, what follows is more than a mere extension of the completed study; it also serves to highlight some of the positive and negative factors affecting my theory of the 'Three Dimensions of Success' referred to in the introduction. The main findings have been grouped into six sections:

Corporate Identity
Trends towards International Advertising
Agency and Media Scenes
The Regulatory Situation
Training
1993 and beyond

CORPORATE IDENTITY

This is a vast subject, and countless books have been written about it, so that I do not intend to elaborate on it. However, as part of the function of corporate advertising is to prepare the ground for advertising of specific products and services and as several of the companies discussed here are paying special attention to it, a few words should be said on the subject.

In some of these cases, the growing importance of corporate advertising can be explained by the problems arising from the restrictions and regulations that increasingly inhibit companies in their direct communications with consumers. However, there are other considerations that encourage companies to present themselves to the public as honest and responsible bodies with a special interest in the general welfare of the community and in the environment. These include a dearth of innovative breakthroughs and the frequent tendency for increasing numbers of companies to compete in already saturated markets.

So, in addition to direct product advertising, many of the companies discussed in this book do make a genuine social contribution, the nature of which is often of immediate relevance to their own business. For example, Apple wishes to be seen as a pioneer in education and makes thousands of its computers available to schools, universities and campuses; while Colgate runs extensive programmes to teach proper habits for brushing the teeth and other basics of good dental care. Similarly, Philip Morris runs corporate citizen programmes, many in the field of education but others in support of the arts and to provide grants for projects such as the despatch of a parchment copy of the American Bill of Rights to more than one-and-a-half million Americans[2]. Finally, Levi Strauss has its own Foundation, conducting social responsibility programmes and making special grants to universities.

TRENDS TOWARDS INTERNATIONAL ADVERTISING

It will have come as a disappointment to those who created the advertising for the products and services reviewed in this book that the creative function has not been specifically discussed. Of course, without the film star in the advertisements for Lux or the cowboy in those for Marlboro, this book could never have been written, but it should be borne in mind that the aim here was to discuss the management of international advertising – in other words, the international exploitation of an advertising idea that had already been successfully used somewhere.

This raises the interesting observation that not one of the brands or services in this book started on an international scale: all began in one country and then gradually expanded into others. In ten years' time, we may well see an entirely different pattern; this study already clearly confirms the trend towards greater internationalization and centralization. Of course, brands such as Marlboro are already as international in terms of the concept and execution of their advertising as they are ever likely to be, but consider Mercedes, Club Med, Miele, and Nescafé. Their managements are all urging the agencies responsible for their advertising to form 'centres of excellence'[3], where basic creative ideas can be developed for international use.

It was of great interest to note that in eight out of the 15 cases discussed in this book, the companies concerned employ one international advertising agency on a worldwide or on a European basis. The remaining seven employ one agency to develop a basic advertising idea to be used in many countries, but in all 15 cases the adaptation of the basic advertising idea to local conditions is, in varying degrees, left to the national offices of the advertiser and the advertising agency. In view of the long-standing success of the eight cases employing one international advertising agency, it is tempting to conclude that this way of operating is preferable both in terms of effectiveness and efficiency. However, as, in each case, such a decision depends upon a number of different circumstances, I would prefer to reserve judgement; let me instead sum up the reasons given by participating companies to explain why they had decided to employ one international advertising agency for the handling of their business everywhere:

---

1. To achieve optimal results, it is vital to have a thorough knowledge and long experience of the product and its usage, its advertising development and its position versus competitors in those countries where it is on the market.

2. It is essential that this knowledge and experience is vested in an established team of people from the staffs of the advertiser and the advertising agency, who co-operate at national and international levels, exchange experiences, and complement and assist each other, in order to execute agreed policies as effectively and efficiently as possible in every individual country.

3. Although changes in personnel are unavoidable, under the leadership of capable and internationally trained managers a fund of experience will be accumulated that will provide a guarantee for consistency of policy and execution.

4. The economies of scale to be achieved can be considerable, depending upon the number of countries in which one basic theme and its (adapted) presentation can be used.

Looking to the future, it may well be that companies such as Nestlé, which still gives much authority for the advertising of its products to its national offices, will go further in centralizing their operations. However, instead of indulging in vain predictions, it is preferable to examine the criteria that must be considered before starting operations of an international nature, so let us review some of the points that arose in this connection from our discussions with the companies involved in this study:

1. Decisions regarding the advertising of products or services on an international scale can never be taken in isolation. They will have to conform to the general structure and procedures of the company concerned, and to the level of responsibilities of its affiliates. For example, are the affiliates accountable for the financial results of their operations? If so, one would expect the views of the local managements on the content and execution of the advertising of the products or services to be taken into account. Consultation will indeed take place, in most cases, but striking the balance between international policy and national interests is clearly one of the most difficult aspects of international operations of this kind. It requires considerable professional and managerial skills from all concerned.

2. Another factor is the extent to which the positioning, strategy, basic consumer promise and presentation of that promise can be based upon the same consumer profile and the same consumer habits in the countries concerned. The brands and services described in this book happen to have a more or less universal appeal and consumer profile in many markets, but even when brands have the same name everywhere, their appeal and profile need not always be the same everywhere. Needless to say, research is vital at this phase of an international operation.

3. Of similar importance are a product's market position in each of the countries in which it is sold and the timing of the introduction of the international advertising campaign. In other words, is the product's position in all markets sufficiently uniform to enable one advertising campaign to be run everywhere?

4. A final consideration is the availability and quality of local advertising agency personnel and, for that matter, the quality of the company's own staff and its experience of running international operations.

These were just four of the many factors that emerged from our discussions. Clearly they are interrelated and serve no other purpose than to highlight some of the aspects vital to 'going international'.

There remains one important negative factor, which, unfortunately, cannot be ignored. Some companies suffer from it more than others, but the malaise has not yet died out. It is, of course, the 'Not Invented Here' syndrome, which, on occasion, manages to infiltrate a company or advertising agency and halt its progress. The diagnosis is not difficult, but the therapy can be long and painful.

AGENCY AND MEDIA SCENES

As already observed, among the companies that participated in this study there is a clear tendency towards greater centralization of advertising. This could have a number of consequences for the agency business, and my discussion of this point with the executives of the companies that I visited, produced the following conclusions:

(1) As we have seen, the basic creative work is often done in one of the larger offices of the advertising agency concerned, while its adaptation to the circumstances of individual countries is left to the affiliates of the company and the agency in those countries.

(2) As the headquarters of companies have often already paid for the development of the basic advertising idea, their national offices tend to negotiate the terms of remuneration for work still to be done in their territories with the local agencies. In such cases, the usual 15 per cent commission rate has virtually ceased to exist.

(3) Because of the reduced income from such international accounts, and in order to remain viable, the agencies concerned will try to attract purely local business on a more profitable basis.

(4) Such business may be obtained from local companies that are trying to find 'niches' in a market that they can exploit successfully and profitably. However, it can only be hoped that the number of such purely local advertisers will not decrease to the point where the future of local agencies might be in jeopardy.

(5) Most of the companies visited leave media decisions to their national affiliates; in cases where, in addition to its national campaigns, the company also has advertisements in international media, the latter are always the responsibility of headquarters. KLM and Seiko are interesting cases in point. The use of satellites as an advertising medium is still limited, but those advertisers, such as Levi's, who employ non-verbal commercials show considerable interest in this medium. So too do other advertisers, such as Club Med, Martini and Marlboro, whose advertising messages are based on vision and sound.

General media developments

Despite the fact that media buying is still largely a national responsibility, expected developments in the field of communications could have such significant consequences for international advertisers that the subject must be discussed here.

Although in 1989, according to Initiative Media International, 63 per cent of total advertising expenditure in Europe was still spent on print and 25 per cent on television, total volume is rising sharply and so is the availability of media; for example, there will soon be no less than 150 TV channels. It is not only media moguls, such as Bertelmanns (who owns 75 per cent of Grüner & Jahr), Berlusconi and Maxwell, who are creating turbulent times for sellers and buyers alike; so too are specialized media agencies and, of course, advertising agencies now that they have started their own media-buying operations.[4]

However, there are other factors involved. It is quite evident that important changes are taking place, not only in the many ways in which advertisers will be able to buy the time or space that they need, but even more in the way in which they will use that time and space to convey their messages to consumers. Fantastic developments, not only in electronic and computer technology related to the dissemination of information, but also in bar coding and other electronic methods for collecting data and information from individual consumers, will enable advertisers both to cover an entire continent with one advertising message and, at the same time, also to exploit precise segmentation of audiences with their many different tastes and preferences. As the chairman of Initiative Media International puts it:

> One can clearly detect the development of a new trend, which derives from market segmentation, the fragmentation of media audiences and technological developments, which will enable the manufacturer to move from mass, to individual production and marketing, and the agency from mass communication to addressing individuals, about their specific needs in their own language.
> All of this at a reasonable cost.[5]

This is not all. Because of these developments there will be a strong case for giving a new meaning to an old concept used in marketing or advertising operations, that of 'integrated communications'. The need to think in terms not only of all the traditional media, but also of disciplines such as direct marketing, sponsorship and consumer promotions will become much greater in the years to come; the new key words might well become 'personalized precision marketing'.

After this short digression, we should now deal with an aspect of international operations that, at present, is of more concern to some companies than to others, but that might well affect many industries in the future.

THE REGULATORY SITUATION

During the mid-1970s, consumer programmes and 'directives' (discussed extensively in other publications[6]) were at their most prolific. The majority emanated from the Commission of the EC in Brussels and constituted a serious threat to companies' freedom to advertise products or services.

The scope of this book does not allow for a detailed analysis of the regulatory developments in the mid-1980s, which have been well described in presentations made by the directors of advertiser and advertising agency associations.[7] Suffice it to say that, since the Berlin Wall came down, in November 1989, not only accelerating progress towards European unification but also opening up new markets in Eastern Europe, a new wave of regulatory activities has hit industry and the advertising business alike. Unfortunately, the Commission is seeking uniformity – in itself highly desirable – by regulating at the maximum, rather than at the minimum. Tobacco and alcoholic products are bearing the brunt of this activity.

There is a strange paradox in this situation, which Mr Paul de Win, director of the World Federation of Advertisers (WFA) put as follows:

> Everywhere today, Governments are seeking to improve the well-being of their people by encouraging individual development. But these Governments are also passing regulations, restrictions and even bans that are detrimental to the development of local, national and international industries and commerce. They forget that this industrial development is fundamental to the improved well-being of both the individual and the nation.
> So, while these new democracies in Eastern Europe are well on their way to deregulation and a free market economy, those countries which have a long established tradition in this respect are contemplating more and more restrictions.[8]

In the chapters on Marlboro and Martini much attention was paid to this problem and to the response of the industries concerned. However, the Commission is not likely to give up its efforts to regulate much of Europe's advertising and once this practice spreads, it could easily have a 'domino-effect' highly detrimental to the interests of the business world.

As a final resort, there is still the option of bringing a case before the Council of Europe's Court of Justice, to which we referred in the context of Marlboro, but, to date, no industry has taken this step – though the patience of the business community is gradually being stretched to the limit.

Apart from this what else can be done to curtail governmental regulation of the free flow of ideas throughout Europe? It will stop if the entire business world gives its unwavering support to national and international trade associations defending the common interests of industry and the advertising business at both national and international levels; it will stop, if the voices of the 'captains of industry' and of distinguished academics ring out loud and clear in defence of freedom of speech; and it will stop if, at the same time, international voluntary codes and other international self-regulatory systems are introduced or strengthened, promoted and adhered to.

The case for self-regulation

The case for advertising self-regulation has been extensively argued elsewhere[9], so it should suffice to say here that self-regulatory codes have existed for many decades and have always been seen as a quick, simple, flexible and efficient system of ensuring that dishonesty in advertising will be spotted and stopped.

Since the International Chamber of Commerce introduced the first 'International Code of Advertising Practice', in 1937, industry and the advertising business have co-operated closely in drawing up the codes needed to protect consumers against any malpractice on the part of advertisers. In European countries, these systems have been working for many years to the satisfaction of all parties concerned, including consumers, making governmental interference superfluous. However, in spite of the efficiency and effectiveness of self-regulatory systems, politicians do not like them; hence my renewed plea for active support from industry and the advertising world for bodies such as the European Advertising Tripartite, referred to in the chapter on Marlboro, that are making such a convincing case for self-regulation as the best way to ensure the right balance between freedom of choice and protection of consumers' interests against any dishonesty in advertising.

One final point needs to be made on this subject: prevention is better than cure. The earlier that an industry presents the positive case for the advertising of its products to governments and the public at large, the better it will be. This is clearly shown by the steps taken by the coffee industry described in the chapter on Nescafé.

TRAINING

As we have seen, communication with consumers throughout Europe is becoming increasingly complex and specialized; no wonder, therefore, that all the companies participating in this study accept the need for proper training of both existing and new staff.

Training on the job is, of course, essential, so most companies run seminars, workshops or conferences for the training of their employees; others prefer to organize regular exchange-visits or job rotation schemes; and some use all these methods. However, preparation for a job in the communications business should start earlier, preferably at secondary school and advanced levels. Unfortunately, opportunities for advanced study of communications are still limited in Europe. Unlike in the USA, where advertising is included in the curriculum of many universities, this is not yet the case in most European countries.

On the positive side, the number of private colleges or institutes running advertising programmes is increasing, and the International Advertising Association also has a diploma course in international advertising. Nonetheless, it is to be hoped that industry and the advertising business will not only join together to bring about better opportunities for those who wish to make a career in communications, but will also exert greater pressure on governments to finance the introduction of advanced advertising programmes at a university level. Particular attention should be given to inculcating the knowledge needed for the sort of international operations described in this book; and providing the necessary resources will put a considerable burden on both the business world and governments.

1993 AND BEYOND

Readers will have noticed that the question of what will happen after 1993 has been posed at the end of every chapter. The answers were more specific in some cases than in others, but, generally speaking, there was hardly any company that was not reviewing some aspects of its international advertising operations. Naturally, in this book, I have devoted most attention to managerial and organizational aspects of advertising throughout Europe and to the trends toward greater internationalization. As my visits to the companies studied happened to coincide with important political developments in Europe, I was able also to include questions about the companies' plans to expand their businesses into the Eastern Bloc. Virtually all of them were preparing themselves for this new opportunity. However, they were hurrying slowly! The general expectation was that Eastern Germany, Czechoslovakia, Hungary and Poland would be the first countries where consumers would respond (and could afford to respond) to the kind of marketing and advertising methods that have proved to be so successful in Western Europe. But there was no optimism about the time needed to achieve one European market-place, embracing East and West.

In preparing this book, I visited family businesses, such as Miele, Levi Strauss and Martini & Rossi, conglomerates, such as Nestlé, Unilever and Mercedes, and the visionary computer company, Apple – and I came away from all of them impressed with the dedication, professionalism and single-minded action-oriented ambitions of the executives that I had met.

I was, of course, particularly pleased to find that my 'Three Dimensions' thesis, discussed in the Introduction, was confirmed and reinforced at every visit. All these practitioners, these 'doers', were dedicated to the interests of consumers and totally committed to the quality of their brands and services and to the way these were presented to the public – my first dimension. They had inquisitive minds and were alert to changing circumstances, but, in spite of that, they firmly believed in the consistency of the basic advertising policies for their brands, which they defended, maintained and developed – my second dimension. Finally, they had the rare ability to make other people act in accordance with their wishes – my third dimension.

I sincerely hope that the cases described in this book, and the recorded experiences of so many executives will help those advertising men and women who are already involved in communications on a European scale, or who wish to become involved in such activities, to achieve unqualified success. After 1992, the enlarged European market-place will offer great opportunities to those who combine entrepreneurial spirit with acceptance and understanding of new communications technologies and their infinite potential and who have thus become real experts in managing international advertising.

Notes

1. Bellow, Saul (1984), *Him with His Foot in His Mouth and Other Stories*. London: Alison Press/Secker & Warburg, p. 102.
2. *Annual Report 1989*, Philip Morris Companies Inc., New York, p. 56.
3. Personal discussion with A. Bernard, Chairman of Initiative Media International, Brussels, 28 November 1990.
4. *The Changing World of Media – Integrated Marketing Communication: Myth or Reality* (1990), a report from Initiative Media International, 12 March.
5. *Ibid.*, p. 21.
6. Rijkens, Rein, and Miracle, G. E. (1986), *European Regulation of Advertising*. Amsterdam: Elsevier Science Publishers.
7. Beatson, Ronald, Director-General of the European Advertising Agency Association, Brussels, 'EC Regulations/Product Category Bans in Europe,' a presentation at the Annual General Meeting of the Danish Advertising Agency Association, Copenhagen, 1 February 1990; and 'Europe 1993', a presentation at the Point-of-Purchase Advertising Institute Marketplace, New York, 31 October – 2 November 1989. See also note 8.
8. Win, Paul de (1990/1991), 'Win – ning formula,' *Media and Marketing Europe*, December/January.
9. Rijkens and Miracle, pp. 40–46.

ACKNOWLEDGEMENTS

Dino Aiassa	Central Director, General Beverage Management (Martini & Rossi), Geneva, Switzerland
Allan Allbeury	PR Manager, Nestlé UK, Croydon, UK
John Ankeny	Marketing Director, Levi Strauss Europe, Brussels, Belgium
Ronald Beatson	Director-General, European Association of Advertising Agencies, Brussels, Belgium
Pierre-Xavier Becret	Marketing and Planning Department, Club Méditerranée, Paris, France
Howard Belton	Senior Marketing Member, Detergents Co-ordination Unilever, London, UK
Alain Bernard	Associate Director, Nestec Ltd., Vevey, Switzerland
André Bernard	Chairman, Initiative Media International, Brussels, Belgium
Peter de Boer	Managing Director, Club Méditerranée B.V., Heemstede, Netherlands
Victor Bos	Market Communication Department, Mercedes-Benz Nederland B.V., Utrecht, Netherlands
F. David Bottomley	International Advertising Executive, Rowntree PLC, York, UK
Julian Boulding	International Account Director, DMB & B Advertising B.V., Amsterdam, Netherlands
Josiane Bourguignon	Public Relations Manager, Levi Strauss Europe, Brussels, Belgium
Mike Bowman	Multinational Accounts Director, Lintas: Worldwide, London, UK
Michael Bronsten	Advertising Specialist, Foods Executive, Unilever, London, UK
G.L. de Bruin	Area Director, Benelux, Philip Morris EEC Region, Amstelveen, Netherlands
Jeremy Bullmore	Director, WPP Group PLC, London, UK
Antoine Cachin	Secretary-General, Club Méditerranée, Paris, France
Simon Derungs	Account Director, Gold Greenless Trott Advertising, London, UK
M. van Dijk	Advertising Manager, Philip Morris Holland B.V., Amstelveen, Netherlands
Margret Dixon	Marketing Manager, Lever GmbH, Hamburg, Germany
Just Donker	Director, PMSvW/Y & R Advertising, Amsterdam, Netherlands
J.W.M. van Doorn	Head of Communication, Planning and Research Department, PMSvW/Y & R Advertising, Amsterdam, Netherlands
Mike Dowdall	Member of the Board, and Detergents Co-ordinator, Unilever, London, UK

Hans Eggerstedt	Member of the Board, and Frozen Foods Co-ordinator, Unilever, Rotterdam, Netherlands
Ronald C. Flens	Account Manager, Noordervliet & Winninghof/Leo Burnett, Amsterdam, Netherlands
Silas M. Ford	Executive Vice-President, Colgate-Palmolive Company, New York, USA
Esther Gan	Advertising and Public Relations Department, Philips Singapore Pte Ltd
Peter Gilson	Associate Director, Réflexions, Boulogne, France
Leendert Goedman	Marketing Manager, Lever GmbH, Hamburg, Germany
Helen Goossens	Corporate Communications Manager, Apple Computer Europe Inc., Paris, France
Simon P. Hardy	Drinks Department, Nestec Ltd., Vevey, Switzerland
G.J.J.M. Hayen	Director, Corporate Bureau of External Relations, Philips International B.V., Eindhoven, Netherlands
J.J. Hermans	International Advertising Manager, Domestic Appliances & Personal Care Division, Philips International B.V., Groningen, Netherlands
Sylvaine Hervet	RSCG Advertising, Issy-Les-Moulineaux, France
Peer Hilbig	Advertising Manager, Miele & Cie GmbH & Co., Gütersloh, Germany
Michel van Honk	Account Director, Lintas: Amsterdam, Netherlands
Ies Hoogland	Head of Advertising and Sales Promotion Department, KLM, Amstelveen, Netherlands
Michael Horst	President Corporate Services Inc., Philip Morris EEC Region, Lausanne, Switzerland
Bonno Hylkema	General Manager, Philips Singapore Pte Ltd
Alexander Kemner	Member of the Board, and Chairman Foods Executive, Unilever, Rotterdam, Netherlands
Jan Willem van Kleef	Advertising Manager, BMW Nederland B.V., Rijswijk, Netherlands
David Lamb	Former Advertising Executive, Rowntree PLC, York, UK
Jean Max Lenormand	Senior Vice-President, McCann Erickson, Paris, France
R. Loader	Director of Information Services, INFOTAB, Brentford, UK
Mathieu Lorjé	Marketing Communications Manager, Domestic Appliances & Personal Care Division, Philips International B.V., Groningen, Netherlands
Anders Malmfält	General Manager, Levi Strauss Nederland B.V., Amsterdam, Netherlands
Martin Marsh	General Manager, Nestec York Ltd., York, UK
Helmut Maucher	Managing Director, Nestlé S.A., Vevey, Switzerland
David Mayers	International Account Director, DMB & B Advertising, London, UK
M.C.J. Meijer	Head of Marketing Communication Department, Mercedes-Benz Nederland B.V., Utrecht, Netherlands
Rudolf Miele	Director, Miele & Cie GmbH & Co., Gütersloh, Germany
Serge Milhaud	Senior Vice-President, Nestec Ltd., Vevey, Switzerland
Gordon E. Miracle	Professor, Department of Advertising, Michigan State University, East Lansing, USA
Keith Monk	Former International Advertising Adviser to Nestlé, Vevey, Switzerland

ACKNOWLEDGEMENTS

Marieke de Mooij	Consultant and Secretary of IAA Education Committee, Badhoevedorp, Netherlands
Tom O'Connell	Account Director, J. Walter Thompson, Hamburg, Germany
Leo van Os	International Account Director, Lintas: Worldwide Amsterdam, Netherlands
Eliza Oxley	Former Account Director, J. Walter Thompson Company, London, UK
John Pattman	International Account Director, Lintas: Worldwide, London, UK
Jon L. Peterson	Chief Executive, Lever Europe, Brussels, Belgium
Manuel Ramiro	Chairman, Lintas: Madrid, Spain
Lucia Ransom	J. Walter Thompson Company, London, UK
Michel Reinarz	Director of Visual Communications, Nestec Ltd., Vevey, Switzerland
Peter Rijntjes	Account Director, PMSvW/Y & R, Amsterdam, Netherlands
Robert Riphagen	Director of Corporate Planning & Marketing Support, Philips International B.V., Eindhoven, Netherlands
W.S. Roijers	Head of Advertising & Sales Promotion Department, Miele Nederland B.V., Vianen, Utrecht, Netherlands
David Roussel	Account Director, J. Walter Thompson Company, London, UK
H.-J. Schultz-Hector	Director, Marketing Communication, Mercedes-Benz Commercial Vehicles, Stuttgart, Germany
Kenneth S. Sirlin	Director of Finance, Levi Strauss Europe, Brussels, Belgium
Gees-Ineke Smit	Head of Historic Archives, KLM, Amstelveen, Netherlands
J.F. de Soet	President, KLM, Amstelveen, Netherlands
Bill Taylor	Consultant, Scan, Sevenoaks, UK
Clay S. Timon	Vice-President, Worldwide Advertising, Colgate-Palmolive Company, New York, USA
J.C. Tollenaar	General Manager, Domestic Appliances and Personal Care Division, Philips International B.V., Groningen, Netherlands
Adriaan Vinju	General Manager, Martini & Rossi Nederland N.V., Gouda, Netherlands
Robert Wilson	Marketing Manager, Seiko Europe Ltd., Maidenhead, UK
Paul de Win	Director-General, World Federation of Advertisers, Brussels, Belgium
M. de Wolff	Marketing Director, Apple Computer B.V., Zeist, Netherlands
T.H. Woltman	General Manager, KLM Nederland, Amstelveen, Netherlands
Robin Worth	Senior Vice-President, McCann-Erickson Worldwide, London, UK
Ingo Zuberbier	Chairman, Lintas: Europe, Hamburg, Germany

BIBLIOGRAPHY

Functions held at the time

Aaker, David A., and Myers, J.G. (1975) *Advertising Management*. Hemel Hempstead: Prentice-Hall.

Bartlett, Christopher A., and Ghosal, S. (1989) *Managing across Borders – The Transnational Solution*. London: Hutchinson Business Books.

Boddewyn, Jean J., Soehl, R., and Picard, J. (1986) 'Standardization in international marketing: is Ted Levitt in fact right?' *Business Horizons*, November/December, no. 86611.

Cecchini, Paolo, Catinat, M., and Jacqemin, A. (1988) *The European Challenge – 1992 – the Benefits of a Single Market*. Hants: Wildwood House.

Clark, Terry (1990) 'International marketing and national character: A review and proposal for an integrative theory,' *Journal of Marketing*. October, pp. 66–80.

Day, Barry (1989) (ed.) *Perspectives: Europe 1992*. New York: The Interpublic Group of Companies.

Douglas, Susan, and Craig, S. (1989) 'The evolution of global marketing strategy: Scale, scope and synergy,' *Columbia Journal of World Business*, Fall.

Geier, Philip (1986) 'Global products, localized messages,' *Marketing Communications*, December.

Greffe, Pierre, and Greffe, Francois (1990) *La Publicité et la loi*. Paris: Librairie de la Cour de Cassation. Paris, France.

Grüner + Jahr A.G. & Co. (1989), *The European Internal Market, 'The Great Occasion'*. Hamburg, July.

Grüner + Jahr A.G. & Co. (1990), *Quantities – Potentials and Structures*. Hamburg, July.

Grüner + Jahr A.G. & Co.; and Initiative Media Hamburg (1991) *The Media Scene in Europe 3*. Hamburg, January.

International Advertising Association (1988) *Regulatory Intervention Calls for a Global Answer*. 31st World Advertising Congress, Sydney, Australia, 3 May.

Keegan, Warren (1989) *Global Marketing Management*. Hemel Hempstead: Prentice-Hall.

Kotler, Philip (1967) *Marketing Management*. Princeton, NJ: Prentice-Hall.

Levitt, Theodore (1983) 'The globalization of markets,' *Harvard Business Review*, May–June.

Maskulka, Thérèse, and Ryans, John K. Jr. (1990) 'European corporate communications: Preparing to cope with EC 1992?', *International Journal of Advertising*, 9 (2), pp. 159–167.

Millar, Carla (1989) 'Globalisation and the management of marketing and advertising in "Europe 1992",' *EIASM Conference Proceedings*, Brussels, May.

Miracle, Gorden E., Rijkens, R., and Tempest, A. (1988) 'The saga of the directive on misleading advertising,' *International Journal of Advertising*, 7, pp. 118–129.

Monk, Keith (1989) *Go International*. Maidenhead: McGraw-Hill.

Mooij, Marieke de, and Keegan, W. (1991) *Advertising Worldwide*. Hemel Hempstead: Prentice-Hall.

Naisbitt, John (1982) *Megatrends*. New York: Warner Books.

Naisbitt, John, and Aburdene, P. (1988) *Megatrends 2000*. New York: William Morrow.

Oliver, Daniel (1988) 'Who should regulate advertising, and why?' *International Journal of Advertising*, 7, pp. 1–9.

Peebles, D.M., and Ryans, J.K. (1984) *Management of International Advertising – a Marketing Approach*. Boston: Allyn and Bacon.

Peters, Thomas J., and Waterman Jr., R.H. (1982) *In Search of Excellence*. New York: Harper & Row.

Rossiter, John R., and Percy, L. (1987) *Advertising and Promotion Management*. Maidenhead: McGraw-Hill.

Roth, Robert F. (1982) *International Marketing Communications*. Chicago: Crain Books.

Rijkens, Rein, and Miracle, G.E. (1986) *European Regulation of Advertising*. Amsterdam: Elsevier.

Schultz, Don E. (1981) *Essentials of Advertising Strategy*. Chicago: Crain Books.

Sundberg Baudot, Barbara (1989) *International Advertising Handbook, a User's Guide to Rules and Regulations*. Lexington, KY: Lexington Books.

The Tom Peters Group (1990) *Prometheus Barely Unbound: A Quick Overview of the New Business Logic*. Palo Alto, CA: T.P.G. Communications.

Tugendhat, Christopher, *The Multinationals*. Harmondsworth: Pelican Books.

UNESCO, Paris (1990) *Rapport sur la Communication dans le Monde*.

Wells, William, Burnett, J., and Moriarty, S. (1989) *Advertising Principles and Practice*. Hemel Hempstead: Prentice-Hall.